WHAT WE *Believe* AND WHY

Volume 3

Lester Hutson

What We Believe and Why - Volume 3

All scripture is from the King James version of the Bible, which is public domain.

ISBN: 978-1-7324282-9-4

www.lesterhutson.org

Acknowledgments

What We Believe and Why 3 is the third volume in what has become a set. I have spent hundreds of hours studying, researching and writing (and rewriting) this material; but I have not been alone. So many have helped me: with ideas, with proofreading, with layout and design and with the many details necessary in the publishing of a book.

I especially owe a deep debt of gratitude to my dear and precious wife, Margaret. She has given me time and space to think, study and write. It takes time, lots of time, especially for a book of this size to become reality. She has also sheltered me; you can't spend too much of your time on the phone, in counselling sessions or returning texts and emails; and still finish work like this. A writer must have a sizeable amount of quiet time. Margaret has helped make that happen for me. She has also proofread every word, and held me to a high standard of excellence.

I am so blessed to have a dedicated, God-fearing team of proofreaders. Margaret is my first proofreader; but there is Julia Kovach, James Peterson and Nancy Sims. Of course, there is my final line of defense, Philip Rice. Each of these looks for any mistake or way to improve; however, each has a particular line of expertise. One specializes in seeing that my Scripture quotes are correct and correctly referenced. Another specializes in grammar, particularly in punctuation. There is a specialized eye on biblical correctness; are the points made truly sound? Then, there is the dedication to flow. Is everything laid out well, logical, easy-to-read and clear? This team worked diligently to made sure this book is well-written and that the truths therein are enunciated well. To each of you, I express my sincere and deep gratitude.

I am most grateful to our great God who lets me be a spokesman for Him. This is His work. He is the fountain-head of truth. I have nothing of my own, and I am a very ordinary human; yet, He lets me be a part of what He is doing. I am dependent on Him for everything.

Furthermore, He keeps extending my time and giving me the health I need and presence of mind to write. I am a truly blessed man, and I am thankful!

I also want to acknowledge you who read the materials I write. Thank you. I also thank you for the feedback, the great encouragement I receive from so many of you.

Table of Contents

Foreword

You are holding in your hands one of the most resourceful reference materials available. This third installment of *What We Believe and Why* tackles a variety of important biblical issues. Issues that are relevant for today but also clarifies misunderstood matters from the past. Bro. Hutson explains key subjects clearly for the man in the pew while also expounding in detail for the seasoned pastor. This is an excellent tool which helps its readers understand the full meaning of the material presented with sound biblical explanations.

There are many commentaries printed but there is none better than the Bible itself. *"What We Believe and Why 3"* is a commentary written from a Biblical point of view. You will not find a better commentary available on the subjects given. Bro. Hutson has labored in putting together topics from hard to understand or even preach to topics that are simple. In both cases he has put together a thorough commentary. He exegetes' scripture so not to distort the meaning giving a solid foundation to each chapter. He illustrates clearly so confusion is alleviated.

To help you to understand the author's heart, he has a quote "*Take what you can and can what you can't.*" He has two concerns: the lost person and the Bible reader. His desire is for the reader to draw closer to the LORD and have a better understanding of the heart of GOD. He believes the Bible is the most trusted sacred book that should be read daily. He reads the Bible from cover to cover yearly and believes it's GOD's infallible Word. He is a friend to all he meets with a spirit of excellence in all he inspires to do.

I believe *"What We Believe and Why 3"* will help everyone achieve a closer walk with the LORD GOD of Heaven. I have many of Bro. Hutson's books in my personal library. The "*What We Believe and Why*" series has been and is a treasured resource when studying GOD's Holy Word. It has helped draw me into a deeper understanding of GOD's word and being more concise when preaching. Having this tool will help dig deeper into the mysteries of GOD.

Chase Finch

Preface

Bible doctrine has never been highly popular. It has a way of harnessing people, changing their lifestyles and bringing them into a lifestyle that separates them from many people. Even the word *doctrine* is viewed by many with caution. Doctrine is simply the teachings of God, and His teachings are set forth in the Bible. *Doctrine* is not some strange, secretive system of beliefs. No! It's the thinking of God. Doctrine is the whole Bible; but it was especially set forth and clarified by Jesus Christ and His apostles. Doctrine tells us what is right and wrong, and how to live. It touches every nook and cranny of life in general, and our lives in particular.

I have written and published on many areas of doctrine. My first two volumes of *What We Believe and Why* are given to doctrine as in my book: *Great Bible Truths Revisited.* In those three volumes, more than 150 doctrinal issues are addressed. There are so many more. In my journey through life, more and more doctrinal issues seem to assert themselves. Therefore, I keep writing and addressing additional doctrinal issues. Sometimes, the truth on a particular issue remains so needed. That drives me to occasionally repeat an essay, or address an issue from a different perspective.

That need has driven me to write *What We Believe and Why 3.* My prayer is that you will find it useful, that it will strengthen your faith and that it will equip you to do a better job at *earnestly contending for the faith.*

Chapter 1

The Spirit of Christ

Philippians 2:5-8

"Let this mind be in you." That smites me. Each and every one of us should take a good look at the thinking of Jesus Christ and the spirit that marked Him, and then take a look at our own.

What a command! Be mentally disposed, earnestly in a certain direction. Be of the same disposition as Christ. You, which are in Him, keep on thinking this.

This passage is talking about a mindset, an attitude, a certain kind of spirit, specifically the spirit that was in Jesus Christ. He was always *"meek and lowly in heart,"* **Matthew 11:29**. Never was anyone as humble or had a better spirit or disposition than Jesus Christ. His is the ideal model of what our spirit should be like. He never sought His own, but *"humbled himself,"* **Philippians 2:8**. Christ is the ultimate example of humility.

The spirit that characterized Jesus Christ is sadly rare in believers. It is very hard to find in large measure in anyone, including those who posture themselves as strong, mature Christians. Strangely, often the more knowledgeable people become of the Bible, the more eager and ready they are to *straighten out* other people who don't see things exactly as they do.

Listening is seldom a strong characteristic of learned people, especially preachers; a large percentage of them *"already know most everything."* They act as though people ought to listen to them, not visa-versa. Most of them are prone to jump in with corrections and answers before they hear enough to understand the other person. Reasoning together, coming to understandings and openly discussing matters particularly where there are differing viewpoints seldom happens. Instead, sparks fly, anger rises, people (yes, even preachers and *"mature"* Christians) get *catty,* sarcastic and ugly. Parties square off. Divisions and hatred develop; good brothers and sisters who are in 99% agreement on basic issues criticize, carry grudges and talk negatively about each other especially behind their backs. They say they want to reason together, understand and be corrected; until they don't agree or until they touch a real nerve or sore spot! Suddenly, you realize that the *spirit of Christ* is more lofty talk than it is reality.

It's so much easier to talk about our doctrinal positions than it is to look at our attitudes and our own spirit. Christians as a whole have a reputation for being hard, stiff and not reasonable; not all, but too many. They know how to argue and get mad. They know plenty of ugly language even though it's not full of profanity. They know how to bully and straighten-out people. They know how to hold grudges, and go to civil war with their own brothers and sisters.

Most of us know far too little about *the spirit* that epitomized Jesus Christ. The Bible says, *"Let this mind be in you, which was also in Christ Jesus,"* **Philippians 2:5**.

THE SPIRIT OF CHRIST WAS AND IS CLEAR AND EASY TO IDENTIFY AND SEE

A. This is not an essay about the Holy Spirit.

1. Jesus Christ is God. Bible students know that God is one: Father, Son and Holy Spirit. Yes. They are all one.

2. Jesus was, *"Full of the Holy Ghost,"* **Luke 4:1**. He performed His miracles through the power of the Holy Spirit. *"I cast out devils by the Spirit of God,"* **Matthew 12:28.**

3. I am speaking about Jesus' attitude and approach. As you look at Him in the Word, His personality/spirit becomes clear. He had a very defined and distinct spirit. It's the kind

of thinking and mind we should have in ourselves. This spirit should characterize every believer. *"Let this mind be in you!"*

B. It's not hard to see it in Jesus Christ.

1. Talk about humility and submission. *"Let this mind be in you, which was also in Christ Jesus: Who, being in the form of God, thought it not robbery to be equal with God: But made himself of no reputation, and took upon him the form of a servant, and was made in the likeness of men: And being found in fashion as a man, he humbled himself, and became obedient unto death, even the death of the cross,"* **Philippians 2:5-8**.

   You're not going to find a better summary statement of the spirit of Christ than that one.

2. At the time of greatest trial and agony any person has ever endured, Jesus' spirit of godliness never wavered. There was never malice, hatred, evil, ugly or revenge in His spirit. *"For even hereunto were ye called: because Christ also suffered for us, leaving us an example, that ye should follow his steps: Who did no sin, neither was guile found in his mouth: Who, when he was reviled, reviled not again; when he suffered, he threatened not; but committed himself to him that judgeth righteously: Who his own self bare our sins in his own body on the tree, that we, being dead to sins, should live unto righteousness: by whose stripes ye were healed,"* **1 Peter 2:21-24**.

3. Every moment Jesus Christ was on this earth, He had a perfect spirit. He was *"holy, harmless, undefiled and separate from sinners."* **Hebrews 7:26**. He **never** had a bad attitude, **never** had a temper fit, **never** gossiped and **never** told a lie. **Not once** was He deceitful, corrupt or ugly in His dealings, even with vicious enemies who were bent on His destruction. Imagine Him on the cross saying, *"Father, forgive them; for they know not what they do,"* **Luke 23:34**!

4. He was always *"just,"* **Romans 3:26**, *"holy,"* **Luke 4:34**, *"good,"* **Matthew 19:16-17**, and *"forgiving,"* **Colossians 3:13**.

5. He was the picture of *"compassion,"* **Matthew 9:36**, His love *"passeth knowledge,"* **Ephesians 3:19**, and though He had all power, He was never pushy or a bully. He's the one who gave *the golden rule*. *"And as ye would that men should do to you, do ye also to them likewise,"* **Luke 6:31**. He's the author of these

gracious words of **Luke 6:35-38**, *"But love ye your enemies, and do good, and lend, hoping for nothing again; and your reward shall be great, and ye shall be the children of the Highest: for he is kind unto the unthankful and to the evil. Be ye therefore merciful, as your Father also is merciful. Judge not, and ye shall not be judged: condemn not, and ye shall not be condemned: forgive, and ye shall be forgiven: Give, and it shall be given unto you; good measure, pressed down, and shaken together, and running over, shall men give into your bosom. For with the same measure that ye mete withal it shall be measured to you again"*

6. His own words were *"I am meek and lowly in heart,"* **Matthew 11:29**. *"Never man spake like this man,"* **John 7:46**. *"All bare him witness, and wondered at the gracious words which proceeded out of his mouth,"* **Luke 4:22**.

7. Even Old Testament Isaiah gave us a preview of the absolutely gracious and beautiful spirit of Jesus Christ. *"He shall grow up before him as a tender plant, and as a root out of a dry ground: he hath no form nor comeliness; and when we shall see him, there is no beauty that we should desire him. He is despised and rejected of men; a man of sorrows, and acquainted with grief: and we hid as it were our faces from him; he was despised, and we esteemed him not. Surely he hath borne our griefs, and carried our sorrows: yet we did esteem him stricken, smitten of God, and afflicted. But he was wounded for our transgressions, he was bruised for our iniquities: the chastisement of our peace was upon him; and with his stripes we are healed. All we like sheep have gone astray; we have turned every one to his own way; and the LORD hath laid on him the iniquity of us all. He was oppressed, and he was afflicted, yet he opened not his mouth: he is brought as a lamb to the slaughter, and as a sheep before her shearers is dumb, so he openeth not his mouth. He was taken from prison and from judgment: and who shall declare his generation? for he was cut off out of the land of the living: for the transgression of my people was he stricken. And he made his grave with the wicked, and with the rich in his death; because he had done no violence, neither was any deceit in his mouth,"* **Isaiah 53:2-9**.

8. Jesus did not have the spirit He had because we are gracious, understanding, great listeners, reasonable, free of emotions or easy to talk to about any subject at any time. His spirit was a living testimony of who He was.

THE SPIRIT OF EVERY ONE OF US SHOULD ALWAYS BE A REFLECTION OF *THE SPIRIT OF CHRIST*

A. Far too many Christians are more interested in their own *great self,* what they have to say, and who they can *straighten out* than in their attitudes and spirits.

1. One man, who thought he was one of God's favorites, stood before God and prayed, *"God, I thank thee, that I am not as other men are,"* **Luke 18:11**. Doubtless, he is indicative of far more of God's people than we'd like to admit. Pride is an insidious enemy, and there's too much of it in every one of us. *"A man's pride shall bring him low: but honour shall uphold the humble in spirit,"* **Proverbs 29:23**.

2. Many *Christians* seem to have the notion that great Bible knowledge and strict adherence to outward Christian practices are enough and makes them great with God.

   a. They faithfully attend church, pay the tithes, give offerings, serve in church ministries and don't cheat on their mate. Or cuss! Or *straighten out those who've gotten it wrong!*

   b. They work hard, are good citizens, never steal or cheat, faithfully pay their taxes, know lots of truth and Scriptures and make good soldiers. They're doctrinally sound; and they're good, sincere, respectable people.

3. Is there no more to Christianity than going faithfully to church, and deeply participating in all that goes with that package? Is it all about keeping exacting moral standards, giving money and having a head full of great Bible knowledge?

B. No amount of *good stuff* is ever enough in a Christian without the spirit of Christ.

1. When speaking about some very good things like paying tithes, Jesus once said to a group of very well-entrenched *religious men, "These ought ye to have done, and not to leave the other undone,"* **Matthew 23:23**. In the rest of the verse, you will see that Jesus was speaking about what He called, *"the weightier matters of the law, judgment, mercy, and faith."*

2. As surely as you read these words, there are some things more important than winning an argument, showing how smart or tough you are, impressing those around and vanquishing a foe. Or friend!

3. Apart from walking with the Lord and having the day-to-day Lordship over our spirits, we will hurt and offend brothers and sisters in Christ, turn away baby and immature believers, divide brethren and churches, gain an infamous reputation as being hypocrites and bullies and be empty when we don't know we are.

4. No amount of sincerity, work (according to the letter of the law) or faithful service will count with God when the heart and spirit are not right.

a. That message glares in Old Testament Isaiah. God challenged them (and all of us), *"To what purpose is the multitude of your sacrifices unto me? saith the LORD: I am full of the burnt offerings of rams, and the fat of fed beasts; and I delight not in the blood of bullocks, or of lambs, or of he goats. When ye come to appear before me, who hath required this at your hand, to tread my courts? Bring no more vain oblations; incense is an abomination unto me; the new moons and sabbaths, the calling of assemblies, I cannot away with; it is iniquity, even the solemn meeting. Your new moons and your appointed feasts my soul hateth: they are a trouble unto me; I am weary to bear them. And when ye spread forth your hands, I will hide mine eyes from you: yea, when ye make many prayers, I will not hear: your hands are full of blood. Wash you, make you clean; put away the evil of your doings from before mine eyes; cease to do evil; Learn to do well; seek judgment, relieve the oppressed, judge the fatherless, plead for the widow,"* **Isaiah 1:11-17**.

b. It's very hard to miss God's point to the exactingly religious people before Him in days of Old Testament Amos. *"I hate, I despise your feast days, and I will not smell in your solemn assemblies. Though ye offer me burnt offerings and your meat offerings, I will not accept them: neither will I regard the peace offerings of your fat beasts. Take thou away from me the noise of thy songs; for I will not hear the melody of thy viols. But let judgment run down as waters, and righteousness as a mighty stream,"*

Amos 5:21-24. There's a message here for every one of us. The spirit in which we conduct ourselves matters.

c. King David once said, *"For thou desirest not sacrifice; else would I give it: thou delightest not in burnt offering. The sacrifices of God are a broken spirit: a broken and a contrite heart, O God, thou wilt not despise,"* **Psalm 51:16-17**.

With God, apart from a right spirit of humility, submission, brokenness and tenderness (*the spirit of Jesus Christ*) all of the letter-perfect performances do not count. Until the heart and the spirit get right, a whole lot of other things don't really count.

C. Nothing could be clearer than the fact that Jesus Christ wants *His* spirit in you and in me.

1. *"Let this mind be in you, which was also in Christ Jesus,"* **Philippians 2:5**. What could be clearer? *"This mind,"* this thinking, this spirit. Renown Greek scholar A. T. Robertson wrote on this passage, "Keep on thinking this in you which was also in Christ Jesus (ho kai en Christōi Iēsou). What is that? Humility. Paul presents Jesus as the supreme example of humility."[1] Should not every one of us *"follow his steps,"* **1 Peter 2:21**?

2. Our great God wants every child of His to be *"Conformed to the image of his Son,"* **Romans 8:29**. His *spirit* should be in every one of us. Bystanders who know the spirit of Christ and who know us should be able to *see* it. Yes! *"See"* it. *"The disciples"* in Antioch could *"see"* it and thus *"called"* them *Christians,"* **Acts 11:26**. Though not intended as such, what a compliment! Sadly, in current times, too many *Christians* have a negative impact on bystanders. Even their own kind.

3. It would be wise for each of us to realize that our spirit is always a testimonial of who we are. Our God is not interested only in how much we know and how rigidly we toe the line; His

[1] A.T. Robertson, *Word Pictures in the New Testament*, vol. 4, (Nashville, Tennessee: Broadman Press, 1931), 444.

eye is on our heart and He is **more interested** in how much of His spirit has become a part of us.

Dear brothers and sisters, I challenge each of us. Is the spirit of Christ *seen* in your spirit. Are you humble, meek, compassionate and submitted? Is tenderness, goodness and forgiveness a routine part of your lifestyle? Even when you're under pressure? Or when you have the upper hand? **They were a part of Jesus' spirit**. Do you have His spirit of lowliness, giving, forbearance and genuine love? Could it be that your attention has been so sharply focused on keeping the letter of church attendance, tithing, serving in some ministry and **doctrinal correctness** that your spirit is a reproach?

2 Corinthians 3:6 says, *"The letter killeth, but the spirit giveth life."* How true! Beloved, the letter of the law is not enough. The spirit of Christ must be there too. Jesus personally said so. *"God is a Spirit: and they that worship him must worship him in spirit* ***and*** *in truth,"* **John 4:24**.

Chapter 2

You and Your Worldview

Proverbs 23:7

"As he thinketh in his heart, so is he"

As people enter this world, they begin to learn and develop ideas, beliefs, opinions. Before long, people see things as good or bad, normal or abnormal, possible or impossible. With time, learning grows and beliefs become systems. These systems broaden and intensify. With time, basic belief systems develop which increasingly dictate decisions and behavior.

A person's comprehensive belief system is his/her worldview. The Merriam-Webster dictionary defines a worldview as *"a comprehensive conception or apprehension of the world especially from a specific standpoint."*[1] It is *"a particular philosophy of life or conception of the world."*[2] Wikipedia says a worldview *"is the fundamental cognitive orientation of an individual or society encompassing the whole of the individual's or society's knowledge, culture, and point of view."*[3]

AS PEOPLE LEARN AND GROW UP, THEY ALL DEVELOP WORLDVIEWS

Life demands decisions and actions. Making those decisions and taking action requires information and opinions, a database. The mind

---

1 https://www.merriam-webster.com/dictionary/worldview

2 *Google's English Dictionary* by Oxford Languages, https://languages.oup.com/google-dictionary-en

3 https://en.wikipedia.org/wiki/Worldview

constantly receives and processes information, and forms opinions. Beliefs and opinions grow stronger; people become increasingly entrenched in their mental positions. It is impossible to not have worldviews. Views on matters of life are vital.

Even a short conversation will quickly uncover the fact that people have ideas and opinions on all kinds of things: what they like and don't like, whether it's a good or bad day, what's moral and what's immoral, politics, what constitutes good character, on fairness, on religion and even the issue of God. A person's views come through in their conversations, in their behavior and especially in their responses. Just because a person doesn't express his/her views doesn't mean he/she doesn't have them. Even young children have surprisingly strong views on multiple issues. Their worldviews are taking shape well before they reach their teens.

A WORLDVIEW THAT INVOLVES GOD EMERGES IN PEOPLE AT A VERY EARLY POINT IN LIFE

As people mentally develop, they cannot escape the issue of God. How did the Universe originate? How do we explain intelligent design and the precision and fine-tuning of the Universe? How did life originate? What is the purpose and meaning of life? From where did man come? Why is man here? What is man's purpose? Is there any accountability? Why do people die? What happens after death? For man, is there anything beyond mortal life?

Is there really a God? Is He a mythological creature? What evidence says He exists? Did God create man or did man create God? Is the Universe, including life and man, merely a cosmic accident? Is man accountable to anyone?

Consciously or subconsciously, every human must deal with these questions and everyone has opinions on them. They are inescapable. Consider science with all its *"ologies;"* and ultimately, they always come back to *"how did it all start?"* Could *the beginning* be the result of mere *chance*; and if so, how can we explain it, especially its complexity which is beyond comprehension: it's mind-staggering original complexity and the absolute intricacy required for continued existence? It is not necessary for a person to be an academic or highly intelligent and educated scholar to face these questions. They're there for all people. Subconsciously, the issue of God is always there. Look around the world. Read the histories of the people who have lived here. All of them have faced the issue of God. Until the relatively-recent atheistic movement sprang up in the name of *intellectualism* and *science,* from the most primitive and backward people to the most brilliant and scholarly, there has been enormous belief in the existence of a god of one sort or another. Humanity has overwhelmingly been *theistic* (belief in the existence of a god), and not *atheistic* (belief that no god exists). The intensity of belief on this matter varies; but everybody has an opinion. Agnostics attempt to be neutral and say they don't know; but there really is no neutral ground. On the issue of God's existence, He either exists or He doesn't exist. The only alternative to belief in His existence is to believe that He doesn't exist.

A PERSON'S WORLDVIEW ON THE ISSUE OF GOD WILL ULTIMATELY DOMINATE HIS LIFE

A Theistic Worldview (There is a God)

This worldview sees all things to have originated by God. *"In the beginning God created the heaven and the earth,"* **Genesis 1:1**. Consequently, all things, including people are under His jurisdiction and authority. *"In the beginning was the Word, and the Word was with God, and the Word was God. The same was in the beginning with God. All things were made by him; and without him was not any thing made that was made,"* **John 1:1-3**. By right of creation and ownership, God has the right to make the rules, the power to enforce them and the final say in all matters. *"The earth is the LORD'S, and the fulness thereof; the world, and they that dwell therein. For he hath founded it upon the seas, and established it upon the floods,"* **Psalm 24:1-2**. They are also under His control. *"He is before all things, and by him all things consist,"* **Colossians 1:17**.

All things, including people, exist only because of Him. *"In him we live, and move, and have our being,"* **Acts 17:28**. He has ultimate power. King David said of Him, *"Blessed be thou, LORD God of Israel our father, for ever and ever. Thine, O LORD, is the greatness, and the power, and the glory, and the victory, and the majesty: for all that is in the heaven and in the earth is thine; thine is the kingdom, O LORD, and thou art exalted as head* *above all. Both riches and honour come of thee, and thou reignest over all; and in thine hand is power and might; and in thine hand it is to make great, and to give strength unto all,"* **1 Chronicles 29:10-12**. This is a good example of how a person with a proper worldview of God sees both God along with himself or herself. In light of God, he sees himself as a totally dependent being. God is the one in charge, and all of the existence and strength he/she has comes only at the goodness and benevolence of God.

God is *"the Almighty God,"* (highest possible power), **Genesis 17:1**, and *"The blessed and only Potentate, the King of kings, and Lord of lords; Who only hath immortality, dwelling in the light which no man can approach unto; whom no man hath seen, nor can see: to whom be honour and power everlasting,"* **1 Timothy 6:15-16**.

At the heart of a theistic worldview is authority and accountability. God sees and knows all things, *"For the word of God is quick, and powerful, and sharper than any twoedged sword, piercing even to the dividing asunder of soul and spirit, and of the joints and marrow, and is a discerner of the thoughts and intents of the heart. Neither is there any creature that is not manifest in his sight: but all things are naked and opened unto the eyes of him with whom we have to do,"* **Hebrews 4:12-13**. God, who has absolute authority and power holds all people accountable for their thoughts, motives, decisions and actions. Jesus said, *"That every idle word that men shall speak, they shall give account thereof in the day of judgment,"* **Matthew 12:36**. Accountability and judgement are an inseparable part of the concept of God. *"For God shall bring every work into judgment, with every secret thing, whether it be good, or whether it be evil,"* **Ecclesiastes 12:14**. *"Be sure your sin will find you out,"* **Numbers 32:23**. *"It is written, As I live, saith the Lord, every knee shall bow to me, and every tongue shall confess to God. So then every one of us shall give account of himself to God,"* **Romans 14:12-13**. This *"is written"* in **Isaiah 45:23**. People who believe there's a God are naturally aware of and concerned about their motives, thoughts, words and behavior.

Interwoven in the belief that there's a God is the idea that every person was made by God, belongs to God and is accountable to God. In this worldview is the belief that God deliberately created man for the purpose of honoring and exalting God with his/her life. *"Glorify God in your body, and in your spirit, which are God's,"* **1 Corinthians 6:20**. Life is not all about *self;* it's about living God's way which is where true joy and fulfillment are. *"Thou wilt shew me the path of life: in thy presence is fulness of joy; at thy right hand there are pleasures for evermore,"* **Psalm 16:11**. *"He that dwelleth in the secret place of the most High shall abide under the shadow of the Almighty. I will say of the LORD, He is my refuge and my fortress: my God; in him will I trust,"* **Psalm 91:1-2**. In the theistic worldview, life has purpose and meaning. We're here to do good, help people and take care of the planet. We came from God and shall return to God where we will spend eternity in a sin-free, immortal body where pain, aging, sorrow and death do not exist.

God has made His views about living in His world very clear. In His written Word (the Bible), they are spelled-out in great detail. They are summarized in these words: *"What doth the LORD thy God require of thee, but to fear the LORD thy God, to walk in all his ways, and to love him, and to serve the LORD thy God with all thy heart and with all thy soul, To keep the commandments of the LORD, and his statutes, which I command thee this day for thy good?"* **Deuteronomy 10:12-13**. Those words were given to Israel, the nation through whom God would give His written Word and His Messiah; but God wants all people to fully give themselves to Him. Jesus made that clear when He later said, *"Thou shalt love the Lord thy God with all thy heart, and with all thy soul, and with all thy mind. This is the first and great commandment. And the second is like unto it, Thou shalt love thy neighbour as thyself. On these two commandments hang all the law and the prophets,"* **Matthew 22:37-40**. A theistic, Christian worldview is about love, caring, giving and forgiving. It's about doing unto others as you would have them do unto you. It's about honesty in word and deed, kindness, humility and pure hearts and motives. It's about integrity, morality, respect and doing right. It's against hatred, prejudice, pride, corruption and every evil way.

This kind of worldview places value on life, peace and harmony. It reduces crime; and condemns oppression, bullies and corrupt politicians. It promotes reconciliation, builds friendships and strong relationships of all sorts and produces clear consciouses. It is the fountainhead of civilized, free, law-abiding societies where people live in safety.

An Atheistic Worldview (There is no God)

Take away God, and life has no purpose. None! If there is no God, we came from nowhere, and have absolutely no reason for being here. We're going nowhere; this brief existence is it. There's nothing past death; no eternal life, no resurrection, no new body or reunion with family. There is no hope! Nothing! It's all right here; right now!

If there's no God, there's no accountability other than what man might impose: parents, bosses, civil authorities and the State! Morality doesn't exist; there is no right or wrong. Outside of human authority, nobody is going to punish you for anything. Why not bully and capitalize on people? Murder your mother, your wife or your baby; who says it's wrong? What makes their opinion any better than yours? Without God, who is to say that Adolph Hitler, Joseph Stalin or the cannibals of Papua, New Guinea were wrong? By what authority do you say a school shooting, ploughing a car into a crowded street, an airplane into New York's Twin Towers or a cold-blood premeditated murder is evil? Without God, every man becomes a self-made authority, and a law unto himself. Who rules is determined by who has the most power; usually the most guns or other weapons.

Everything is touched and impacted by what he believes about there being no God. Leaving God out means there are no natural restraints, only manmade restraints. Sex is whatever you want it to be including rape, sex outside of marriage, homosexuality and bestiality. Who's to say that child or wife abuse is wrong? Without God, there is no central moral code. Standards are only what society determines them to be. If you can *"get away with it"* with people, then do whatever you want to do. After all, nothing is right or wrong, and you'll never have to answer to anybody for anything.

The removal of the belief in God literally rips restraint, integrity and lawful behavior right out of a person and a society. It is not difficult to see why God said, *"The fool hath said in his heart, There is no God. Corrupt are they, and have done abominable iniquity: there is none that doeth good,"* **Psalm 53:1**. Denial of God lays the groundwork for corruption and the proliferation of evil. Thus, God concluded, *"The fool hath said in his heart, There is no God,"* **Psalm 14:1**. Belief in God is the foundation for restraint, sane behavior, morality, lawfulness, hope, responsible living and all things that promote the common good and can be considered positive to human welfare both personally and corporately. On a colossal scale, denying God is somewhat akin to sawing off the limb upon which you are standing. It simply doesn't make sense.

THE STRENGTH OF A PERSON'S VIEW OF GOD

Earlier, I spoke of different stages in the development of worldviews. Some who have a basic belief in God have not seriously given themselves to learning His ways. Still others have not committed themselves to yielding or submitting to Him. Hence, countless and needless evils continue at breakneck speed. The strength of a theistic (God) worldview will determine how often and enthusiastically a person thinks, decides and acts in accordance with God's position on the issues he/she faces. Furthermore, the weaker a person's belief in and commitment to God, the more often he/she will think, decide and act out of harmony with God's position on the issues he/she faces. You would think that all people who embrace a theistic worldview would all be on or close to the same page on most issues. Sadly, such is not the case. Not all God-believers believe in the same God. Too many who embrace the God of the Bible know very little of what He teaches; the vast majority of them have never read His Word (Bible) even one time. They believe He created the Universe, that He's all-powerful and that there is good and evil/right and wrong; and that constitutes great restraint and accountability; but they know very few of His details. They're really not serious about God.

The result is lives that generally do not reflect the thinking of God. Self is the basis of most thinking, decisions and behavior. Being man's constant adversary, Satan ever exploits man's propensity to do things his own way. God warns us against the destructive influence of Satan on our lives, *"Be sober, be vigilant; because your adversary the devil, as a roaring lion, walketh about, seeking whom he may devour,"* **1 Peter 5:8**. If they have weak and undisciplined ways combined with Satan's destructive efforts in this evil world, those that embrace a theistic worldview may look like atheists. We profess that we believe there's a God, but act like He doesn't exist. It is glaringly obvious that Satan has made great inroads in the theistic community. Jesus described multitudes of people with corrupted theistic worldviews when He said, *"This people draweth nigh unto me with their mouth, and honoureth me with their lips; but their heart is far from me,"* **Matthew 15:8**. Jesus once asked some of His close followers, *"Why call ye me, Lord, Lord, and do not the things which I say?"* **Luke 6:46**. The wide gap between those who profess a theistic, Christian worldview and their words and lifestyle has done great harm to Christianity.

Even a weak theistic worldview (belief in God) is a tremendous restraint against evil. This is true in individuals and in nations. Consistent with a biblical worldview of God are over-riding beliefs such as the sanctity of life, freedom of religion, freedom of speech, personal liberty of conscience, a justice system and the right of self-defense. The United States of America continues to move away from a theistic worldview; but since her inception, her belief in God has produced enormous benefits. Her belief in a higher power and set of standards, and her voluntary submission to divine laws has kept her free.

When men and nations embrace a truly well-developed atheistic worldview, there are no restraints. Despots like Joseph Stalin and Adolph Hitler do whatever they please. To people like them who believe there is no right, wrong or accountability life is meaningless. They are guided by no higher power, and life is meaningless. However heinous and macabre, there is no reason not to do whatever they wish.

How sobering are the words of God: *"The wicked shall be turned into hell, and all the nations that forget God,"* **Psalm 9:17**.

GIVE THE CORRECT WORLDVIEW ABOUT GOD TO THE NEXT GENERATION

God insists on it! Here is how He put it: *"Hear, O Israel: The LORD our God is one LORD: And thou shalt love the LORD thy God with all thine heart, and with all thy soul, and with all thy might. And these words, which I command thee this day, shall be in thine heart: And thou shalt teach them diligently unto thy children, and shalt talk of them when thou sittest in thine house, and when thou walkest by the way, and when thou liest down, and when thou risest up. And thou shalt bind them for a sign upon thine hand, and they shall be as frontlets between thine eyes. And thou shalt write them upon the posts of thy house, and on thy gates,"* **Deuteronomy 6:6-9**. Obviously, God is serious about passing on a proper view of who He is to each new generation.

God knows how fickle people are, especially from generation to the next generation. By nature, the heart is wicked. The lyrics of a great hymn put it well:

Oh, to grace how great a debtor

Daily I'm constrained to be

Let Thy goodness like a fetter

Bind my wandering heart to Thee

Prone to wander, Lord I feel it

Prone to leave the God I love

Here's my heart, oh take and seal it

Seal it for Thy courts above

It has been very rare in the history of people from generation to generation for children to retain the rich treasures their parents had. The young children of ancient Israel saw firsthand their deliverance from Egyptian bondage. They also saw God's delivering hand in Joshua. The Bible records what happened when Joshua died. *"And the people served the LORD all the days of Joshua, and all the days of the elders that outlived Joshua, who had seen all the great works of the LORD, that he did for Israel,"* **Judges 2:7**. As people always do, this generation died. Listen to these sad words about the next generation. *"Also all that generation were gathered unto their fathers: and there arose another generation after them, which knew not the LORD, nor yet the works which he had done for Israel,"* **Judges 2:10**. What a sad, but typical story: *"There arose another generation after them, which knew not the LORD!"* It happened at the Ivy League schools in America. They started as God-fearing, Bible-believing colleges; now they generally reject God and divine inspiration. It's probable that you know a long list of *preacher's kids* who grew up in a God-fearing, Bible-believing home. Now they are a long way from God.

People drift. God tells parents, especially parents, to ***"teach"*** their children. *"And what nation is there so great, that hath statutes and judgments so righteous as all this law, which I set before you this day? Only take heed to thyself, and keep thy soul diligently, lest thou forget the things which thine eyes have seen, and lest they depart from thy heart all the days of thy life: but teach them thy sons, and thy sons' sons,"* **Deuteronomy 4:8-9**. God also tells parents to ***"train"*** their children. *"Train up a child in the way he should* *go: and when he is old, he will not depart from it,"* **Proverbs 22:6**. This admonition to pass truth on to your children is repeated in the New Testament: *"Fathers, provoke not your children to wrath: but bring them up in the nurture and admonition of the Lord,"* **Ephesians 6:4**.

The idea of passing truth, especially a theistic worldview or belief in the God of the Bible particularly stands out in the **78th Psalm**. *"Give ear, O my people, to my law: incline your ears to the words of my mouth. I will open my mouth in a parable: I will utter dark sayings of old: Which we have heard and known, and our fathers have told us. We will not hide them from their children, shewing to the generation to come the praises of the LORD, and his strength, and his wonderful works that he hath done. For he established a testimony in Jacob, and appointed a law in Israel, which he commanded our fathers, that they should make them known to their children: That the generation to come might know them, even the children which should be born; who should arise and declare them to their children: That they might set their hope in God, and not forget the works of God, but keep his commandments: And might not be as their fathers, a stubborn and rebellious generation; a generation that set not their heart aright, and whose spirit was not stedfast with God,"* **Psalm 78:1-8**.

One's worldview, especially about God, seems to be one of life's unspoken (and generally un-noticed and neglected) realities. Everyone has a worldview. Its power and influence on one's thinking, decisions and behavior are profound. Every one of us would do well to work on and strengthen our own worldview, and help develop the worldviews of those around us, particularly our children and children's children.

Worldviews will continue to develop and strengthen, with or without deliberate efforts. God's people are *"Ambassadors,"* (deliberate mentors), *"Now then we are ambassadors for Christ,"* **2 Corinthians 5:20**. It is part of our divine purpose to mentor people, help them come to a knowledge of God. We are commanded to *"Sanctify the Lord God in your hearts: and be ready always to give an answer to every man that asketh you a reason of the hope that is in you with meekness and fear,"* **1 Peter 3:15**. That involves giving reasons why we believe there's a God, and why we are committed to Him and His Word, the Bible. We are commanded to *"study to shew thyself approved unto God, a workman that needeth not to be ashamed, rightly dividing the word of truth,"* **2 Timothy 2:15**.

God *"will have all men to be saved, and to come unto the knowledge of the truth,"* **1 Timothy 2:4**. For that to happen, a person must come to a theistic worldview. May every one of us who knows God work to represent Him better in both word and testimony. That means a true and serious commitment to Him and His Word.

I challenge every person who reads these lines to take a look at your worldview. Is it theistic? If so, on a scale of 1 to 10 with 10 being very strong, where do you place yourself?

Chapter 3

Thinking for Yourself

Acts 17:10-11

"Dad, if a black cat crosses the road in front of you, something bad will happen to you." "Son, what makes you think that?" "Uncle John told me, and I believe everything he says."

Believing trusted people is about as common as things get. To some degree, we all do it. Beware! Trust is a marvelous thing, but it can be betrayed. Let the buyer beware. When it's your trust, you'd better pay attention.

Most of us have heard about the Pied Piper. In the legend out of the Middle Ages, he's the lead character from the town of Hamelin, in Saxony, Germany; The Rat-Catcher of Hamelin. The piper, dressed in multicolored ("pied") clothing was hired by the town to lure rats away with his magic pipe. When the citizens refused to pay for this service as promised, the Pied Piper retaliated by using his instrument's magical power on their children, leading them away as he had the rats. The phrase "pied piper" has become a metaphor for a person who attracts a following through charisma or false promises.[1]

The deception need not be intentionally. Some deceive others on purpose, but most people who deceive others have no intentions of doing so. Furthermore, they're unaware of what they're doing. They

[1] https://en.wikipedia.org/wiki/Pied_Piper_of_Hamelin

believe lies, so they pass them on along to their children, students and circle of friends including those at church. Lies and other falsehoods are replicated from one generation to the next for many generations. Very few ever escape the spell; and often when they do, they become outcasts.

A very old type of argument is commonly used in debates and courtrooms. The Latin word is **ad hominem** meaning *"to the person"* (directed at the person). It's a persuasion that appeals to feelings or prejudices rather than to intellect.[2] As in the case of the Pied Piper who directed his attack at the parents of Hamelin by deceiving their children, people attack other people with subtle lies, by apparent harmlessness and innocence and by an assassination of the character of an honest and upright person. Character assassination is a common practice in courtrooms. Focus is taken off the guilt or innocence of the defendant and placed on whether or not a witness on the stand is fit to testify. It really stood out in the O. J. Simpson trial.

In everyday real life, the validity of long-standing beliefs, positions and claims are rarely called into question. They've usually been entrenched for generations. Most people don't know or believe they have wrong or flawed views. They have no problem passing them down to their children, students or other people of the next generation. Furthermore, who is going to call into serious question mom or dad, the preacher, the teacher, *"that's what I've always been taught," the way it's always been done*, science or especially the professor who has written several textbooks and has at least one Ph. D? It's a whole lot less messy to simply *go with the flow. Don't rock the boat.*

Someone has well said, *"It does make a difference what you believe."*[3] How true! Lies blind and damn people. Truth frees. Through the centuries multitudes have suffered untold agony due to their own ignorance and blindness. Talk about the potential consequences of blind following, the infamous *Judas Sheep* makes it eerily vivid. For centuries butchers kept one old sheep which all the other sheep trusted and would follow. All the sheep to be slaughtered were put in a big pen with a ramp to the killing gate at one end. At the end of the ramp

---

[2] https://www.scribbr.com/fallacies/ad-hominem-fallacy

[3] For many years, this was the slogan on the front of Berean Baptist Church in Houston, Texas

butchers were stationed with sharp knives. At a signal from a butcher, the *Judas Sheep* would walk up the ramp with the flock following. The *Judas Sheep* would jump off the ramp and go his way. One by one the butchers would slit the throats cutting the carotid arteries of the sheep which followed and leave them to bleed to death.[4]

THE WAY OF BELIEVING THAT REQUIRES LITTLE THINKING FOR YOURSELF IS VERY COMMON

A. **This type of approach to moving other people is far more common than you might think.**

1. Find yourself in or gain a position of trust. Strengthen it all you can. From that platform, make known and convince others of what you believe. In societies, it's the easiest and most natural of ways to do it.

2. The higher and more trusted and respected you are, the more people trust and follow you. Usually, with little or no serious questions. Charismatic preachers can sell nearly anything. Their beliefs and position easily get through our filters because they come from our best, most respected and trusted information sources.

3. Most of us just *take their word for it.* We're predisposed to take the word of *experts, authorities on the subject.* Because we like and trust the person and not because we've truly thought-through the matter and seen it for ourselves, we *buy into* the thinking of somebody else. I suspect much of what most of us believe is based largely on the thinking of other people.

4. As some people begin to grow up, they encounter "new" beliefs such as Darwinian Evolution, socialism and progressive thinking. Family and old friends are often shocked at the transformation that takes place. Very often old beliefs and positions are being replaced with new beliefs and positions because of a highly charismatic and credentialed professor, another popular figure or even a transforming book. The transformation rarely occurs because he/she truly thought it through and saw it for himself/herself.

---

[4] https://wordhistories.net/2019/08/30/judas-sheep-judas-goat

5. The book of Acts in the New Testament gives a historical account of early church times and speaks of a very renown leader by the name of Gamaliel. He led a Rabbinical School, **Acts 5:34-40**. Once he spoke his thinking on the matter before them, *"They all agreed."* This day, many young preachers come out of seminary in some professor's pocket with a case of Calvinism, universal theology, Lordship salvation, compromised worship fads and practices and no convictions about Bible translations.

6. The age (new or old) is not the deciding factor in whether or not a belief or practice is bad or good. It's easy to get caught up in what someone believes and teaches without really understanding it at all. Don't let yourself buy into anything that you cannot knowingly embrace because you made it yours.

7. A great old story illustrates the point: "Mother, why do you always cut off the ends of the roast before you cook it?" "My daughter, that's the way Granny always did it." "Granny, why did you cut the ends off your roast?" "If I didn't, they wouldn't fit in my roaster."

B. The Bible is far from silent on the issue of thinking for yourself.

1. Very early in His Word God said, *"Thou shalt not follow a multitude to do evil; neither shalt thou speak in a cause to decline after many to wrest judgment,"* **Exodus 23:2**. God knows the weaknesses of the human heart, and how easily it can be duped, deceived and led astray. It's pretty obvious that when God warned about mindlessly following big majorities, He knew about the Pied Piper metaphor.

2. Jude spoke of how some exercise great persuasion and control over others with their words and influence. *"These are murmurers, complainers, walking after their own lusts; and their mouth speaketh great swelling words, having men's persons in admiration because of advantage,"* **Jude 16**. The combination of personal admiration and trust with lofty words has obviously influenced blind people to follow for a long time.

3. The Old Testament tells of two prophets in the ancient city of Bethel, one young and very godly and the other old and very shrewd. Because of the respect he had for the old prophet, the young prophet believed the old prophet even when he lied on God. You would have thought that the young prophet would have believed God over anyone, but he didn't. What a sad, but accurate picture of how trust and respect can blind! It's been a very successful trick of Satan for thousands of years. See **1 Kings 13**.

4. It was King David's charismatic, favorite son Absalom who cunningly turned the men of Israel against his father and convinced them to make him king in his father's stead. It was an underhanded, divisive, bloody rebellion; but his cunning and power of persuasion was enough to get it done. The Bible records this sleezy report. *"And on this manner did Absalom to all Israel that came to the king for judgment: so Absalom stole the hearts of the men of Israel,"* **2 Samuel 15:6**. Under the guise that he loved and cared for his family and the people of Israel, Absalom overthrew and tried to murder his own father.

5. One of the most striking expressions of the ruinous effects of erroneous teaching combined with gullible, mindless thinking was given directly by Jesus Christ. He said, *"This people draweth nigh unto me with their mouth, and honoureth me with their lips; but their heart is far from me. But in vain they do worship me, teaching for doctrines the commandments of men. And he called the multitude, and said unto them, Hear, and understand: Not that which goeth into the mouth defileth a man; but that which cometh out of the mouth, this defileth a man. Then came his disciples, and said unto him, Knowest thou that the Pharisees were offended, after they heard this saying? But he answered and said, Every plant, which my heavenly Father hath not planted, shall be rooted up. Let them alone: they be blind leaders of the blind. And if the blind lead the blind, both shall fall into the ditch,"* **Matthew 15:8-14**.

   It is sickening to realize how many are blind to the reality of what they believe, where they spiritually stand and where they and their children are headed. *The blind leading the blind.* What a mental picture! Some know they're there, but most don't. Furthermore, most are not really interested in waking up from their blind swoon. For now, they're too comfortable, secure and wed to their old blind buddies. Talk to me about preachers. I've been one for over six decades. Even sitting down for an open, honest discussion not dominated by emotions and interruptions on issues where we don't see things exactly the same is too risky for some of us. It might be embarrassing and dislodge us out of our old peer groups.

6. Recently, I read about a blind man in Cincinnati who introduced another man to his blind friend. The blind man explained, *"I'm showing him to the city."* I marvel that there are so many people with 20 X 20 vision who can see and hear only what they've been taught and told to be true.

FAILURE TO THINK FOR YOURSELF IS VERY POWERFUL AND DANGEROUS

A. It usually leads to dire consequences and multiplies evil.

1. There have been and are huge numbers of impressive people who have played havoc with their gullible, unthinking comrades. Those who would do you harm are always out there. King David prayed, *"Be merciful unto me, O God: for man would swallow me up; he fighting daily oppresseth me. Mine enemies would daily swallow me up: for they be many that fight against me, O thou most High."* He went on to explain how they did it: *"Every day they wrest my words: all their thoughts are against me for evil. They gather themselves together, they hide themselves, they mark my steps, when they wait for my soul,"* **Psalm 56:1-2, 5-6**. The primitive Hebrew root verb here for *"wrest"* is **'âtsab** (aw-tsab'). It literally means *"to carve,"* that is *"to fabricate or fashion."* More people among us than most of us suspect are good at carving up truth and fashioning it to something very different.

2. The apostle Peter also used the word *"wrest."* In a reference to the letters written by the apostle Paul, Peter acknowledged that Paul wrote some things which were hard and difficult to understand. Peter promptly mentioned that the *"unlearned and unstable wrest"* (twist or pervert) Scriptures from Paul and *"also the other scriptures."* Peter said they did this twisting of truth *"unto their own destruction."* He then warned,

"Ye therefore, beloved, seeing ye know these things before, beware lest ye also, being led away with the error of the wicked, fall from your own stedfastness," **2 Peter 3:16-17**. Peter used the Greek word **strebloō** (streb-lo'-o) meaning *"to pervert."* People who pervert truth capitalize on those who do not think for themselves. Following anybody with your *mind out of gear* is a formula for disaster and continued ignorance. Ignorance brings lots of grief with it. Nobody can afford to remain a mindless robot.

3. God spoke to Jeremiah, and to all of us when He warned about deception and those who are not paying attention: *"Then the LORD said unto me, The prophets prophesy lies in my name: I sent them not, neither have I commanded them, neither spake unto them: they prophesy unto you a false vision and divination, and a thing of nought, and the deceit of their heart,"* **Jeremiah 14:14**.

4. Jesus warned, *"False Christs and false prophets shall rise, and shall shew signs and wonders, to seduce, if it were possible, even the elect,"* **Mark 13:22**. He also warned, *"Beware of false prophets, which come to you in sheep's clothing, but inwardly they are ravening wolves,"* **Matthew 7:15**.

5. Gullible! Fall in line behind the Pied Piper. *He's handsome, smart and charismatic. Everybody thinks he's right.* Talk about a formula for false doctrine. That's how most of the mainline *Christian* Churches were born. That's how Adolph Hitler came to power. Over the past 2,000 years in the name of *Christianity,* every imaginable heresy has flourished because people blindly followed Constantine, Valentinus, Origin, John Calvin, Martin Luther, Brigham Young, Alexander Campbell, a parade of popes and a host of others.

6. Good, intelligent people can go to sleep with their eyes wide open. Unsaved and saved people do it routinely. Blindness puts lost people in hell, and it freezes saved people in error. It's not enough to say you're a Christian because a preacher, your mother or some other persuasive person says He's the Savior. You have to see that it's true for yourself. You have to accept Him in your heart. You have to personally think about your sin and its penalty. In your own heart, you must

face the impossibility of your ever being saved by your own efforts including any number or form of works. Jesus Christ, who died, was buried and rose again for you, is your only hope. You must see that for yourself. You must trust Him; not merely believe that He exists and did the work for you. You must depend on Him and Him alone as your only hope beyond the grave. *"The word is nigh thee, even in thy mouth, and in thy heart: that is, the word of faith, which we preach; That if thou shalt confess with thy mouth the Lord Jesus, and shalt believe in thine heart that God hath raised him from the dead, thou shalt be saved. For with the heart man believeth unto righteousness; and with the mouth confession is made unto salvation,"* **Romans 10:8-10**.

B. Respect, trust and following people of understanding and wisdom are straight from God; but you must always be cautious and think for yourself!

1. God put respect and honor for older people of learning, experience and wisdom right in His Ten Commandments. *"Honour thy father and thy mother: that thy days may be long upon the land which the LORD thy God giveth thee,"* **Exodus 20:12**. Open your ears; listen to your elders, those of wisdom. Pay attention. Ascribe value and weight to what they say and do. *"Children, obey your parents in the Lord: for this is right. Honour thy father and mother; (which is the first commandment with promise;) That it may be well with thee, and thou mayest live long on the earth,"* **Ephesians 6:1-3**. It's REAL important! *"The hoary head is a crown of glory, if it be found in the way of righteousness,"* **Proverbs 16:31**. Though it is not always the case, *"Days should speak, and multitude of years should teach wisdom,"* **Job 32:7**.

2. Yet, regardless of who is speaking, God never gives us the right to turn off our brains. He says, *"But let every man prove his own work, and then shall he have rejoicing in himself alone, and not in another,"* **Galatians 6:4**. *"Thou shalt not follow a multitude to do evil; neither shalt thou speak in a cause to decline after many to wrest judgment,"* **Exodus 23:2**.

   That includes all of your teachers and professors, the great theologians, the charismatic preachers, the old people, the clever people, the famous people, the brilliant people, all of those news reporters, your dearest and most trusted friends and your own mother and dad. (I didn't think I had to include politicians.)

Think for yourself. ALWAYS keep your mind in gear. Following Pied Pipers is a risky and dangerous business.

THE POSITION OF THE BIBLE IS THAT EVERY ONE OF US THINK FOR HIMSELF

A. Make truth your own.

1. *"Buy the truth, and sell it not; also wisdom, and instruction, and understanding,"* **Proverbs 23:23**. That means continual listening, paying attention, looking for inconsistencies, cautious of agendas, checking out references, and most of all continuously measuring the inflow against the divine standard of the Word of God, the Holy Bible.

2. Jesus said, *"Search the scriptures; for in them ye think ye have eternal life: and they are they which testify of me"* **John 5:39**. It's not enough to simply take the word of mother, daddy, the Sunday school teacher, the preacher, a well-known and trusted religious authority and celebrity or to simply take the church stance on the matter.

B. Here is a godly method for developing beliefs and convictions.

1. First, make God's Word the ultimate standard for all things.

   a. *"Let God be true, but every man a liar,"* **Romans 3:4**.

   b. *"For ever, O LORD, thy word is settled in heaven,"* **Psalm 119:89**.

   c. *"Heaven and earth shall pass away, but my words shall not pass away,"* **Matthew 24:35**.

2. Second, build your knowledge and understanding of God's Word; build a grid of truth into your life.

   a. Study God's Word. *"Study to shew thyself approved unto God, a workman that needeth not to be ashamed, rightly dividing the word of truth,"* **2 Timothy 2:15**.

b. Hide it in your heart. *"Thy word have I hid in mine heart, that I might not sin against thee"* **Psalm 119:11**.

c. It takes time to have it instantly available for use.

3. Examine/analyze all things in light of God's Word.

a. Listen to the Apostle John. *"Beloved, believe not every spirit, but try the spirits whether they are of God: because many false prophets are gone out into the world,"* **1 John 4:1**.

b. That's exactly what the Bereans did. *"They received the word with all readiness of mind, and searched the scriptures daily, whether those things were so,"* **Acts 17:11**.

C. Nowhere does the Bible highlight and magnify the importance of thinking for yourself better than in the example of the Berean.

1. *"The brethren immediately sent away Paul and Silas by night unto Berea: who coming thither went into the synagogue of the Jews. These were more noble than those in Thessalonica, in that they received the word with all readiness of mind, and searched the scriptures daily, whether those things were so,"* **Acts 17:10-11**.

2. The Bereans speak of a way of thinking; one that could rightfully be called ***the Berean Spirit***. The Bereans thought for themselves; analyzed, evaluated, checked out everything. No **ad hominem** thinking; not even when the speaker was Paul. Unless they could see it for themselves, they bought into nothing.

3. They were open-minded and looked, but what they heard rose or fell on its own merits. Everything had to square with the Scriptures.

There's a great old story of a pastor and guest preacher standing at the main door of a church shaking hands as people exited the building after a revival service. As a very well-known, talkative and outspoken young lady passed by, she said to the guest, *"I didn't like that sermon at all."* The guest preacher was visibly stunned. The lady worked the crowd a bit, got back in line and said, *"I believe that's the worst sermon I ever heard."* The big guy was now mesmerized. The young woman worked the crowd again and returned. This time, she said, *"You're the worst preacher I ever heard, and I hope you never come back here again."* Finally, the old pastor said to his guest, *"Don't pay any attention to her. She just repeats what she hears."*

This story strikes closer to home than most of us would dare to admit. Too many of God's people (like most of the world) basically believe what they've been taught and *repeat what they hear* from those who raised them or some lofty professor. Sadly, that's what they're passing on to the next generation.

Think for yourself, friend. Make it a lifestyle. Don't be conceited and proud about it; but listen, think for yourself, learn and stand on your own two feet.

Chapter 4

What God Wants from Every Person

This chapter is designed to synthesize major elements of true biblical Christianity. Though we rightfully study those elements individually, God's idea for His children is that they personify many elements of truth functioning simultaneously and in harmony. Christology is the cornerstone of Christianity; but a deep study of Christ apart from His work in Soteriology (the doctrine of salvation) will not help fallen sinners. The work of eternal redemption was never intended to be divorced from holy living and ecclesiology (the study of churches). Christ's First Coming is intricately tied to His Second Coming. *"No prophecy of the scripture is of any private interpretation,"* **2 Peter 1:20**. That simply means all Scripture is connected without contradiction or variance. It is not intended to be taken alone. Truth is inter-related.

God wants all people to be saved, but He also wants them to be baptized and become functional in one of His churches. He has a multifaceted, unified plan for all people; every person. He is not satisfied with any person until His plan is implemented in that person. He constantly works on people to bring them to be what He wants.

This chapter is quite simple; not at all profound. It is not high, lofty or sterile; but it is the heart of true Christianity. You're probably not going to read anything you don't already know. Hopefully you will gain a perspective that you do not yet have.

You read the title right. God wants these things for *"**every** person."* This sermon is for everybody; those who read this book, and those who don't. I am quite aware that most people will never be what God wants. They have their own ideas and plans for their lives. They will never submit themselves to the plan God has for them. That's sad. They will be the losers. Not only eternal life, but true joy and fulfillment in life come only in knowing and doing the will of God for your life. In this chapter, we will first look at three things God wants from every person. We will then put a face on what it means to become a mature Christian.

You should be aware that the key verse for this chapter is addressed to saved people, but it also reflects God's plan for those who are not saved. After exhorting God's people to pray for civil leaders, the divinely inspired apostle Paul expressed the will of God for all men. Hear it for yourself. *"For this is good and acceptable in the sight of God our Saviour; Who will have all men to be saved, and to come unto the knowledge of the truth,"* **1 Timothy 2:3-4**.

GOD WANTS THREE THINGS FROM EVERY PERSON

They are stated in writing. *"Jesus came and spake unto them, saying, All power is given unto me in heaven and in earth. Go ye therefore, and teach all nations, baptizing them in the name of the Father, and of the Son, and of the Holy Ghost: Teaching them to observe all things whatsoever I have commanded you: and, lo, I am with you alway, even unto the end of the world. Amen,"* **Matthew 28:19-20**.

A. God first wants every person to be saved.

1. *"Go ye therefore, and teach all nations"* is God's expressed desire that all people hear the gospel message and be saved. The gospel message is *"that Christ died for our sins according to the scriptures; And that he was buried, and that he rose again the third day according to the scriptures,"* **1 Corinthians 15:3-4**. It is this work of Jesus Christ that enables God to forgive and save condemned sinners. This work *"is the power of God unto salvation to every one that believeth; to the Jew first, and also to the Greek,"* **Romans 1:16**. No doubt about it; God wants every person to be saved, to be forgiven and receive eternal life. *"The Lord is not slack concerning his promise, as some men count slackness; but is longsuffering to us-ward, not willing that any should perish, but that all should come to repentance,"* **2 Peter 3:9**.

2. Because of sin, people who are not saved will spend eternity in the Lake of Fire. God doesn't want that to happen to anyone. God made that fact unmistakably clear, *"For God so loved the world, that he gave his only begotten Son, that whosoever believeth in him should not perish, but have everlasting life. For God sent not his Son into the world to condemn the world; but that the world through him might be saved,"* **John 3:16-17**. *"The Son of man is come to seek and to save that which was lost,"* **Luke 19:10**.

3. Though not every person is saved or ever will be, God wants all of them to be saved. Listen to Him: *"Come unto me, all ye that labour and are heavy laden, and I will give you rest,"* **Matthew 11:28**. *"And the Spirit and the bride say, Come. And let him that heareth say, Come. And let him that is athirst come. And whosoever will, let him take the water of life freely,"* **Revelation 22:17**. Being saved simply means coming in the heart to the realization and admittance that you are a sinner before God. It also means facing the fact that sin carries the death penalty. A lost person must see Jesus Christ as his only hope, so that person must give up on self (all personal efforts to merit the help of God). Jesus paid the death penalty, did all of the work to save sinners when He died, was buried and rose again. To be saved, a person must trust Christ. Yes, trust Him; not just believe the facts, but rely on Him as the only hope.

B. The second thing God wants from every person is that he be baptized.

1. Water baptism is God's way of identifying a person publicly with Him. Baptism is a public picture (a pantomime) of the death, burial and resurrection of Jesus Christ. *"We are buried with him by baptism into death: that like as Christ was raised up from the dead by the glory of the Father, even so we also should walk in newness of life,"* **Romans 6:4**. By your baptism you say the gospel is your only hope.

2. Baptism can't happen before you're saved, and still be valid. It must follow the point of salvation, the time when in the heart a person trusts Christ as personal Savior. With baptism, a person publicly affirms the gospel work of Christ as his only hope. The biblical example of the conversion of the Ethiopian man leaves no doubt as to the order of salvation

and baptism. Salvation had to be first. *"As they went on their way, they came unto a certain water: and the eunuch said, See, here is water; what doth hinder me to be baptized? And Philip said, If thou believest with all thine heart, thou mayest. And he answered and said, I believe that Jesus Christ is the Son of God. And he commanded the chariot to stand still: and they went down both into the water, both Philip and the eunuch; and he baptized him,"* **Acts 8:36-37**.

3. Baptism is the picture of a death, burial and resurrection. It must be by immersion for the picture to be right. The aforementioned example makes this fact clear. *"And he commanded the chariot to stand still: and they went down both into the water, both Philip and the eunuch; and he baptized him. And when they were come up out of the water, the Spirit of the Lord caught away Philip, that the eunuch saw him no more: and he went on his way rejoicing,"* **Acts 8:38-39**.

4. Baptism must be administered by a church doctrinally connected to the church which Jesus gave authority to baptize. He gave the authority to baptize to His church as a corporate organization, not to individuals. *"Go ye therefore, and teach all nations, baptizing them in the name of the Father, and of the Son, and of the Holy Ghost,"* **Matthew 28:19**. Through the centuries, individuals have come and gone. His corporate organization (the church) has endured, and will continue until He returns. *"Unto him be glory in the church by Christ Jesus throughout all ages, world without end. Amen,"* **Ephesians 3:21**. Note well the promise: *"throughout all ages, world without end."* That's a guarantee that His corporate body would continuously endure and make converts and baptize them until His return.

5. As in the case of the Jerusalem Church, baptism adds the new believer to the church which administers the baptism. *"They that gladly received his word were baptized: and the same day there were added unto them about three thousand souls . . . And the Lord added to the church daily such as should be saved,"* **Acts 2:41, 47**.

C. The third thing God wants for every person is that he grow-up to maturity.

1. That was evident when Jesus gave His purpose statement to His newly-formed church. *"Teaching them to observe all things whatsoever I have commanded you,"* **Matthew 28:20**. The

teaching that is to be done in the church should bring about growth to maturity.

2. The idea of natural growth and spiritual growth are parallel. The right path for every child is growth to natural maturity with maturity being the point where the child learns to do it for himself. The growth of a new believer should never stop short of maturity. Growth to maturity is the heart of discipleship and mentoring.

3. God's plan for every person is pretty straightforward and clear-cut: get saved, be baptized and then grow up to become a mature Christian.

A BRIEF VIEW OF WHAT IT MEANS TO BECOME A MATURE CHRISTIAN

A. To become a mature Christian means membership in one of the Lord's churches.

1. Jesus personally established His church as custodian of His spiritual work until His return. He said to Simon Peter, *"I say also unto thee, That thou art Peter, and upon this rock I will build my church; and the gates of hell shall not prevail against it. And I will give unto thee the keys of the kingdom of heaven: and whatsoever thou shalt bind on earth shall be bound in heaven: and whatsoever thou shalt loose on earth shall be loosed in heaven,"* **Matthew 16:18**. He gave the commission and the authority to His first church. Paul called it, *"The pillar and ground of the truth,"* **1 Timothy 3:15**. He also said that the work of God is to be done in and through it. *"Unto him be glory in the church by Christ Jesus throughout all ages, world without end. Amen,"* **Ephesians 3:21**.

2. Maturity means covenant relationship with other believers in a church; becoming a part of a church. It means joining a specific church, not merely attending or helping in it. Every church in the Bible was made up of members, people in covenant relationship and a part of the body. At least twelve times the word *"members"* is used to identify people who were in churches. It is impossible to be a mature Christian or what God wants from you apart from membership.

B. Maturity means becoming functional in one of the Lord's churches.

1. It means becoming involved, serving, giving of yourself to the welfare of the church. That means seeing yourself as a necessary part to a body much bigger than you. It means carrying your weight, contributing your part to it. *"Till we all come in the unity of the faith, and of the knowledge of the Son of God, unto a perfect man, unto the measure of the stature of the fulness of Christ: That we henceforth be no more children, tossed to and fro, and carried about with every wind of doctrine, by the sleight of men, and cunning craftiness, whereby they lie in wait to deceive; But speaking the truth in love, may grow up into him in all things, which is the head, even Christ: From whom the whole body fitly joined together and compacted by that which every joint supplieth, according to the effectual working in the measure of every part, maketh increase of the body unto the edifying of itself in love,"* **Ephesians 4:13-16**.

2. The Bible likens church members to members of the natural human body. *"For the body is not one member, but many. If the foot shall say, Because I am not the hand, I am not of the body; is it therefore not of the body? And if the ear shall say, Because I am not the eye, I am not of the body; is it therefore not of the body? If the whole body were an eye, where were the hearing? If the whole were hearing, where were the smelling? But now hath God set the members every one of them in the body, as it hath pleased him. And if they were all one member, where were the body? But now are they many members, yet but one body. And the eye cannot say unto the hand, I have no need of thee: nor again the head to the feet, I have no need of you. Nay, much more those members of the body, which seem to be more feeble, are necessary,"* **1 Corinthians 12:14-22**. In both the natural body and the church body, it is vital that all members work together in harmonious concert as a team with each member doing his or her part. Failure here can be devastating to both a physical body and to a church body.

3. God wants from all people deep engagement in the life of one of His churches. He wants church engagement in both worship and service.

C. Maturity also means becoming a practicing Christian.

1. God expects Christians to practice what they preach; to behave like a Christian. He says, *"So speak ye, and so do,"* **James 2:12**.

2. God wants no hypocrites. He wants all people to be saved and manifest true godly, holy living. He wants people to see integrity, good character, godly values and attitudes that reflect the spirit of Christ. He wants Bible Christianity to become our lifestyle, our way of living; not just an occasional Christian act. Here are His words: *"As he which hath called you is holy, so be ye holy in all manner of conversation,"* **1 Peter 1:15**.

D. Maturity means passing Christianity on to others.

1. Maturity is reproduction. People having children is an unquestionable mark of maturity. God said, *"Be fruitful and multiply,"* **Genesis 1:28**. God wants every person to reproduce both physically and spiritually.

2. Having spiritual children is bringing people to Christ, teaching others the truths of God and helping others to grow up in the Lord.

3. The concept of reproduction and spiritual maturity is everywhere in the Bible. Perhaps Paul said it best, *"The things that thou hast heard of me among many witnesses, the same commit thou to faithful men, who shall be able to teach others also,"* **2 Timothy 2:2**. Four generations of spiritual reproduction.

Obvious spiritual maturity is how maturity (the third aspect of the Great Commission) looks. Apart from membership and serious participation in one of the Lord's churches, Christlike day-to-day living and spiritual reproduction, it's hard to be identified as a mature Christian.

Be reminded that this chapter is about ***"What God Wants from Every Person."*** Yes, ***every person***. That means you. God wants you to be saved, to be baptized and to grow up to maturity. You have just seen the face of Christian Maturity. It is not vague, mystical or hard to see. It is (1) membership in one of His churches and (2) functional participation in that church. It is (3) living a godly Christian lifestyle and (4) reproducing yourself in the lives of others.

Everything God wants for every person is good, edifying and uplifting. Everything He wants gives meaning and purpose to life. Nothing He wants is unreasonable, evil or hard. God expressed His sentiments quite well in the first three verses of his hymnal. *"Blessed is the man that walketh not in the counsel of the ungodly, nor standeth in the way of sinners, nor sitteth in the seat of the scornful. But his delight is in the law of the LORD; and in his law doth he meditate day and night. And he shall be like a tree planted by the rivers of water, that bringeth forth his fruit in his season; his leaf also shall not wither; and whatsoever he doeth shall prosper,"* **Psalm 1:1-3**.

When it comes to what God wants from every person, where do you stand? Jesus said, *"If ye know these things, happy are ye if ye do them,"* **John 13:17**. Doing these simple things is what Paul called, *"doing the will of God from the heart,"* **Ephesians 6:6**. This is where fulfillment in life really is. I challenge every person reading these words to do what God wants from you: (1) trust Him as your Savior and be saved. (2) Identify with Him in baptism and become a part of one of His churches. (3) Grow up and become a mature Christian. That means (1) membership in a church, (2) active function in your church, (3) a godly lifestyle and (4) reproduction of yourself in others.

Chapter 5

Who We Are

Those who follow Jesus Christ are given this command. *"But sanctify the Lord God in your hearts: and be ready always to give an answer to every man that asketh you a reason of the hope that is in you with meekness and fear,"* **1 Peter 3:15**. Volumes of commentaries have been written on the Bible. Each of the 66 individual books of the Bible have several volumes of their own commentaries. The fact is that one chapter in any book can at best be a mere peek at the belief and practice system of a true Bible Christian.

Gaining a functional understanding of some things is a huge challenge; but with time, it can be done. People grow from babies to adults, and in that relatively short time they learn to function and compete well in society. Obviously, no person knows everything; but as people grow up, proficiency usually comes pretty quickly. Intelligent people have the capacity to comprehend and assimilate a working knowledge of most things necessary to their flourishing in a society. When a summary of a general concept or belief system is presented, without having to know a great many details, the big picture emerges in a comprehendible way. Whether or not the concept is fully embraceable may remain in question; however, it encourages further investigation.

This chapter gives a cursory overview of the Bible and of many who embrace God, the Bible and a serious approach to Christian living. While a great many questions will not be answered, a clear and definitive direction will be established. With one broad stroke, this chapter is going to define us, tell you who we are, give you an unmistakable answer for our identity: how we think, our world view and what guides our behavior.

MOST OF US WHO EMBRACE THIS MINDSET IDENTIFY WITH A CHURCH

A. During His earthly lifetime, Jesus personally established the institution which He called *"my church."*

1. He personally said, *"I will build my church; and the gates of hell shall not prevail against it,"* **Matthew 16:18**. The first Christian church to ever exist was in Jerusalem, Israel. All other legitimate churches find their roots in that church.

2. The Bible promised churches of that kind would continuously exist until the Second Coming of Jesus Christ. *"Unto him be glory in the church by Christ Jesus throughout all ages, world without end. Amen,"* **Ephesians 3:21**.

3. We who embrace the concepts set forth in this chapter seek membership in a church of this sort, and become a part of the institution Jesus established.

B. His church is not the property and buildings; it's the people who compose the church.

1. God owns everything including the property and people.

2. Jesus Christ is the head of this Church; He runs it and His Word is final. The Bible says, God has *"put all things under his feet, and gave him to be the head over all things to the church,"* **Ephesians 1:22**.

C. God defines His church as an ecclesia or called-out assembly. If it can't assemble, it can't be a *"church."*

1. To be a member, you must be a believer in the person and redemptive work of Jesus Christ. People who have not trusted Christ cannot be church members.

2. Water baptism is one's action statement of identification with Christ who died, was buried and rose again.

3. Baptized believers have covenanted together as one local, united body.

4. Churches exist for the specific purpose of getting people (1) saved, (2) baptized and (3) trained to maturity. Jesus commanded the first members of His first church, *"Go ye therefore, and teach all nations, baptizing them in the name of the Father, and of the Son, and of the Holy Ghost: Teaching them to observe all things whatsoever I have commanded you: and, lo, I am with you alway, even unto the end of the world. Amen,"* **Matthew 28:19-20**.

5. As a member of a church, every member is to be a functional part. *"From whom the whole body fitly joined together and compacted by that which every joint supplieth, according to the effectual working in the measure of every part, maketh increase of the body unto the edifying of itself in love,"* **Ephesians 4:16**.

THE BEDROCK CONVICTION THAT CONTROLS ALL WE BELIEVE, SAY AND DO IS THE BIBLE

"Thy word is true from the beginning: and every one of thy righteous judgments endureth for ever," **Psalm 119:160**.

A. **We believe the Bible is God's Word, and it is infallible.** *"All scripture is given by inspiration of God, and is profitable for doctrine, for reproof, for correction, for instruction in righteousness,"* **2 Timothy 3:16**.

   1. God used men to pen it, but it is His revelation. The apostle Paul said the Bible was given to him, the other apostles and the prophets by divine revelation. *"God hath revealed them unto us by his Spirit: for the Spirit searcheth all things, yea, the deep things of God,"* **1 Corinthians 2:10**.

   2. Furthermore, we believe He preserved it, and got accurate copies to us. Jesus said, *"Heaven and earth shall pass away, but my words shall not pass away,"* **Matthew 24:35**.

B. **The Bible is our final authority.**

   1. It controls us; we yield to it.

   2. We study diligently to get the author's intended message. Once we do, it's end of discussion. In a sound church, men are not guided by the opinions of men.

C. We know that we have a sound English translation of the Bible.

1. We refuse watered-down translations that vary from and defy the original Hebrew and Greek manuscripts.

2. We reject any translation that was not rooted in and translated from the Old Testament Masoretic Texts and the standardized Greek New Testament text, **Textus Receptus**.

THE TEACHINGS OF THE BIBLE ARE THE BASIS OF OUR BELIEFS ON ALL SUBJECTS

A. They are our doctrine, our worldview.

1. We don't know everything, and we are still learning; however, our fundamentals are set.

2. We will reason with anybody, but only in light of the Bible.

B. The great truths of the Bible are summarized under the headings of *"ologies."*

1. *"Ology"* refers to a subject of branch of knowledge.

2. *"Ology"* is a suffix. *Ology* added to a word indicates the branch of knowledge being studied.

C. The Bible is the greatest book of knowledge in existence. It addresses all subjects. An ancient way of approaching the Bible is by its major areas of knowledge. Since all of the Bible is ultimately about God, (there is no place where God is not), then the entire Bible is a book of theology.

1. *Theology* proper is the study of God. **Theos** is the chief Greek word for God. Hence, *theology* is the study of God.

   a. We believe God is one being in three persons. When Jesus was baptized, *"the Holy Ghost descended in a bodily shape like a dove upon him, and a voice came from heaven, which said, Thou art my beloved Son; in thee I am well pleased,"* **Luke 3:22**.

   b. We are aware that all we know of God comes from His self-revelation, the Bible. All other ideas of God are mere speculation.

2. *Bibliology* is the study of the Bible.

   a. We believe all of the Bible **is** the inspired Word of God. It does not merely contain the Word of God.

   b. We believe the Bible gives us all of the information we need to know and serve God acceptably. *"All scripture is given by inspiration of God, and is profitable for doctrine, for reproof, for correction, for instruction in righteousness: That the man of God may be perfect, throughly furnished unto all good works,"* **2 Timothy 3:16-17**.

3. *Christology* is the study of Jesus Christ.

   a. We believe Jesus Christ was fully God in flesh. Of Christ, the Bible says, *"In him dwelleth all the fulness of the Godhead bodily,"* **Colossians 2:9**.

   b. We believe Jesus Christ was the only person in all eternity who qualified to reconcile sinners to God. *"There is none other name under heaven given among men, whereby we must be saved,"* **Acts 4:12**.

4. *Pneumatology* is the study of the Holy Spirit of God.

   a. We believe the Holy Spirit is fully God with all of the powers of the Father and Son.

   b. We believe the Holy Spirit lives in every believer. *"If any man have not the Spirit of Christ, he is none of his,"* **Romans 8:9**.

5. *Angelology* is the study of angels.

   a. We believe God uses angels in many ways including to insure the welfare of believers. *"The angel of the LORD encampeth round about them that fear him, and delivereth them,"* **Psalm 34:7**.

   b. Angels are heavenly beings which are not mortal.

   c. Satan is a fallen angel who hates God, and he is the enemy of God and His people.

   d. Satan is the instigator of evil, and exploits the sinful nature of man. The Bible says, *"Your adversary the devil, as a roaring lion, walketh about, seeking whom he may devour,"* **1 Peter 5:8**.

e. Demons are fallen angels who do the bidding of Satan.

f. Demons are also enemies of God and His people.

6. *Soteriology* is the study of salvation.

a. Shortly after creation, man sinned and fell into condemnation. *"By one man sin entered into the world, and death by sin; and so death passed upon all men, for that all have sinned,"* **Romans 5:12**.

b. Consequently, all men are fallen creatures who are unable to save themselves from eternal damnation. *"For there is not a just man upon earth, that doeth good, and sinneth not,"* **Ecclesiastes 7:20**.

c. *Soteriology* is the study of how God brought believers back into a just relationship to Himself. *"When the fulness of the time was come, God sent forth his Son, made of a woman, made under the law, To redeem them that were under the law, that we might receive the adoption of sons,"* **Galatians 4:4-5**.

7. *Hamartiology* is the study of sin.

a. It's the study of what sin is, and of its consequences. *"All have sinned, and come short of the glory of God,"* **Romans 3:23**.

b. Sin entails the study of evil, pain and suffering, selfishness and death.

8. *Anthropology* is the study of man.

a. It's about man's sin and fall, and his fallen nature. *"They are all gone aside, they are all together become filthy: there is none that doeth good, no, not one,"* **Psalm 14:3**.

b. *Anthropology* is especially about man's need for a Savior.

9. *Ecclesiology* is the study of the church.

a. We believe Jesus personally established His church in His earthly lifetime. In speaking of Himself, He said, *"Upon this rock I will build my church; and the gates of hell shall not prevail against it,"* **Matthew 16:18**.

b. We believe that it is a called-out assembly of baptized believers who are covenanted together to carry Christ's great commission, and keep the ordinances: baptism, the Lord's Supper and the Lord's Day.

c. We believe churches will continue until He returns, and that it will constitute His bride when He returns. The Bible says, *"Unto him be glory in the church by Christ Jesus throughout all ages, world without end. Amen,"* **Ephesians 3:21**.

10. *Eschatology* is the study of events on God's prophetic calendar.

a. We believe that Jesus Christ is coming back. Jesus personally said, *"Let not your heart be troubled: ye believe in God, believe also in me. In my Father's house are many mansions: if it were not so, I would have told you. I go to prepare a place for you. And if I go and prepare a place for you, I will come again, and receive you unto myself; that where I am, there ye may be also,"* **John 14:1-3**. This is the glorious hope of all of us who know Jesus Christ as personal Savior. Those who do not know Him have no hope. None!

b. When He returns, dead believers will be raised from the dead, and get new bodies. Living believers will be transformed and given new, eternal bodies. *"For this we say unto you by the word of the Lord, that we which are alive and remain unto the coming of the Lord shall not prevent them which are asleep. For the Lord himself shall descend from heaven with a shout, with the voice of the archangel, and with the trump of God: and the dead in Christ shall rise first: Then we which are alive and remain shall be caught up together with them in the clouds, to meet the Lord in the air: and so shall we ever be with the Lord,"* **1 Thessalonians 4:15-17**.

c. God will banish Satan and *"cast him into the bottomless pit,"* **Revelation 20:3**, *"and there shall be no more curse,"* **Revelation 22:3**.

d. God's people will spend eternity with Him. *"And so shall we ever be with the Lord,"* **1 Thessalonians 4:17**.

D. These *ologies* address every area of existence.

1. They address Creation, the Great Flood and the coming destruction of the world by fire.

2. They address the family, government and the church.

3. They talk about heaven, hell, eternity past and eternity future.

4. They deal with good and evil, right and wrong and motives and the heart.

5. They are right on the cutting-edge of freedom, slavery, truth and the spiritual realm as well as the natural realm.

6. As King David marveled, *"O LORD, thou hast searched me, and known me. Thou knowest my downsitting and mine uprising, thou understandest my thought afar off. Thou compassest my path and my lying down, and art acquainted with all my ways. For there is not a word in my tongue, but, lo, O LORD, thou knowest it altogether. Thou hast beset me behind and before, and laid thine hand upon me. Such knowledge is too wonderful for me; it is high, I cannot attain unto it. Whither shall I go from thy spirit? or whither shall I flee from thy presence If I ascend up into heaven, thou art there: if I make my bed in hell, behold, thou art there,"* **Psalm 139:1-8**. The Apostle Paul mused, *"O the depth of the riches both of the wisdom and knowledge of God! how unsearchable are his judgments, and his ways past finding out!"* **Romans 11:33**.

WE BELIEVE OUR NUMBER ONE REASON FOR EXISTING IS TO REPRESENT JESUS CHRIST

A. He is our Savior. He said it clearly, *"I am the way, the truth, and the life: no man cometh unto the Father, but by me,"* **John 14:6**.

B. He's the only hope beyond the grave for any person.

C. We're committed to Him and what He's about.

1. We belong to Him, and our business is to be about what He's about. To all of us who know Him, He said, *"Ye shall be witnesses unto me both in Jerusalem, and in all Judaea, and in Samaria, and unto the uttermost part of the earth"* **Acts 1:8**.

2. This chapter has been about what real biblical Christianity is; not the shallow variety when the lifestyle shows little if any evidence of reality.

3. Knowing Christ personally in the heart is where real life is. It's about coming to the end of self, and embracing by faith Jesus Christ who died, was buried and rose again as your only hope. He will change your life both here and hereafter.

4. My earnest hope is that you will seriously look at who real Christians are, and that you come to Christ in your heart as your Savior and Lord. We would love for you to be a part of us.

Chapter 6

"When the Fullness of the Time Was Come"

(The Strategic Land of Israel in Jesus' Day)

Galatians 4:3-5

The land of Israel is the most unique and extra-ordinary piece of real estate on earth. It was especially that way at the time Jesus was here in bodily person. The Bible says, *"But when the fulness of the time was come, God sent forth his Son, made of a woman, made under the law, To redeem them that were under the law, that we might receive the adoption of sons,"* **Galatians 4:4-5**. Every word of Scripture is inspired of God and is important to the whole. There is far more to the claims and statements God makes than first meets the eye.

Why did Christ come to this place when He did? Notice the Galatians text mentions *"the fullness of the time,"* **Galatians 4:4**. The use of the article *"the"* denotes a particular time, not just any time. God had in mind a particular time to come. Jesus arrived at exactly the right time, a time like no other either before or since. To understand something of the gravity of this statement, it is necessary to know things about this land of Israel and about the conditions that prevailed when Jesus arrived.

THE LAND OF ISRAEL IS THE MOST UNIQUE PIECE OF REAL ESTATE ON EARTH

It was especially so at the time Jesus was here in bodily person.

A. At that time, there existed the most remarkable arrangement of population and economic centers of all of time.

(See maps at the end of the chapter)

1. Rome and its importance.

   a. The City of Rome is where the government of the whole Mediterranean world was centered, and it was the nerve center of the Western world at that time.

   b. There was always traffic within the City of Rome, and throughout the empire. Taxes were brought in from the entire empire. Roman officials and military personnel were constantly traveling between Rome and every province under her power. Reports, messages, news and commerce constantly flowed back and forth to and from Rome.

2. Egypt and its importance.

   a. Before and during the time of Christ, Egypt was one of the oldest and richest civilizations in the world. Her richness and wonders predate even Rome by over 2,000 years.

   b. The mighty Nile River with its fertile basin and temperate climate made Egypt a consistently prosperous and rich society. The rest of the world looked to her for agricultural products, paper and other commodities. The Genesis story of Joseph sheds much insight into the huge influence Egypt had over the civilized Western world of the day.

   c. Egypt connected the Roman and Mid-eastern societies to the rest of Africa, particularly Ethiopia and Northern Africa.

   d. Egypt was one of the greatest trade centers of the world in Jesus' day.

3. Mesopotamia and its importance.

a. The Tigris and Euphrates Rivers form what is known as *The Fertile Crescent.* According to the Bible and ancient history, civilization started and centered here following the Great Flood. From Nineveh to Babylon civilization and on to Shushan of Persia, this region flourished with riches and commerce. This was the West's connection to India and China.

b. From far before the time of Christ, the cultural and economic centers along the Mesopotamia Valley connected and maintained heavy contact with the centers in Egypt, Rome and Asia Minor.

4. Asia Minor and its importance.

a. This is the area along the north-eastern Mediterranean. In Bible days this area was known primarily as Galatia. Today this area is Turkey.

b. This area connects to the Balkan States. It reaches Greece toward the west and Russia toward the north. In Jesus' time, leading towns in this area were Tarsus, Antioch, Ephesus, Athens, Thessalonica and Corinth. These were heavy population centers with much commerce.

c. This is a rich Mediterranean area, especially along the coastal areas and up and down the many river basins.

B. The population dynamic and impact that existed in Jesus' day is without parallel.

1. This dynamic has never existed at any other time in the history of the world, and could never exist again. The emergence of steam and internal combustion engines have resulted in sea-worthy vessels, automobiles, trains and now air travel. Travel as it existed in Jesus' day has long been obsolete.

2. Furthermore, the population conditions which existed reached their zenith in Jesus' day and diminished thereafter. With changing travel, communication and other dynamics, even with a recovery of populations, conditions wouldn't be the same. In the history of mankind, the situation that existed in Jesus' day was a one-time occurrence.

THE *LAND BRIDGE* FACTOR

Israel was truly in the bull's-eye of the Roman picture.

A. Trade and trade routes.

1. All of these trade centers were in constant contact and commerce with each other. There was a large and continuous flow of people back and forth between them.
2. People travelling between these centers followed established roads and trade routes.
3. There are major reasons why so much traffic came through Israel.
   - **a.** A massive desert and an ocean formed a boundary around Israel. The Mediterranean Sea was to the West. The Arabian Desert was directly to the East. These huge travel obstacles forced traffic through the narrow strip of land which is Israel.
   - **b.** The modes of transportation in that day produced serious ramifications.
     - **1)** Boats were not highly sea-worthy. This forced more land traffic. It also forced ships to stay close to shore lines.
     - **2)** There was no motorized traffic. All land traffic was by foot or by beasts such as burros, camels, mules and horses.

B. Note the obvious. In Jesus' day most commerce between Egypt, Mesopotamia, Rome and Asia Minor was forced through Israel.

1. Because of its unique location and its connecting of three continents (Africa, Asia and Europe), in those days Israel was one of the busiest places on earth.

2. Jesus and His followers did not need to travel great distances to get His message out. The world literally came to Him. In His entire earthly life, Jesus never travelled much more than 100 miles from His birth-place. He didn't need to go anywhere. People from around the world came to Him and took His message back to their people. He truly was in the right place at the right time.

3. In a unique way that only God could arrange, the whole world came to Him. Truly, "*When the fulness of the time was come, God sent forth his Son, made of a woman, made under the law,*" **Galatians 4:4**.

4. Every word of Scripture is inspired of God, and is important to the whole of Scriptures. There is far more to the claims and statements God makes than first meets the eye. Don't miss the obvious. The Bible is trustworthy. In it the hand of God is constantly seen at work. You can believe what it says on all things including why Jesus came. Jesus came for a purpose. Note well, *"We . . . were in bondage under the elements of the world,"* but Jesus came *"to redeem them that were under the law, that we might receive the adoption of sons,"* **Galatians 4:3, 5**. The time and place are simply proof that the whole matter was and is of God.

THE POLITICAL CONDITIONS IN JESUS' DAY

A. There was only one ruling government over the whole Mediterranean world.

1. Rome ruled the entire Mediterranean world.

   a. Rome had no major rival at the time of Christ. Except for local uprisings, she ruled uncontested.

   b. The power of Rome to keep the peace. *Pax Ramano;* Latin for Roman Peace. It was a state of comparative tranquility throughout the Mediterranean world from the reign of Augustus (27 BC) to the reign of Marcus Aurelius (180 AD). Augustus laid the foundation for this period of concord, which also extended to North Africa and Persia.[1]

1) Rome ruled with an iron fist; conquered and eliminated all resistance.

2) The Roman Empire was made up of thousands upon thousands of small ethnic societies and regions. There was no single, large, unified power to be kept in check. Rome's careful vigil kept subdued parties from unifying.

3) Rome was ruthless, void of sympathy for any resistance. At the first sign of resistance, Rome moved to crush it. Roman soldiers were powerful. They were mostly above the law. They had standing authority to identify and strike down any person or group of persons who might pose any threat to Rome's authority.

4) Rome stationed fortresses and legions of soldiers in strategic spots which she suspected as trouble spots. The Antonia Fortress overlooking the Temple Mount is a case in point.

2. Rome was highly feared throughout the empire. Romans made spectacles and scapegoats out of offenders. They ruled by fear and wanted everybody to see what happened to anyone foolish enough to challenge her might. Thus, Rome crucified offenders; and she did it along-side the most heavily travelled highways. She let offenders hang there a long time for all to see.

3. It is not difficult to see the prevailing fear and attitude toward Rome. It was obvious in Ephesus. When an unlawful uprising occurred, the town clerk sternly warned the people that they were in jeopardy of being called into question by Rome. *"When the townclerk had appeased the people, he said, Ye men of Ephesus, what man is there that knoweth not how that the city of the Ephesians is a worshipper of the great goddess Diana, and of the image*

[1] https://www.britannica.com/event/Pax-Romana

which fell down from Jupiter? Seeing then that these things cannot be spoken against, ye ought to be quiet, and to do nothing rashly. For ye have brought hither these men, which are neither robbers of churches, nor yet blasphemers of your goddess. Wherefore if Demetrius, and the craftsmen which are with him, have a matter against any man, the law is open, and there are deputies: let them implead one another. But if ye enquire any thing concerning other matters, it shall be determined in a lawful assembly. For we are in danger to be called in question for this day's uproar, there being no cause whereby we may give an account of this concourse. And when he had thus spoken, he dismissed the assembly," **Acts 19:35-41.** Note well, *"We are in danger to be called in question for this day's uproar."* Such was the nature of Rome toward lawbreakers, including protesters.

B. The result was stability.

1. As a result of this heavy-handed approach, there was generally a prevailing stability throughout the entire Mediterranean world.

2. The brute force and muscle of Rome was able to keep relative peace and stability.

3. Adding to the stability is the fact that the Greeks ruled immediately before the Romans. When Rome conquered the Greeks, they adopted most of the Greek culture. It was called Hellenism. The Romans embraced the Greek gods, the Greek language and many other aspects of the Greek culture. This tended to produce even greater stability.

4. Thus, when Jesus entered the scene, He was in the one place on earth where the whole civilized world passed right by where He was in an era of unprecedented stability.

THE UNIQUE ROLE OF THE GREEK LANGUAGE IN JESUS' DAY

A. When Jesus arrived, Greek was the universal language.

1. There were many other languages, and they were spoken in various regions of the empire; but in addition to their native tongues, nearly everyone also spoke Greek.

2. It is not at all hard to grasp what this universal language did for communications and the spread of any message.

3. The particular form was Koine Greek. Many scholars agree with *The Illustrated Davis Dictionary of the Bible* which says, *"It excels in power of full and precise expression."* [2] There were several forms of Greek, including Classical Greek. Koine means *"common."* Koine Greek was the Greek of the common man, the *everyday* language of the Roman Empire. It was the form of Greek speaking and writing known and used by everybody.

B. The New Testament Scriptures were written in Koine Greek.

1. It is this common Koine Greek that is used in the Septuagint, the New Testament and the writings of the early church fathers.

2. No matter where the Scriptures went in the Roman world, they could be understood.

3. Furthermore, the Word of God does not belong only to the elite; it belongs to all men. The use of this marvelous language expresses God's love and concern for the common man as well as the sophisticated man.

C. The story and message of Christ spread like wildfire.

1. It happened in a unique way that only God could arrange for the whole world to come to Him.

2. Roman political power was so effective that it discouraged crime and made travel relatively safe.

3. The universal language provided just the right tool for the message of Jesus Christ to spread. The message of Christ soon *"turned the world upside down,"* **Acts 17:6**.

4. Jesus was truly in the right place at the right time with the perfect means for spreading His message. These conditions

---

[2] J. D. David, *Illustrated Davis Dictionary of the Bible,* Old Time Gospel Hour edition, s.v. "Greek," (Nashville, Tennessee: Royal Publishers, Inc. 1973), 293.

> never existed at any other time in the history of the world and they could never exist again. He truly came *"when the fulness of the time was come."*

There are multitudes of reasons to recognize that Jesus Christ was the Messiah, the only Savior there is. Reasons like these cannot be legitimately discounted.

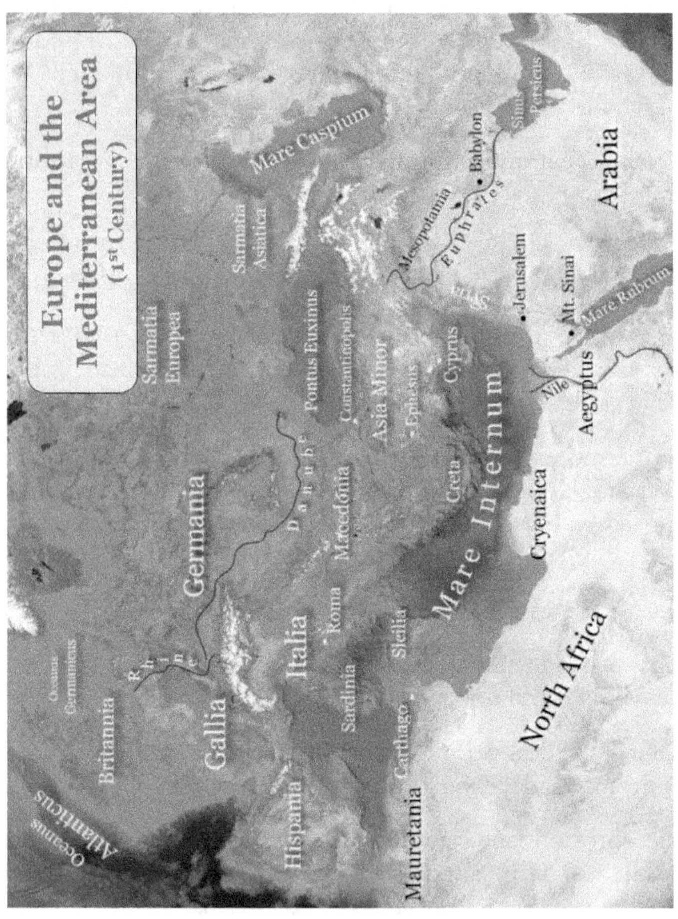

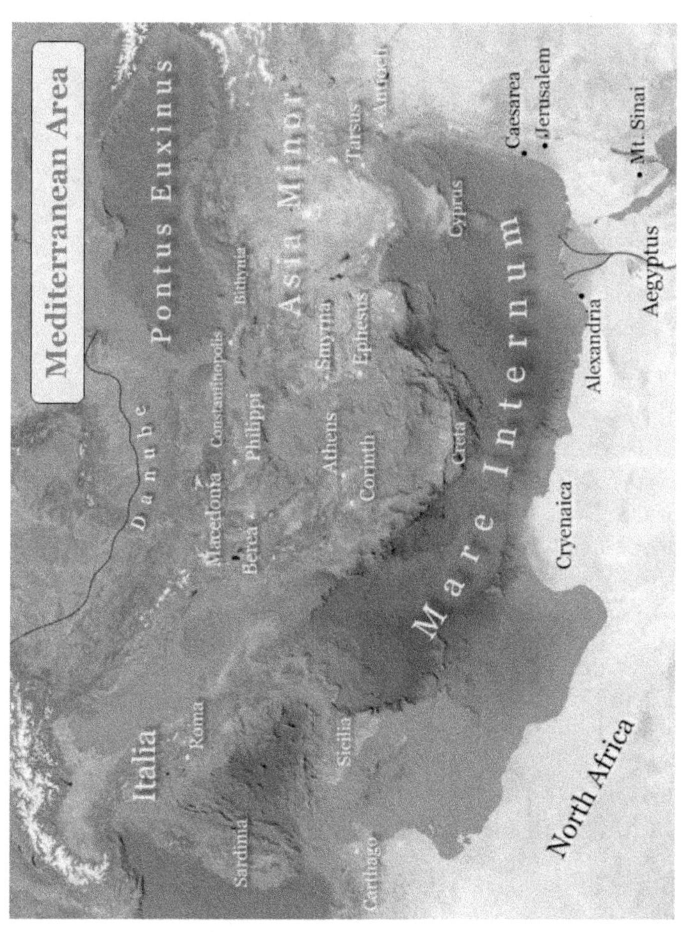
Mediterranean Area
Pontus Euxinus
Asia Minor
Mare Internum
Danube
Italia
Roma
Sardinia
Sicilia
Carthago
Macedonia
Berea
Philippi
Constantinopolis
Bithynia
Athens
Corinth
Smyrna
Ephesus
Creta
Tarsus
Antioch
Cyprus
Caesarea
Jerusalem
Mt. Sinai
Aegyptus
Alexandria
Cryenaica
North Africa

Chapter 7

A Chosen Land and a Chosen People

Deuteronomy 11:11-12

The land of Israel is the most unique and extra-ordinary piece of real estate on earth. To the people whom He chose for specific purposes God said of that land, *"But the land, whither ye go to possess it, is a land of hills and valleys, and drinketh water of the rain of heaven: A land which the LORD thy God careth for: the eyes of the LORD thy God are always upon it, from the beginning of the year even unto the end of the year,"* **Deuteronomy 11:11-12**.

This chapter is designed to give you a better understanding of how integral the Land of Israel and the Jewish people are in at least a few of God's plans. This is only a small glimpse of a much broader scope.

THE LAND OF ISRAEL IS A VERY SMALL PLACE

A. Its width is 85 miles at its widest point with a length of roughly 290 miles.[1]

1. It is 289 miles from Galveston, Texas to Dallas. Before you could drive from Houston to Beaumont, you'd cross Israel.

---

[1] https://embassies.gov.il/MFA/AboutIsrael/Maps/Pages/Israel-Size-and-Dimension.aspx

2. Israel has 8,630 square miles and is about the size of New Jersey. It would fit into the state of Maine almost four times.

3. Because of its small size, Israel is commonly viewed as a *Postage Stamp* country.

B. Israel is uniquely bordered on every side.

1. Located at the eastern end of the Mediterranean Sea, Israel is very Mid-eastern; yet European too. It is on the border of two worlds, the western and the eastern.

2. Three continents touch in Israel: Africa, Asia and Europe.

3. Israel is bordered by a big sea on the west (the Mediterranean) and by a big desert on the east (the Arabian). On its southern boundary is a large, barren wilderness (the Negev and Sinai). To its immediate north and northeast are powerful political Syrian enemies.

ISRAEL IS VERY SMALL, YET SHE HAS GREAT CLIMATIC AND GEOLOGICAL DIVERSITY

A. No place of its size on earth comes even close to its diversity.

1. The climate is distinctly Mediterranean, very nice and pleasant.

   a. It is in the Northern Hemisphere with almost the exact same latitude as Austin, Texas; 31 degrees.

   b. The air is dry and cool, with a mountainous feel.

2. On the west, its elevation is sea level with lovely Mediterranean beaches and coastal plains.

3. Along Israel's eastern border, which is only 20 to 70 miles inland from the Mediterranean Sea, is a part of the deepest rift on earth. Through this deep depression flows the Jordan River, which from start to finish is less than 156 miles. The Jordan River starts with three springs coming out from the foot of Mount Herman to the north. It empties into the Dead Sea to the south. Mount Herman is 9,232 feet high, and is generally covered at its top with snow year-round. The

surface of the Dead Sea is 1,368 below sea level. This is the lowest place on earth's surface.

4. In the center of the country, running north to south, is a ridge or backbone of mountains rising to over 3,000 feet above sea level. They are full of valleys, springs and lush pastures. This is some of the greatest sheep-raising country in the world.

5. To the south in Israel is the barren, rugged Judean Wilderness.

6. Where the hills break into the Jordan Rift is an unparalleled formation of canyons, cliffs, gorges, caves and badlands.

7. In the north is a triangular valley, approximately 35 miles on a side; it is the greatest single farming spot on earth. Climate, water, soil, temperature and everything there is just right for farming and agriculture.

B. The land itself preaches many messages.

1. When God was ready to bring Israel out of Egyptian bondage, He said to Moses, *"I am come down to deliver them out of the hand of the Egyptians, and to bring them up out of that land unto a good land and a large, unto a land flowing with milk and honey,"* **Exodus 3:8**. This land is truly a spiritual picture of God's provision for those who follow Him and dwell where He wants them to dwell.

2. Before bringing them into this land, God informed the people of Israel, *"the land, whither ye go to possess it, is a land of hills and valleys, and drinketh water of the rain of heaven: A land which the LORD thy God careth for: the eyes of the LORD thy God are always upon it, from the beginning of the year even unto the end of the year,"* **Deuteronomy 11:11-12**. The message is that life will always be a series of ups and downs, with very few level places. Even so, God always knows where we are in life; and His grace will always be sufficient. He promises His people, *"There hath no temptation taken you but such as is common to man: but God is faithful, who will not suffer you to be tempted above that ye are able; but will with the temptation also make a way to escape, that ye may be able to bear it,"* **1 Corinthians 10:13**.

3. Nothing lives in the Dead Sea. The Jordan River flows into it, but the Dead Sea has no outlet. This Dead Sea speaks of those who take in, but who never give.

4. God said, *"And of Zion it shall be said, This and that man was born in her: and the highest himself shall establish her. The LORD shall count, when he writeth up the people, that this man was born there. Selah. As well the singers as the players on instruments shall be there: all my springs are in thee,"* **Psalm 87:5-7**. God gives Israel early and late rains, and the wonderful waters of the Sea of Galilee are sufficient to water the whole country.

   All around her is desert and a salty sea, yet this little place blooms like a rose in the desert. What a picture of the difference water makes! Jesus said, *"Whosoever drinketh of the water that I shall give him shall never thirst; but the water that I shall give him shall be in him a well of water springing up into everlasting life,"* **John 4:14**. He is the water of life; and without Him, there is no spiritual life.

5. Jerusalem is the highest place in the land and is called *"the city of God,"* **Psalm 46:4**. What a message! You can go no higher than the presence of God. When you dwell where He is, you are at the top.

FOR RICHNESS, ISRAEL IS UNPARALLELED BY ANY NATION CLOSE TO ITS SIZE

A. This is the place where the desert truly blooms.

1. Israel is the breadbasket of Europe. Her tomatoes, oranges, bananas, wheat, melons and other produce have fed much of Europe for centuries.

2. In Israel you will see citrus fruits such as the famous Jaffa orange growing side by side with peaches and apples. There are grapes, avocados, almonds, olives, figs, persimmons and pomegranates.

3. Poultry is big in Israel. Winter flowers from the Jordan Valley are exported world-wide.

4. Her farming techniques such as drip irrigation, plastic sheeting use in farming, agricultural genetic research and communal farming concepts are the envy and export of the world.

5. In winter the Jordan Valley below the Sea of Galilee is uniquely warmer than all its surroundings, often by as many as 20 degrees. While it is too cold to farm the higher elevations, in the dead of winter this rich valley flourishes with produce and flowers.

B. This little nation has had an enormous impact on the world.

1. Despite tremendous obstacles and opposition since its birth as a modern state, the GNP of Israel has grown at close to 10% annually.

2. Most years close to 4 million tourists visit Israel.

3. Though there are no diamond mines in Israel, approximately 50% of the cut diamonds sold in the world are cut in Israel.

4. There is enough potash in the Dead Sea to meet all the world's fertilizer needs for many years. Israel is one of the world's largest producers of potassium salts, including table salts. One of the biggest salt works in the world is at the southern end of the Dead Sea.

5. The Jews are leaders in technology which has impacted the modern world. Most people are aware of her famous Uzi machine gun. Israel is big in computers including programming, extracting minerals from salt water, producing fresh water from salt water, steel manufacturing and cement works.

6. The whole world is keenly aware of Israel's military might and of her strategic role in world affairs.

GOD HAS NOT ONLY BLESSED THIS LAND, HE HAS ALSO BLESSED THIS PEOPLE

A. God specifically raised up this people to be His own in a unique way. Here is one of the oldest prophecies in the Bible. It is God's promise to Abraham, the father of the Jews. *"Now the*

LORD had said unto Abram, Get thee out of thy country, and from thy kindred, and from thy father's house, unto a land that I will show thee: And I will make of thee a great nation, and I will bless thee, and make thy name great; and thou shalt be a blessing: And I will bless them that bless thee, and curse him that curseth thee: and in thee shall all families of the earth be blessed," **Genesis 12:1-3**. Here is another promise from God, *"For thou art an holy people unto the LORD thy God, and the LORD hath chosen thee to be a peculiar people unto himself, above all the nations that are upon the earth,"* **Deuteronomy 14:2**.

1. **To this people God gave the land of Canaan.** *"The LORD made a covenant with Abram, saying, Unto thy seed have I given this land, from the river of Egypt unto the great river, the river Euphrates,"* **Genesis 15:18**.

2. **To this people God gave the holy Scriptures.** *"What advantage then hath the Jew? or what profit is there of circumcision? Much every way: chiefly, because that unto them were committed the oracles of God,"* **Romans 3:1-2**.

3. **The greatest honor of all to Israel was Jesus Christ**, God in flesh, the Savior. When God came into the world in flesh to save sinners, He came to the Jews. *"He came unto his own, and his own received him not,"* **John 1:11**.

B. The preservation of the Jewish people is one of the most remarkable stories in all of history.

(This is not a detailed account; it is a brief summary. Nothing like this has ever happened with any other people.)

1. Beginning with Abraham, God raised up this people from a world of paganism. Remember **Genesis 12:1-3**.

2. Jacob who was Abraham's grandson took Israel to Egypt. There God nurtured them into a great people. **Genesis** tells the story.

3. When they grew strong, God brought Israel out of Egypt with a strong arm and planted them in this land of Canaan. He brought them to power and glory as the envy of all the nations around them.

4. In spite of all His goodness to them, this people rejected God and all His ways. Listen to the Bible's description: *"But they mocked the messengers of God, and despised his words, and misused his prophets, until the wrath of the LORD arose against his people, till there was no remedy,"* **2 Chronicles 36:16**.

5. God then brought enemy after enemy until this people were removed from the land in shame and bondage. They spent 70 years in exile in Babylon. Finally, they came back to the land, but remained under foreign dominance past the time of Christ.

6. In A.D. 70 these Jews rebelled against their Roman rulers. Under the Roman general Titus, Roman troops destroyed Jerusalem, killed multitudes of Jews and exiled all the rest. Jews fled in every direction, especially throughout Europe. The land was taken by Arabs.

7. For centuries that followed, Jews had no place to call home. They were hated everywhere they went. They were driven out of many countries and persecuted mercilessly.

- **a.** When the Bubonic Plague struck Europe, the Jews were blamed. Because of their adherence to the sanitation and food laws of Moses, they suffered least from the plague. Because they were prosperous, they were resented. These factors made multitudes see them as the source of the plague. Massive rounds of persecutions were the result.
- **b.** Long before Nazi Germany, Jews suffered atrocities.
- **c.** The Holocaust of Nazi Germany is a well-documented fact.

8. It was only in 1948 that a modern Jewish state was re-established and the Jews had a place to call home. For 1,878 years the Jews had neither a center of government nor a homeland, yet they managed to keep their identity, maintain their heritage and preserve a nationality.

- **a.** In all other cases where a people has been uprooted and thrown in with other peoples for long periods of time, that people has lost its identity.
- **b.** Inter-racial marriages, a mixing of cultures, a loss of nationalism and loss of nationalistic vision and hope

have dissolved nationalities. They have been swallowed up in other societies, and ceased to exist as a distinct and pure people.

c. That did not happen with the Jew. Against tremendous odds over vast centuries of time, the Jew survived and is again flourishing in his land this very day.

The eye of God is on this place and this people. He has preserved them and smiled on this land. They are God's chosen people and this is God's chosen land. God forbid that any one of us or America ever turn against Israel! God said to them, *"For thou art an holy people unto the LORD thy God: the LORD thy God hath chosen thee to be a special people unto himself, above all people that are upon the face of the earth,"* **Deuteronomy 7:6**. Nowhere has God rescinded that statement.

He loves the Gentiles, but Israel is still His natural branch, His people according to the flesh. One day, this people shall rule as the head of all nations in a great Millennial Reign. God's promise to Abraham was unconditional and immutable. God reaffirmed it to Moses and those who God had freed from Egypt: *"Ye stand this day all of you before the LORD your God; your captains of your tribes, your elders, and your officers, with all the men of Israel, Your little ones, your wives, and thy stranger that is in thy camp, from the hewer of thy wood unto the drawer of thy water: That thou shouldest enter into covenant with the LORD thy God, and into his oath, which the LORD thy God maketh with thee this day: That he may establish thee to day for a people unto himself, and that he may be unto thee a God, as he hath said unto thee, and as he hath sworn unto thy fathers, to Abraham, to Isaac, and to Jacob. Neither with you only do I make this covenant and this oath; But with him that standeth here with us this day before the LORD our God, and also with him that is not here with us this day,"* **Deuteronomy 29:10-15**.

The Jews are a great people in a great land. Let us never forget who they are. May every one of us respect them highly.

Chapter 8

"He Made Himself of No Reputation"

(The kenosis)

Philippians 2:7

"In the beginning was the Word, and the Word was with God, and the Word was God...And the Word was made flesh, and dwelt among us, (and we beheld his glory, the glory as of the only begotten of the Father,) full of grace and truth," **John 1:1-14**. What a wonderful statement; but what a complex, mind-challenging affirmation! God as man! How can that be?

The Bible says, *"Let this mind be in you, which was also in Christ Jesus: Who, being in the form of God, thought it not robbery to be equal with God: But made himself of no reputation, and took upon him the form of a servant, and was made in the likeness of men: And being found in fashion as a man, he humbled himself, and became obedient unto death, even the death of the cross. Wherefore God also hath highly exalted him, and given him a name which is above every name: That at the name of Jesus every knee should bow, of things in heaven, and things in earth, and things under the earth; And that every tongue should confess that Jesus Christ is Lord, to the glory of God the Father,"* **Philippians 2:5-11**.

When Paul wrote that Jesus *"made himself of no reputation"* (vs. 7), he used the Greek word **kenoo** (ken-o'-o). The Greek combination **heauton ekenose** literally means *emptied himself.* This is generally known as the **kenosis**. Both *The Interlinear Greek-English New Testament*[1] and *The Zondervan Parallel New Testament in Greek and English*[2] literally translate *"made himself of no reputation"* as *"himself emptied."*

HOW COULD JESUS GIVE UP ANYTHING AND STILL BE GOD?

A. God, by His very nature, is perfect, complete, lacking in nothing.

1. God is immutable.

a. That means He does not and cannot change. His own words are, *"I am the LORD, I change not,"* **Malachi 3:6**. Jesus Christ was God, and thus it is said of Him, *"Jesus Christ the same yesterday, and to day, and for ever,"* **Hebrews 13:8**. The same book says He has *"an unchangeable priesthood,"* **Hebrews 7:24**.

b. God is unchangeable in duration. He is eternal. *"Now unto the King eternal, immortal, invisible, the only wise God, be honour and glory for ever and ever. Amen,"* **1 Timothy 1:17**.

c. God is unchangeable in His nature. James spoke of Him *"with whom is no variableness, neither shadow of turning,"* **James 1:17**.

d. God is unchangeable in His will. Job said, *"...he is in one mind, and who can turn him?"* **Job 23:13**.

e. God is unchangeable in His character. His *justice* never changes, **Romans 2:2**, His *truth* never changes, **2 Timothy 2:13**, His *holiness* never changes, **Job 34:10**, His *knowledge* never changes, **Isaiah 40:13-14**, and His *mercy* never changes, **Lamentations 3:22-23**. Aren't you glad!

2. It is impossible to improve on that which is perfect and to diminish anything is to make it less than perfect. God never

[1] George Ricker Berry, *The Interlinear Greek-English New Testament,* (Grand Rapids: Zondervan, 1974), 515.

[2] The Committee on Bible Translation, *The Zondervan Parallel New Testament in Greek and English,* (Grand Rapids: Zondervan, 1981), 578-579.

improves. To say that He does implies that before He improved, He was something less. God was or is never less than perfect, and He never learns anything. To say God learned is to imply that there was a time when He didn't know; however, God is omniscient. He always knows all things. *"Neither is there any creature that is not manifest in his sight: but all things are naked and opened unto the eyes of him with whom we have to do,"* **Hebrews 4:13**.

(Hebrews says of Jesus that *"Though he were a Son, yet learned he obedience by the things which he suffered,"* **Hebrews 5:8**. He *"learned"* in the sense of *personally experienced*, not in the sense that He acquired knowledge of something He didn't previously know. When verse 9 of the same chapter says He was *"made perfect,"* the passage is establishing the fact that He personally executed His own plan of redemption and thereby became experimentally qualified in all regards as the perfect redeemer. Previously, He was not lacking perfection in any sense of who He was, but He had not yet personally executed His eternal plan of redemption of which He had forever known every detail.)

God does not learn, forget, remember or deal with information or knowledge as do mortals. God knows everything possible all of the time. With God there is no past, present or future. God is! God always is! Everything is always present tense with God. When Moses asked His name, God said, *"I AM THAT I AM: and he said, Thus shalt thou say unto the children of Israel, I AM hath sent me unto you,"* **Exodus 3:14**. The Hebrew verb is *to be.* God simply **is**, always perfect in every regard. Jesus who was and is God thus said, *"Verily, verily, I say unto you, Before Abraham was, I am,"* **John 8:58**.

B. If Jesus emptied Himself, gave up anything, was He really God?

1. The Scriptures say He did empty Himself.

a. He *"...made himself of no reputation...,"* **Philippians 2:7**. This Scripture is there, under divine inspiration, and cannot be denied or ignored.

b. To rob Jesus of any attribute of God is to rob Him of deity. He's either all God or no god at all *"For there is"* only *"one God, and"* the Scriptures affirm Him to be *"the man Christ Jesus,"* **1 Timothy 2:5**.

2. Yet! The Scriptures say that Jesus Christ was God.

a. Remember what John affirmed: *"In the beginning was the Word, and the Word was with God, and the Word was God...And the Word was made flesh, and dwelt among us, (and we beheld his glory, the glory as of the only begotten of the Father,) full of grace and truth,"* **John 1:1,14**. There can be no question from the context that the person of this passage is Jesus Christ.

b. Remember also that Jesus affirmed Himself to be the eternal *"I am"* who predated Abraham, **John 8:58**.

c. The first verse of the Bible says, *"In the beginning God created the heaven and the earth,"* **Genesis 1:1**. The Book of Hebrews 1 discusses the same event (Creation) and Jesus Christ. *"And, Thou, Lord, in the beginning hast laid the foundation of the earth; and the heavens are the works of thine hands,"* **Hebrews 1:10**.

d. Jesus was conceived of the Holy Spirit without an earthly father, **Matthew 1:18-25**, and was virgin born, **Luke 1:26-28** with **Luke 2:4-14**. Thus, Jesus is referred to as *"Emmanuel, which being interpreted is, God with us,"* **Matthew 1:23**.

3. Jesus Christ was and is the Jehovah God of the Old Testament. When Jesus came, undiminished deity touched limited humanity, a human nature was experientially added to the divine nature and in Him was perfect God and perfect man.

IN WHAT WAY DID JESUS CHRIST EMPTY HIMSELF WITHOUT DESTROYING HIS DEITY?

A. He veiled His glory.

1. When God became man in Jesus Christ, He hid His glory.

a. No man can see God and live. The Scriptures say, *"No man hath seen God at any time,"* **1 John 4:12**. When Moses desired to see the Lord, God said, *"Thou canst not see my face: for there shall no man see me, and live,"* **Exodus 33:20**.

b. Even so, man can know what God is like. Though he cannot actually *see* God, he can know and experience the presence of God. John put it this way, *"No man hath seen God at any time; the only begotten Son, which is in the bosom of the Father, he hath declared him,"* **John 1:18**. Isaiah did not see God but he experienced God's presence. When he did, he cried out, *"Woe is me! for I am undone; because I am a man of unclean lips, and I dwell in the midst of a people of unclean lips: for mine eyes have seen the King, the LORD of hosts,"* **Isaiah 6:5**. When John had a similar experience on Patmos, he said, *"And when I saw him, I fell at his feet as dead,"* **Revelation 1:17**.

2. John gave the most concise of all statements about the incarnation in which the glory of God was veiled. *"The Word was made flesh, and dwelt among us, (and we beheld his glory, the glory as of the only begotten of the Father,) full of grace and truth,"* **John 1:14**.

a. *"Dwelt"* is translated from the Greek word <u>skenoo</u> which literally means *to tabernacle* or *to pitch one's tent.*

b. Jesus Christ was God *tabernacled* among men, not in a tent of goat or calf skins, but in a tent or body of human flesh. The divine glory of God was veiled in the man Jesus.

c. Even as God dwelt in the Old Testament Tabernacle and men saw the evidence of His reality and presence, likewise God dwelt in the body of Jesus Christ and men saw the evidence of His reality and presence. They saw that evidence in His (1) word and in His (2) works.

3. In the transfiguration of Jesus Christ, **Matthew 17:1-8**, Peter, James and John received a brief glimpse of glory that they had not seen day by day with Jesus. When even a part of the veil was lifted, they could not look on Him, but rather fell on their faces. Jesus, *"was transfigured before them: and his face did shine as the sun, and his raiment was white as the light,"* **verse 2**. It is clear that He possessed glory not routinely revealed in His life on earth. They didn't see it because it was veiled, not because it didn't exist. It was there, but veiled in flesh. Jesus knew it and thus prayed, *"And now, O Father, glorify thou me with thine own self with the glory which I had with thee before the world was,"* **John 17:5**.

4. As the Old Testament tabernacle was the place of legal redemption for the Jews, even so Jesus Christ is the place of eternal redemption for all who come to Him. He was the place where God and man met in one. As one theologian has said, *"If Christ is not in the same person both God and man, he either could not die, or his death could not avail."*[3] How true! Had He been only God and not man, He could never have died. Had He been only man and not God, His death would have been of no avail. As God/man, He could both die and satisfy the demands of the holy God against fallen sinners. This is precisely the point of Hebrews, *"But Christ being come an high priest of good things to come, by a greater and more perfect tabernacle, not made with hands, that is to say, not of this building; Neither by the blood of goats and calves, but by his own blood he entered in once into the holy place, having obtained eternal redemption for us,"* **Hebrews 9:11-12**.

5. Yes! God veiled His glory when He came to earth and He did it that He might redeem us from the curse of sin. There was no other way. Only God/man could do it. In order to do it, He didn't give up anything that God is. Instead, He emptied Himself, veiled His glory in such a way that He could dwell among men without every one of them being destroyed at His glorious presence.

B. He also emptied Himself in that He voluntarily submitted to the limitations of humanity.

1. Before His birth, heaven was His throne and He travelled the universe at will. In the flesh, Jesus was limited to the distance a man can walk. The Son of God, who created water, voluntarily lived in a body and got thirsty.[4] He, who grew the

---

[3] Archibald Alexander Hodge, *Outlines of Theology,* (New York: Robert Carter and Brothers, 1867), 288.

[4] Elmer L. Towns, *Theology for Today,* (Orlando, Florida: Harcourt Custom Publishers, 1999), 140.

tree, was crucified on it. Like other men, Jesus grew hungry, **Matthew 4:2**, got tired and thirsty, **John 4:6-7**, needed sleep, **Mark 4:38**, and felt pressure and pain, **Luke 22:44**.

2. Jesus was born just like other humans, **Matthew 1:18**, and grew up just as other children grow, **Luke 2:40**.

3. In His redemptive work, which necessitated His becoming God/man, God the Son was willing to *humble himself,* **Philippians 2:8**. He willfully *emptied himself,* **Philippians 2:7**, by taking on, for that period of time, the limitations of humanity. He *"was in all points tempted like as we are, yet without sin,"* **Hebrews 4:15**. That does not mean He was any less God. When an agile person agrees to stand still for five minutes, there is no reason for anyone to conclude that he has lost any of his agility or ability to move. When God agreed to the limitations of humanity He was still just as much God as ever.

C. Jesus' emptying of Himself also means that He voluntarily surrendered the use of His comparative attributes during His earthly ministry.

1. There are three attributes of God that are generally known as His comparative attributes.

a. He is *omnipotent* or all powerful. *"Our God is in the heavens: he hath done whatsoever he hath pleased,"* **Psalm 115:3**.

b. He is *omnipresent* or ever present in all places. *"Whither shall I go from thy spirit? or whither shall I flee from thy presence? If I ascend up into heaven, thou art there: if I make my bed in hell, behold, thou art there. If I take the wings of the morning, and dwell in the uttermost parts of the sea; Even there shall thy hand lead me, and thy right hand shall hold me. If I say, Surely the darkness shall cover me; even the night shall be light about me. Yea, the darkness hideth not from thee; but the night shineth as the day: the darkness and the light are both alike to thee,"* **Psalm 139:7-12**.

c. He is *omniscient* or all knowing. *"Remember the former things of old: for I am God, and there is none else; I am God, and there is none like me, Declaring the end from the beginning, and from* *ancient times the things that are not yet done, saying, My counsel shall stand, and I will do all my pleasure,"* **Isaiah 46:9-10**.

2. While God was on earth in a human body, He possessed each of these attributes and periodically exercised each one.

a. The miracles such as calming the storm, **Mark 4:39-40**, and the raising of Lazarus from the dead, **John 11:43-44**, prove his omnipotence.

b. Jesus spoke of His *"abode"* along with the Father in every believer, **John 14:23**. Before His ascension He spoke with some of His disciples and they didn't realize it was Him. Once they recognized Him, *"he vanished out of their sight,"* **Luke 24:31**. He is omnipresent. The meeting with Thomas further verifies that fact, **John 20:24-29**.

c. In the Garden of Gethsemane Jesus demonstrated His omniscience when Judas and the soldiers came for Him. *"Jesus therefore, knowing all things that should come upon him, went forth, and said unto them, Whom seek ye?"* **John 18:4**. *"Knowing all things"* is a statement that He was omniscient.

3. On earth, Jesus Christ possessed and exercised every comparative attribute of God, but He always did so by the power of the Holy Spirit. He never did so by the exercise of His own will independently of the Holy Spirit.

a. He applied the prophecy of **Isaiah 61:1-2** directly to Himself. Note well that He loosely quoted the Isaiah passage using the first person. *"The Spirit of the Lord is upon me, because he hath anointed me to preach the gospel to the poor; he hath sent me to heal the brokenhearted, to preach deliverance to the captives, and recovering of sight to the blind, to set at liberty them that are bruised, To preach the acceptable year of the Lord,"* **Luke 4:18-19**. Note that He said, *"The Spirit of the Lord is upon me."* The Jews present in the synagogue immediately got Jesus' point. For applying that Scripture to Himself, they accused Him of blasphemy and attempted to kill Him.

b. Jesus clearly made the point in **Matthew 12:28**. He said that He cast out devils through the power of the Holy Spirit. *"...I cast out devils by the Spirit of God...."*

On earth Jesus operated by the will of the Father and in the power of the Holy Spirit. He said, *"For I came down from heaven, not to do mine own will, but the will of him that sent me,"* **John 6:38**. He further emphasized that truth: *"When ye have lifted up the Son of man, then shall ye know that I am he, and that I do nothing of myself; but as my Father hath taught me, I speak these things. And he that sent me is with me: the Father hath not left me alone; for I do always those things that please him,"* **John 8:28-29**.

4. Jesus exercised His comparative attributes only at the will of the Father through the Holy Spirit. In view of that reality, He said that a rejection of the mighty works He did through the Spirit was *"blasphemy against the Holy Ghost."* He said that sin would never be forgiven, **Matthew 12:31-32**. Those who saw Him do those mighty works by the Holy Spirit, and accredited those works to Satan committed the unpardonable sin, and that sin would never be forgiven.

God did not give up His comparative attributes when He came to dwell on earth in a tabernacle of flesh. He merely exercised them for that period only through the Holy Spirit.

Jesus *"made himself of no reputation"* or *emptied himself,* **Philippians 2:7**. He did not cease to be God or give up anything God is. He, being God, merely arranged Himself in such a way for it to be possible for man to be in His presence without destruction. Had He not *emptied himself,* every person in His presence would have died. Had He not *emptied himself,* He could not have purchased man's redemption for redemption necessitated the work of God/man and Jesus Christ was God/man. He's the only God/man there has ever been or ever will be.

It is noteworthy that the ascension of Jesus Christ, **Acts 1:9-11**, ended the time of His emptying of Himself. From that point forward (1) His glory is no longer veiled, (2) He is no longer subject to the limitations of humanity and (3) He has personal and full exercise of all of His comparative attributes.

Chapter 9

Was Jesus Really the Messiah, the Son of God?

John 5:31-39

Jesus personally raised the question about who He was: *"Whom do men say that I, the Son of man, am?"* His disciples answered, *"Some say that thou art John the Baptist: some, Elias; and others, Jeremias, or one of the prophets."*

Since Jesus was born of a virgin there has been controversy over who He really was. The Pharisees insinuated that he was *"born of fornication,"* **John 8:41**. *Your mother had you out of wedlock; you're illegitimate.* That's what many "higher critics" still say. Higher criticism does not approach the Scriptures as inspired. Despite the Scripture's claims of divine inspiration, higher critics approach the Bible as they would any other book.[1] For example, though it is clear from the content of the books bearing their names that Matthew, Mark, Luke and John wrote the first four books of the New Testament, based on language styles, suppositions and other subjective considerations, *higher critics* conclude that those books were written by communities of *"Christians"* several generations after Christ; not the apostles. *Naturalists* believe all things can be explained *naturally*. They do not

[1] https://www.encyclopedia.com/philosophy-and-religion/christianity/protestant-christianity/higher-criticism

believe in God or anything *supernatural.* Thus, regardless of the evidence, they do not accept miracles and the divine including *divine revelation.* They rule out the Virgin Birth and the resurrection; and make Jesus nothing more than an ordinary man.[2] Postmodernists bristle at the exclusive claim that Jesus alone can save sinners.

Jesus Christ believed He was the Messiah, God in flesh, the great *"I AM"* of the Bible. On one occasion Jesus met a woman of Samaria at Jacob's Well. She was quite aware that the Scriptures contained many predictions about the coming Messiah. She said to Jesus, *"I know that Messias cometh, which is called Christ: when he is come, he will tell us all things,"* **John 4:25**. Jesus answered her, *"I that speak unto thee am he,"* **John 4:26**. There was no doubt in His mind that He was the Christ, the promised Savior of the world.

Suddenly Jesus was heart-to-heart with His disciples. *"He saith unto them, But whom say ye that I am?"* What do you say? Who was He, just a great moral teacher, an extraordinary man but not God? As this drama unfolded, *"Simon Peter answered and said, Thou art the Christ, the Son of the living God,"* **Matthew 16:16**.

Is there supporting evidence for such a claim? What reason do you have for committing your eternity to Jesus Christ and to no other being? After all, your decision on this matter is the difference between eternal life and eternal death, damnation.

Jesus says *trust me.* He believed and claimed that He was the Messiah, the only Savior there is. He said, *"I am he,"* **John 13:19**. He believed He was the Messiah and claimed to have proof. Jesus healed an impotent man on a sabbath day at the Pool of Bethesda. The Jews were infuriated that He healed a sick person on a sabbath day. They recognized His healing act to be non-naturalistic, a supernatural act of God, **John 5:1-18**.

Immediately after healing the impotent lame man, Jesus proceeded to talk about His relationship with the Father, and assert Himself to be God. He particularly emphasized His power to raise dead people, **John 5:19-30**.

---

[2] https://plato.stanford.edu/entries/naturalism

Jesus followed His assertation of deity with five claims which prove that He was and is the Christ. As you read these words, please keep in mind that these are Jesus' words. This is His own defense that He was and is the Messiah, the Son of the living God. *"I can of mine own self do nothing: as I hear, I judge: and my judgment is just; because I seek not mine own will, but the will of the Father which hath sent me. If I bear witness of myself, my witness is not true. There is another that beareth witness of me; and I know that the witness which he witnesseth of me is true. Ye sent unto John, and he bare witness unto the truth. But I receive not testimony from man: but these things I say, that ye might be saved. He was a burning and a shining light: and ye were willing for a season to rejoice in his light. But I have greater witness than that of John: for the works which the Father hath given me to finish, the same works that I do, bear witness of me, that the Father hath sent me. And the Father himself, which hath sent me, hath borne witness of me. Ye have neither heard his voice at any time, nor seen his shape. And ye have not his word abiding in you: for whom he hath sent, him ye believe not. Search the scriptures; for in them ye think ye have eternal life: and they are they which testify of me,"* **John 5:31-39**.

JESUS' OWN TESTIMONY

Jesus first claimed his own testimony or witness as proof that He really was and is the Messiah. He said, *"If I bear witness of myself, my witness is not true,"* **Verse 31**.

A. Do not misunderstand Jesus' statement and proof.

1. Jewish law required that *"At the mouth of two witnesses, or three witnesses, shall he that is worthy of death be put to death; but at the mouth of one witness he shall not be put to death,"* **Deuteronomy 17:6**.

2. The necessity of two or more witnesses was not limited to death sentence convictions. On other grave matters such as resolving personal conflicts, Jesus clarified that *"in the mouth of two or three witnesses shall every word be established,"* **Matthew 18:16**. (See also **2 Corinthians 13:1**).

3. In the Jewish legal system, Jesus' witness was not enough to conclusively establish His claim. A minimum of two independent witnesses were necessary to establish Jesus' claim that He was the Messiah (Christ).

B. Jesus did claim to be the Messiah.

1. He said, *"I and my Father are one,"* **John 10:30**.

2. In speaking specifically of the predicted Messiah, *"He said unto them Ye are from beneath; I am from above: ye are of this world; I am not of this world. I said therefore unto you, that ye shall die in your sins: for if ye believe not that I am he, ye shall die in your sins,"* **John 8:23-24**. Note well: ***"I am he."***

3. He said, *"I am the bread of life,"* **John 6:35**, *"I am the light of the world,"* **John 8:12**, *"I am the door,"* **John 10:9**, *"I am the good shepherd,"* **John 10:11**, *"I am the resurrection and the life,"* **John 11:25**, *"Before Abraham was, I am,"* **John 8:58**, and *"I am the Son of God,"* **John 10:36**. They thought He wasn't; He thought He was!

4. Jesus' first claim was true; but for it to be legally valid, it had to be corroborated by other independent witnesses.

Even though Jesus said He was the Messiah, He did not expect them (or us) to believe Him on that claim alone; therefore, Jesus offered further witnesses.

THE WITNESS OF JOHN THE BAPTIST

Jesus' second claim or proof that He was the Messiah was the witness of John the Baptist. He said, *"There is another that beareth witness of me; and I know that the witness which he witnesseth of me is true. Ye sent unto John, and he bare witness unto the truth. But I receive not testimony from man: but these things I say, that ye might be saved. He was a burning and a shining light: and ye were willing for a season to rejoice in his light,"* **Verses 32-35**.

A. John the Baptist was specifically raised up by God to identify the Messiah.

1. *"There was a man sent from God, whose name was John. The same came for a witness, to bear witness of the Light, that all men through him might believe. He was not that Light, but was sent to bear witness of that Light.,"* **John 1:6-8**. Note well. This is divine testimony of the purpose of John the Baptist. We know that John was here to witness and bear proof that Jesus really was the Messiah.

2. Old Testament Isaiah predicted specifically of John the Baptist: *"The voice of him that crieth in the wilderness, Prepare ye the way of the LORD, make straight in the desert a highway for our God,"* **Isaiah 40:3**. Under divine inspiration, Luke said John the Baptist was the fulfillment of Isaiah's prophecy. *"Now in the fifteenth year of the reign of Tiberius Caesar, Pontius Pilate being governor of Judaea, and Herod being tetrarch of Galilee, and his brother Philip tetrarch of Ituraea and of the region of Trachonitis, and Lysanias the tetrarch of Abilene, Annas and Caiaphas being the high priests, the word of God came unto John the son of Zacharias in the wilderness. And he came into all the country about Jordan, preaching the baptism of repentance for the remission of sins; As it is written in the book of the words of Esaias the prophet, saying, The voice of one crying in the wilderness, Prepare ye the way of the Lord, make his paths straight. Every valley shall be filled, and every mountain and hill shall be brought low; and the crooked shall be made straight, and the rough ways shall be made smooth; And all flesh shall see the salvation of God,"* **Luke 3:1-6**.

B. John unequivocally claimed that Jesus was the Messiah.

1. Many asked John if he was the promised Messiah. A lesser man might have said, *Yes*. Not John. He answered, *"I am not the Christ,"* **John 1:20**.

2. But, when Jesus came to where John was baptizing, John declared, *"Behold the Lamb of God, which taketh away the sin of the world,"* **John 1:29**. He further affirmed of Jesus, *"I saw, and bear record that this is the Son of God,"* **John 1:34**.

With the independent witness of John the Baptist, there is now a two-fold witness that Jesus is the Messiah: Jesus' own claim plus that of John. For those people in Jesus' day, the evidence was getting stronger. They couldn't just *blow Him off* so easily. But Jesus was not through.

THE MIRACLES JESUS PERFORMED

Jesus made a third claim. He said the miracles He performed were witness and proof that He was the Messiah. He said, *"But I have greater witness than that of John: for the works which the Father hath given me to finish, the same works that I do, bear witness of me, that the Father hath sent me,"* **Verse 36**.

A. **Jesus did a large number of mighty miracles beyond all human or mortal ability.**

   1. These are only a small sampling of Jesus' healing miracles.

      a. He healed the man who had been impotent for 38 years, **John 5:1-18**.

      b. He restored sight to a blind man named Bartimaeus, **Mark 10:46-52**.

      c. He raised a man named Lazarus who had been dead four days, **John 11:1-44**.

   2. Jesus did miracles of many different types.

      a. He walked on water, **Matthew 14:25-26**.

      b. He calmed a raging storm on the Sea of Galilee, **Mark 4:37-39**.

      c. He turned water into wine, **John 2:1-9**.

      d. He cast devils out of a possessed man, **Luke 8:26-39**.

B. **The miracles constituted proof that He was the Messiah.**

   1. He said the Spirit of God enabled Him to do them and constituted evidence that He was the Son of God. *"The works which the Father hath given me to finish, the same works that I do, bear witness of me, that the Father hath sent me,"* **Verse 36**. The miracles were open to public view. Even the skeptics could see that the miracles were not humanly possible.

   2. When antagonists charged Him with blasphemy (they couldn't miss the fact before their eyes that only God could do the miracles Jesus was routinely doing), Jesus reminded them that He had (1) told them He was God and that He (2) did miracles as proof that He was God. He said, *"I told you, and ye believed not: the works that I do in my Father's name, they bear witness of me,"* **John 10:25**.

   3. The miracles were irrefutable evidence, proof that Jesus was really the Messiah.

4. Talk about deliberate, willful rejection of irrefutable proof, rejecting Jesus to be the Christ is it. He made that point very clear when He said, *"If I had not done among them the works which none other man did, they had not had sin: but now have they both seen and hated both me and my Father,"* **John 15:24**. *"No other man"* could do them because only God has the power. Yet, *"have they both* (1) *seen and (2) hated both (1) me and (2) my Father."*

5. What is your explanation for Jesus' miracles? His resurrection? Do you believe He really was and is the Messiah?

Now there is a 3-fold witness: (1) His claim, (2) the witness of John, (3) the miracles. Jesus has more proof.

THE WITNESS OF THE HEAVENLY FATHER

As his fourth proof that He is the Messiah (the Savior, the Christ), Jesus claimed the witness of the Heavenly Father. He made this claim: *"And the Father himself, which hath sent me, hath borne witness of me. Ye have neither heard his voice at any time, nor seen his shape. And ye have not his word abiding in you: for whom he hath sent, him ye believe not,"* **Verses 37-38**.

A. God is the Heavenly Father and Jesus is His Son, His Messiah.

1. Jesus said it. *"I and my Father are one,"* **John 10:30**.

2. When Philip asked about seeing the Father, Jesus said, *"He that hath seen me hath seen the Father,"* **John 14:9**.

3. There can be no greater witness or proof than the testimony of God the Father.

B. God the Father said Jesus was His Son.

1. When Jesus was baptized *"And Jesus, when he was baptized, went up straightway out of the water: and, lo, the heavens were opened unto him, and he saw the Spirit of God descending like a dove, and lighting upon him: And lo a voice from heaven, saying, This is my beloved Son, in whom I am well pleased,"* **Matthew 3:16-17.**

2. God the Father again bore divine witness that Jesus was His Son at Jesus' glorious transfiguration. There Jesus was in all his radiance and glory. Peter, James and John were awe-stricken. *"And there was a cloud that overshadowed them: and a voice came out of the cloud, saying, This is my beloved Son: hear him,"* **Mark 9:7**. Many years later, Peter wrote about that dramatic moment when the Father proved that Jesus was His Son, the Christ. He said, *"For we have not followed cunningly devised fables, when we made known unto you the power and coming of our Lord Jesus Christ, but were eyewitnesses of his majesty. For he received from God the Father honour and glory, when there came such a voice to him from the excellent glory, This is my beloved Son, in whom I am well pleased. And this voice which came from heaven we heard, when we were with him in the holy mount,"* **2 Peter 1:16-18**.

Now there are 4 witnesses that Jesus is the Messiah: (1) His personal claim, (2) the testimony of John the Baptist, (3) the proof of His miraculous works, and (4) the witness of His heavenly Father. Jesus presented one other great proof.

THE WITNESS OF THE SCRIPTURES

Jesus' fifth proof that He was and is the Messiah, the Savior of the world was the Witness of the Scriptures. Here is what He said, *"Search the scriptures; for in them ye think ye have eternal life: and they are they which testify of me,"* **Verse 39**.

A. Go to any book of the Old Testament and there you will find Him.

1. He's the substitutionary sacrifice of **Genesis**, the Passover Lamb of **Exodus**, the Burnt Offering of **Leviticus** and the Kinsman Redeemer of **Ruth**. He's the Rose of Sharon in **the Song of Songs**, the suffering servant of **Isaiah** and the King of kings of **Daniel**.

2. **Micah** said He'd be born in Bethlehem. He was. **Isaiah** said He'd be born of a Virgin. He was. **David** said He'd suffer and die in shame on a cross. He did. **Jonah** prophesied that He'd rise in 3 days. He did. **Zechariah** said that He will come again in glory and He will.

3. Everything the Scriptures said about the Messiah was fulfilled to the exact detail in Jesus Christ! Yes, everything! *"And beginning at Moses and all the prophets, he expounded unto them in all the scriptures the things concerning himself,"* **Luke 24:37**.

B. The Holy Bible.

1. This book constitutes abundant and irrefutable proof that Jesus Christ is the long-promised Messiah, the only Savior for sinners there is.

2. Throughout the centuries, the combined might of every imaginable force of evil has done its collective best to destroy the Messiah, the Savior. It looked like He'd never be allowed to come to this earth and die in the place of sinners, but He did. It seemed absolutely impossible that He would be able to fulfill every Scripture to the exact letter, but He did. It seemed like a pipe dream that He could be killed, and rise again; but He did. Satan did his best to stop the Messiah, the Savior; but he failed. Multitudes of men have tried their very best to smear, discredit and bury Him once and forever; but they've failed.

3. The Holy Bible is still right: full of truth and wisdom, and on a 100% track record. It's an irrefutable testimony and proof that Jesus is the Messiah, the Savior of the world.

4. Despite all of the skepticism and rejection, one day soon Jesus is coming again. After Jesus rose from the grave, He appeared to His disciples, *"To whom also he shewed himself alive after his passion by many infallible proofs, being seen of them forty days, and speaking of the things pertaining to the kingdom of God,"* **Acts 1:3**. A little later, Jesus took them up on the Mount of Olives where *"He was taken up; and a cloud received him out of their sight,"* **Acts 1:9**. While those apostles stood there gazing into the sky in astonishment, *"two men stood by them in white apparel; Which also said, Ye men of Galilee, why stand ye gazing up into heaven? this same Jesus, which is taken up from you into heaven, shall so come in like manner as ye have seen him go into heaven,"* **Acts 1:10-11**. One day, He'll be back.

5. Here is a passage about Jesus Christ right out of His book, the Bible. It is a wonderful look at Him, both backward and forward. It should fill the hearts of people who operate on overwhelming evidence with both gratitude and hope. *"Let this mind be in you, which was also in Christ Jesus: Who, being in the form of God, thought it not robbery to be equal with God: But made himself of no reputation, and took upon him the form of a servant, and was made in the likeness of men: And being found in fashion as a man, he humbled himself, and became obedient unto death, even the death of the cross. Wherefore God also hath highly exalted him, and given him a name which is above every name: That at the name of Jesus every knee should bow, of things in heaven, and things in earth, and things under the earth; And that every tongue should confess that Jesus Christ is Lord, to the glory of God the Father,"* **Philippians 2:5-11**.

Five separate witnesses that Jesus is the Christ. Five irrefutable proofs! Yes, 5! Far more than enough for even the greatest skeptic! No wonder Jesus said to those who continued to reject Him, *"And, ye will not come to me, that ye might have life,"* **John 5:40**. He can't be rejected on the basis of the evidence. It's too strong. To reject Jesus Christ, you must reject His proofs and make an irrational decision against the evidence.

Keep in mind that who Jesus *was* then is who He *is* now. He is the eternal, everlasting God who is *"the same yesterday, and to day, and forever,"* **Hebrews 13:8**. He not only *was* God, He *is* God.

If Jesus is the Messiah, there is no other who can forgive sins and give eternal life. Ultimately, every person must come to the same junction, and answer the same question: *"What shall I do then with Jesus which is called Christ?"* **Matthew 27:22.**

Chapter 10

"By Whose Stripes Ye Were Healed"

1 Peter 2:24

Peter made this statement regarding Christ: *"Who his own self bare our sins in his own body on the tree, that we, being dead to sins, should live unto righteousness: by whose stripes ye were healed,"* **1 Peter 2:24**. This is a divine reference by the Apostle Peter to a prophecy by the Old Testament prophet Isaiah. It is Peter's commentary on the prophecy. Isaiah prophetically said, *"He was wounded for our transgressions, he was bruised for our iniquities: the chastisement of our peace was upon him; and with his stripes we are healed,"* **Isaiah 53:5**.

Please notice that in both references, it is stated that there is a certain kind of *healing* that accrues from the redemptive work of Jesus Christ on the cross. There are those who believe that the healing under consideration in these texts is *bodily healing*. This belief is neither isolated nor hidden in a corner. You can hear it often on most of the religious TV channels. Many of the proponents of this interpretation of these Bible passages guarantee physical healing to all who have *enough faith*. *Healing services* are the big events for the Charismatics. Several Charismatic preachers have built large ministries upon the claim that physical, bodily healing occurs in their services. The Bible tells about an impotent man whom Jesus bodily healed at the Pool of Bethesda, **John 5:3-9**. Many very *successful* preachers use Jesus' example of healing the impotent man as biblical basis for their own supposed powers to physically heal people. They claim that if you believe in your heart that you will be healed from your bodily ailment; and if your ask God to heal you, then you will be bodily healed of your physical infirmity.

This chapter is written to show from the Bible that immediate physical, bodily healing is not in the Atonement, the redemptive work of Christ on the cross. God physically, bodily heals people today, and sometimes He does it miraculously; but there is no religious formula (be it lots of faith, a certain kind of prayer, fasting, a healing service, a special *divine healer*) which can guarantee bodily healing. Sometimes it occurs; sometimes it doesn't. Gaius was one of the most godly and righteous men of whom we have record. He was full of faith, and fully engaged in the work of God, yet he was a very sick man, **3 John 1-2**. "*Epaphroditus... had been sick... indeed he was sick nigh unto death,*" **Philippians 2:25-27**. As godly and devout as the Apostle Paul was, he had an infirmity, "*a thorn in the flesh*" which God refused to take away, **2 Corinthians 12:7-10**. How about Job?

Do you know of one, even one person, who has not either already gotten sick or hurt or died in some catastrophe? If some greatly debilitating or fatal event has not yet occurred, it ultimately will. Do you really believe that anybody is going to beat physical death? It is obvious to even a casual observer that there is no guaranteed means of physical healing to anyone. Universal sickness and death are observable and irrefutable proof of that fact. Jesus, His apostles and those to whom they gave miraculous powers could heal people with physical infirmities of many sorts. For specific purposes, they often did so; however, those special miraculous healing powers ended with the end of the Apostolic Ministry. That special ministry ended when the Bible was finalized. There are other studies by this author which deal at length with this issue.[1]

There is a definite promise of healing in the redemptive work of Christ, a healing which is available to all (without exception). That healing is spiritual, not physical. This chapter is intended to make clear the meaning of the *healing* promise made by Isaiah and confirmed by Peter.

---

[1] See the first two volumes of *What We Believe and Why* by Lester Hutson. They are available from Amazon.com.

A SPIRITUAL SICKNESS IN THE NATURE OF MAN

The healing provided by Christ's death on the cross is of a spiritual sickness in the nature of man. It does not immediately pertain to the body.

A. Consider these directly connected texts: **1 Peter 2:24** and **Isaiah 53:5.**

1. Peter spoke of Christ, "*by whose stripes ye were healed*," **1 Peter 2:24.** In this text, Peter used the Greek word for *"stripes"* is **molops**, (mo'-lopes). One widely accepted Greek scholar, W.E. Vine, says that **molops** means "a wound" or "bruise." He continues that the *wounding* or *bruising* in reference in **1 Peter 2:24** and in **Isaiah 53:5** does not refer to Christ's physical beating and scourging at Calvary. Instead, this is a reference to the *bruise* or *stroke* of divine justice administered vicariously to Christ on the cross because of our sins and iniquities which were laid on Him.[2] There is no mention of bodily illness or bodily healing in the context of **1 Peter 2:24.**

2. The same is true of **Isaiah 53.** The "*bruising*" of Christ on the cross was not merely a physical matter. Isaiah clearly explained that Christ would be *"bruised"* by the Father when "*his soul*" was made "*an offering for sin,*" **Isaiah 53:10.**

Note it well. "*His soul*" was made "*an offering for sin*;" not for our physical sicknesses.

B. The "*healing*" promised in **1 Peter 2:24** and **Isaiah 53:5** is of a spiritual nature and does not pertain to the body.

1. In a judicial sense. lost people are *"dead in trespasses and sins,"* **Ephesians 2:1.** Jesus Christ died on the cross for lost people because without Him, in a spiritual sense, they are *"dead." "For the love of Christ constraineth us; because we thus judge, that if one died for all, then were all dead: And that he died for all, that they which live should not henceforth live unto themselves, but unto him which died for them, and rose again,"* **2 Corinthians 5:14-15.** Note well: without Christ, in a judicial or spiritual sense people are *"all dead."* In speaking to lost people, Jesus said of their spiritual conditions, *"Verily, verily, I say unto you, Except ye eat the flesh of the Son of man,*

[2] W.E. Vine, *An Expository Dictionary of New Testament Words,* s.v. "stripe," (Nashville, Tennessee: Thomas Nelson Publishers, 1985), 604.

and drink his blood, ye have no life in you," **John 6:53**. Without Christ, people *"have no life in you."* They are spiritually dead; but when they come in the heart trusting Christ as their Savior, they are given spiritual life. Listen to the final authority on the matter explain it: *"Verily, verily, I say unto you, He that heareth my word, and believeth on him that sent me, hath everlasting life, and shall not come into condemnation; but is passed from death unto life,"* **John 5:24**.

2. This "*healing*" provided by Christ's death on the cross for the believer heals the spirit of the spiritual diseases it has. This "*healing*" is actually life-giving because the lost are dead in a judicial sense. What God does for them upon the merits of Christ's redemptive work on the cross is give them full spiritual healing from the ruinous, destructive and terminal effects of sin. Those who had the mark of eternal death now have perfect spiritual life, solely upon the merits of what Christ did. Thanks to our great God this "*healing*" is not random; it is universal and without exception to everyone who believes.

3. Don't miss the message of God. What Christ did on the cross of Calvary is not a guarantee of bodily healing; it is an exclusive guarantee of spiritual healing to all who come in "*repentance toward God and faith toward our Lord Jesus Christ,"* **Acts 20:21**.

SPIRITUAL HEALING AT THE POINT OF SALVATION

Seeing how the Bible often uses the language of disease to describe corrupt and degenerate spiritual and moral conditions sheds light on the spiritual healing that comes at the point of salvation.

A. Consider these Bible examples where the language of physical illness is used to speak of spiritual illness.

1. Listen to God's description of Israel's spiritual condition: *"Ah sinful nation, a people laden with iniquity, a seed of evildoers, children that are corrupters: they have forsaken the LORD, they have provoked the Holy One of Israel unto anger, they are gone away backward. Why should ye be stricken any more? ye will revolt more and more: the whole head is sick, and the whole heart faint. From the sole of the foot even unto the head there is no soundness in it; but wounds, and bruises, and putrifying sores: they have not been closed, neither bound up, neither mollified with*

ointment," **Isaiah 1:4-6**. There is nothing pertaining to the physical body here. God is using figurative language to describe the condition of a sin-laden, sin-sick kingdom which was bent on backsliding. If this drastically sick condition had been addressed by their repentance, then *healing* would have been an appropriate word to use in describing the recovery.

This is precisely how the word "*healed*" is used in **1 Peter 2:24** and **Isaiah 53:5** to show that by faith in Christ as Savior, a spiritually sin-sick soul is made whole and healthy. That's true because of the death (*"stripes"* and *"bruising"*) of Christ on the cross.

2. Consider David's cry to the Lord: "*LORD, be merciful unto me: heal my soul; for I have sinned against thee,"* **Psalm 41:4**. It is not difficult to understand that David was earnestly pleading for his soul which needed healing. What he asked had nothing to do with his body.

3. Listen to Hosea. *"When Ephraim saw his sickness, and Judah saw his wound, then went Ephraim to the Assyrian, and sent to king Jareb: yet could he not heal you, nor cure you of your wound,"* **Hosea 5:13**. It is easy to see that *"sickness"* and *"wound"* are words descriptive of a heart problem, not of a physical ailment. The needed *healing* was spiritual, not physical.

B. The purpose of calling these scriptural references to your attention is to make the point that words such as "*sickness*," "*wounds*," *"bruises," "cures"* and "*healing*" do not always relate to the physical body, but can (and often do) speak of spiritual and moral conditions.

1. That is how the word "*heal*" is used in both **1 Peter 2:24** and **Isaiah 53:5**. Physical healing is not a part of the context of either of these verses. The healing under consideration in these verses has to do with the fact that upon the basis of the substitutionary work of Christ:

    a. Dead spirits are made alive. *"And you hath he quickened, who were dead in trespasses and sins,"* **Ephesians 2:1**.

    b. Guilty sinners are forgiven. *"Be it known unto you therefore, men and brethren, that through this man is preached unto you the forgiveness of sins,"* **Acts 13:38**.

c. Corrupt hearts are purified. *"And God, which knoweth the hearts, bare them witness, giving them* (Gentiles) *the Holy Ghost, even as he did unto us* (Jews)*; And put no difference between us and them, purifying their hearts by faith,"* **Acts 15:8-9**.

d. Peace is established between God and the believer, *"And, having made peace through the blood of his cross, by him to reconcile all things unto himself; by him, I say, whether they be things in earth, or things in heaven,"* **Colossians 1:20**.

2. Yes! "*By his stripes ye are healed*" in the very finest of senses, not merely in some short-lived bodily sense; but in an eternal, spiritual sense. He truly is *The Great Physician, "Who forgiveth all thine iniquities; who healeth all thy diseases; Who redeemeth thy life from destruction; who crowneth thee with loving kindness and tender mercies; Who satisfieth thy mouth with good things; so that thy youth is renewed like the eagle's,"* **Psalm 103:3-5**. He is Jehovah-rapha, the God who heals.

COMPLETE FREEDOM FROM ALL BODILY DISEASES AND AFFLICTION

Included in the redemptive work of Christ on the cross is assurance that every believer will someday in the future enjoy complete freedom from all bodily diseases and affliction.

A. In the ultimate sense, just as every believer will be free from physical death, he will likewise be free from all physical imperfections.

1. "*Beloved, now are we the sons of God, and it doth not yet appear what we shall be: but we know that, when he shall appear, we shall be like him; for we shall see him as he is,"* **1 John 3:2**. Once Jesus Christ rose from the dead, He was forever past all mortal suffering and weaknesses. He has now returned to the former glory He had before He came here to suffer and die for us. On the day before He suffered the shame and agony of the cross, Jesus prayed, *"And now, O Father, glorify thou me with thine own self with the glory which I had with thee before the world was,"* **John 17:5**. Jesus is forever past all mortal suffering and death, and John said someday, we will be *"like him."* What a glorious thought! No more physical sickness, suffering or death! *"Now this I say,*

brethren, that flesh and blood cannot inherit the kingdom of God; neither doth corruption inherit incorruption. Behold, I shew you a mystery; We shall not all sleep, but we shall all be changed, In a moment, in the twinkling of an eye, at the last trump: for the trumpet shall sound, and the dead shall be raised incorruptible, and we shall be changed. For this corruptible must put on incorruption, and this mortal must put on immortality. So when this corruptible shall have put on incorruption, and this mortal shall have put on immortality, then shall be brought to pass the saying that is written, Death is swallowed up in victory. O death, where is thy sting? O grave, where is thy victory? The sting of death is sin; and the strength of sin is the law. But thanks be to God, which giveth us the victory through our Lord Jesus Christ. Therefore, my beloved brethren, be ye stedfast, unmoveable, always abounding in the work of the Lord, forasmuch as ye know that your labour is not in vain in the Lord," **1 Corinthians 15:50-58**.

2. Thus, we who know the cleansing, healing power of the redemptive work of Jesus Christ read with great hope, assurance and anticipation, "*And God shall wipe away all tears from their eyes; and there shall be no more death, neither sorrow, nor crying, neither shall there be any more pain: for the former things are passed away,"* **Revelation 21:4**.

B. There are many things which believers have only in prospect. We will enjoy these things experientially only in what Jesus called "*the world to come,*" **Mark 10:30**.

1. Right now, every believer is an "*heir of God*" and "*join-heir with Christ,"* **Romans 8:17**. Each of us has "*an inheritance incorruptible, and undefiled, and that fadeth not away, reserved in heaven,*" **1 Peter 1:4**. It is "*reserved in heaven.*" It is not for now. Now, we're in these mortal bodies which are laced with physical weaknesses and maladies of every imaginable sort; but thanks be unto God, it will not be this way forever for those who know the redemptive work of Christ. Deliverance from all physical illnesses, sufferings, pain, aging and even death is on its way. Peter called it, "*salvation ready to be revealed in the last time,"* **1 Peter 1:5**.

2. Some things believers have in prospect, but they are not in possession just now. One of those is guaranteed physical, bodily healing and freedom from sickness, disease and death.

Misapplying Scriptures is a grievous mistake which leads to a true plethora of false beliefs and teachings. The practice is called **eisegesis** which is *"the interpretation of a text (as of the Bible) by reading into it one's own ideas."*[3] **Eisegesis** reads into the text what the interpreter wishes to find or thinks he finds there. It expresses the reader's own subjective ideas. This practice is the opposite of **exegesis** which is *"the process of discovering the original and intended meaning of a passage of scripture."* **Exegesis** literally means *to lead out of.*[4]

Thinking a Scripture is speaking of something physical when it is speaking of something spiritual totally skews and perverts the Scripture. That bad, corrupt approach to understanding truth has a long, long track record.

Jesus spoke with a very educated and highly regarded Jewish scholar named Nicodemus about being *"born again,"* **John 3:3**. Jesus was talking about the new spiritual birth which results from faith in Him as personal Savior. He said to Nicodemus, *"Verily, verily, I say unto thee, Except a man be born of water and of the Spirit, he cannot enter into the kingdom of God,"* **John 3:5**. Nicodemus missed the whole point. He immediately jumped to the conclusion that Jesus was talking about something physical. Listen to his tattle-tale response, *"How can a man be born when he is old? can he enter the second time into his mother's womb, and be born?"* **John 3:4**. It's obvious that Nicodemus had nothing more in mind than a physical birth.

The same practice of attaching physical applications to spiritual truths is seen in the next chapter of **John**. Jesus went to Jacob's Well where He encountered a woman of Samaria who came to the well to draw water. Jesus offered to give her spiritual, living water: *"If thou knewest the gift of God, and who it is that saith to thee, Give me to drink; thou wouldest have asked of him, and he would have given thee living water,"* **John 4:10**. Look at her immediate assumption and response: *"Sir, thou hast nothing to draw with, and the well is deep: from whence then hast thou that living water?"* **John 4:11**. Jesus was talking spiritual; she was thinking physical. This was the routine response Jesus encountered as He preached and taught the people who were here during His earthly ministry.

---

[3] https://www.merriam-webster.com/dictionary/eisegesis

[4] Henry A. Virkler, *Hermeneutics: Principles and Processes of Biblical Interpretation,* (Grand Rapids, Michigan: Baker Books, 1981), 18.

Treating spiritual messages as though they were speaking of physical things is still a common misuse of the Scriptures and twisting of truth. This is exactly what many do with Isaiah's prophecy of spiritual healing, and Peter's reaffirmation of it. Isaiah and Peter spoke of the promise of God to heal the spirit of every person who comes to Him in repentance and faith in the merits of what Christ did by the sacrifice of Himself on the cross. That promise of healing is without exception and universally extended to all. That is the kind of healing taught in **Isaiah 53:5** and **1 Peter 2:24**. Beware of those who would exploit these and similar passages by reading a foreign, subjective meaning into them.

Chapter 11

Worshipping God in Spirit and Truth

John 4:21-24

Worship has become quite a *religious football*; it really gets kicked around. Everybody seems to worship: some worship ancestors, others animals, many the sun and rivers and still others the works of their own hands: statues, totem poles, gold and silver. It's been going on since Adam and Eve, and people keep coming up with new spins on it.

This chapter is focused primarily on *Christian* worship, and what a broad field that is! Everything from solemn meditations to chants to rip-roaring concerts with smoke filled rooms. This study is not intended to focus on what's weak, bad or wrong with Christian worship. The focus here will be on Christian worship that's right. It is based on the straightforward and simple words of the greatest and final authority on the subject, Jesus Christ. He said, *"Jesus saith unto her, Woman, believe me, the hour cometh, when ye shall neither in this mountain, nor yet at Jerusalem, worship the Father. Ye worship ye know not what: we know what we worship: for salvation is of the Jews. But the hour cometh, and now is, when the true worshippers shall worship the Father in spirit and in truth: for the Father seeketh such to worship him. God is a Spirit: and they that worship him must worship him in spirit and in truth,"* **John 4:21-24**.

The attempt here will be to **exegete** this Bible passage. To **exegete** a passage is to export or bring out of the passage without distortion the meaning which is in the passage. **Exegeses** is the opposite of **eisegeses** which means to import into a passage a foreign meaning that is not in the passage. **Exegeses** means *out of.* **Eisegeses** means *into.* They are opposites.

The number one job of a spokesman for God is to deliver His Word faithfully, without distortion. That's true of all spokesmen and spokeswomen for God whether in private conversations, Sunday school and other teaching sessions or in the pulpit. God expects it of preachers and teachers; but He also expects it of parents talking to their children, people discussing God and the Bible in informal talks with co-workers or neighbors and of writers like me.

It's shocking and saddening to see how much **eisegesis** routinely comes out of the mouths and off the pens of those who talk about God and what He says. Number 3 of God's Ten Commandments is, *"Thou shalt not take the name of the LORD thy God in vain; for the LORD will not hold him guiltless that taketh his name in vain.,"* **Exodus 20:7**. Yet, it is astounding how many do it; not just with curse words, but in telling other people what God thinks is right or wrong. There are lots of self-styled *"authorities"* on God and the Bible; and many of them have never read one whole book of the Bible, let alone the entire Bible. In spite of such profound ignorance of God and His Word, many have no reservations about expressing their opinions. Some of the worst of the worst are preachers. They have a head full of preconceived notions which are out of harmony with the clearly stated positions of God in His Word. They read their own ideas into Bible passages, and make them sound profound, powerful and persuasive. Through the centuries multitudes have been led astray by such abusers of the Word of God. Jesus warned, *"Beware of false prophets, which come to you in sheep's clothing, but inwardly they are ravening wolves,"* **Matthew 7:15**. Books by authors, who are subtly guilty of **eisegeses** of God's Word, are especially dangerous. They often poison pastors, teachers and other preachers, who in turn poison multitudes of others.

With this honest approach to **John 4:21-24**, we shall now examine Jesus' explanation of what true worship of God is.

UNDERSTANDING WHAT *WORSHIP* IS

A. Jesus used the word seven times in these four verses.

1. Additionally, He used *"worshippers"* once.

2. The word *"worship"* is used 60 times in the King James Bible.

B. *Worship* is translated from the Greek word proskuneo (pros-koo-neh'o) meaning *to prostrate one's self in homage; to reverence, adore.*[1]

1. Derived from a word meaning *to slaughter, kill.* The idea inherent in the word is the death of self in the presence of Almighty God.

2. James Strong says it means *"to kiss, like a dog licking his master's hand."*[2]

3. The Blue Letter Bible presents the following outline of Bible usage.

   a. To kiss the hand to (towards) one, in token of reverence.

   b. Among the Orientals, esp. the Persians, to fall upon the knees and touch the ground with the forehead as an expression of profound reverence.

   c. In the New Testament by kneeling or prostration to do homage (to one) or make obeisance, whether in order to express respect or to make supplication.

4. The worship of anyone or anything other than the God of the Bible is strictly forbidden in Scripture. *"Thou shalt have no other gods before me. Thou shalt not make unto thee any graven image, or any likeness of any thing that is in heaven above, or that is in the earth beneath, or that is in the water under the earth: Thou shalt not bow down thyself to them, nor serve them: for I the LORD thy God am a jealous God, visiting the iniquity of the fathers upon the children unto the third and fourth generation of them that hate me,"* **Exodus 20:3-5**. *"Go not*

---

[1] James Strong, *Greek Dictionary of the New Testament,* (Nashville, Tennessee: Abingdon Press, 1958), ref. 4352.

[2] Ibid.

after other gods to serve them, and to worship them, and provoke me not to anger with the works of your hands," **Jeremiah 25:6**.

5. It should be well noted that by definition, if worship of God falls short of focus on Him in true submission and honor, it fails.

6. It should also be noted that nowhere in the concept of worship is it stated or implied that worship must always be a fun, upbeat or emotionally stimulating experience. Several of King David's Psalms (songs) are very somber and painful.

C. Worship can be either private or public.

1. In either case the idea and approach must be the same.

   a. **The heart** must be prostrated before God in homage and adoration. Otherwise, there is no worship.

   b. Words or body posture alone are not enough, and do not constitute true worship. External pretense and formality void of a true heart of submission, adoration and reverence are offensive and rejected by God who knows every heart. *"Wherefore the Lord said, Forasmuch as this people draw near me with their mouth, and with their lips do honour me, but have removed their heart far from me, and their fear toward me is taught by the precept of men: Therefore, behold, I will proceed to do a marvellous work among this people, even a marvellous work and a wonder: for the wisdom of their wise men shall perish, and the understanding of their prudent men shall be hid. Woe unto them that seek deep to hide their counsel from the LORD, and their works are in the dark, and they say, Who seeth us? and who knoweth us?"* **Isaiah 29:13-15**. Jesus personally exposed the vanity of worship without a pure heart that's focused on God: *"This people draweth nigh unto me with their mouth, and honoureth me with their lips; but their heart is far from me. But in vain they do worship me, teaching for doctrines the commandments of men,"* **Matthew 15:8-9**. To the most elite religious leaders of His day, to the ones who were sticklers about ritual, keeping all the letters of the law and showy worship, Jesus *"answered and said unto them, Well hath Esaias prophesied of you hypocrites, as it is written, This people honoureth me with their lips, but their heart is far from me,"* **Mark 7:6**. Keep in mind that Jesus Christ knows more about true *worship* than anybody.

2. For private worship to count with God, the focus and heart must be on Him.

a. Each and all of us should live in a constant state of worship. It should not be merely *a church thing;* worship should be a lifestyle. *"O come, let us worship and bow down: let us kneel before the LORD our maker,"* **Psalm 95:6**. As Abraham's servant searched for a wife for Isaac, in a marvelous way God provided Rebekah. Right there, on the spot, *"the man bowed down his head, and worshipped the LORD,"* **Genesis 24:26**. Obviously, for him worship was a regular practice, not merely *a showy practice on Sundays.* In the Old Testament you will find almost 300 cases of private worship.

b. Some years ago in August, I was fishing a lovely mountain stream in Mineral County, Colorado. It was a wonderful place: high up in the mountains; a cold, clear creek in a steep remote valley with spruce, fir, aspens and willows on both slopes; a cool, sunny, dry day; fresh, clean air with that special alpine smell; a pure blue sky with a few floaty white clouds; a couple of mule deer nearby and *quiet.* Yes. Quiet! After lots of hot days in noisy Houston, it was a gorgeous and refreshing place.

In the middle of Miner's Creek, I sat down on a big rock and worshipped our great God. I praised Him for His handiwork which was all about me. I bragged on Him, and told Him how much I love and appreciate Him. I meditated on where I was, and how great God is. There was no audience and no one to impress. Just God and me. That day, I touched Him. Somehow, my heart lay prostrate before Him, the almighty God of heaven and earth, the one who brought it all into existence by His awesome power and word.

It was a wonderful time of private worship. Not all have been that spectacular, but through the years it has been my delight to be one-on-one with God countless times: in my study, in my morning exercises and on a roadside after a head-on collision which crushed me almost to death. I hope and plan to be worshipping Him on my deathbed.

3. For public worship to count with God, the focus and heart must be on Him.

a. With God, there are no double standards. Whether at home or at church, the requirements are the same.

b. God's idea of public worship in His churches is established by example in the New Testament. Five formal or public acts of worship are seen:

1) Preaching. This is where the messages of God are delivered by God's preachers to His people. Paul told Timothy who was the pastor of the church in Ephesus, *"I charge thee therefore before God, and the Lord Jesus Christ, who shall judge the quick and the dead at his appearing and his kingdom; Preach the word; be instant in season, out of season; reprove, rebuke, exhort with all longsuffering and doctrine,"* **2 Timothy 4:1-2**. That's what pastors are to do when church members come together in one place on Sunday. Preaching exalts and honors God. More *good Christians* than you might think believe that too much time and emphasis is placed on preaching, especially doctrine. In a growing number of churches, preaching is marginalized in favor of music. From a Bible point of view (and that's the point of view that really matters), preaching is the centerpiece of public worship. *"For the preaching of the cross is to them that perish foolishness; but unto us which are saved it is the power of God. For it is written, I will destroy the wisdom of the wise, and will bring to nothing the understanding of the prudent. Where is the wise? where is the scribe? where is the disputer of this world? hath not God made foolish the wisdom of this world? For after that in the wisdom of God the world by wisdom knew not God, it pleased God by the foolishness of preaching to save them that believe. For the Jews require a sign, and the Greeks seek after wisdom: But we preach Christ crucified, unto the Jews a stumblingblock, and unto the Greeks foolishness; But unto them which are called, both Jews and Greeks, Christ the power of God, and the wisdom of God,"* **1 Corinthians 1:18-21**

2) Praying. Prayer is speaking to God. In individual worship, an individual speaks to God for himself. In public prayer in one of the Lord's churches, the prayer is corporate. One individual speaks to God for the whole. The prayer can be one of thanksgiving, praise or petition, or all three. Public prayer must always adhere to the basic rules which govern all worship: (1) focused on God, (2) in complete submission to God and (3) in recognition and appreciation of who He is.

3) Singing expresses emotions. It's poetry in action. When words seem to fail at expressing how one feels, poetry adds a new dimension. When Moses and Israel passed through the Red Sea on dry ground, then watched the mighty Egyptian army sink in the mud and drown as the sea waters covered them, they sang a song, **Exodus 15**. Songs can express feelings of great joy; they can also express feelings of deep sorry, anguish of soul and grief. On the night before Jesus' crucifixion, He met with His apostles who were the first members of the first church to ever exist. In this earliest of church worship services, Jesus with those original members kept the Lord's Supper and sang a hymn: *"And when they had sung an hymn, they went out into the mount of Olives,"* **Matthew 26:30**.

4) Giving. Corporate giving is public testimony that a person's money and material possessions are submitted to God. He owns everything, and all within our possessions came from Him. Paying tithes and giving offerings publicly testify of His lordship over all. Jesus made it very clear that giving, **like all worship**, must be in thanksgiving and praise to God, not to be seen of men. *"Take heed that ye do not your alms before men, to be seen of them: otherwise ye have no reward of your Father which is in heaven. Therefore when thou doest thine alms, do not sound a trumpet before thee, as the hypocrites do in the synagogues and in the streets, that they may have glory of men. Verily I say unto you, They have their reward. But when thou doest alms, let not thy left hand know what thy right hand doeth: That thine alms may be in secret: and thy Father which seeth in secret himself shall reward thee openly,"* **Matthew 6:1-4**.

5) The Lord's Supper is an on-going reminder of God's ultimate sacrifice for mankind: the death, burial and resurrection of His only begotten Son, Jesus Christ. The unleavened bread speak of Christ's broken body, and the wine speaks of His blood which He willingly shed for us. The focus is obvious; on God's greatest gift to us. The Lord's Supper brings God's people to the very pinnacle of worship. It was a regular part of worship in the church in Corinth, **1 Corinthians 11:17-34**.

c. In church we are worshipping God. Get hold of that. Although they, may come as collateral benefit, our primary reason for going to church is not to fellowship with our friends, hear great music or preaching or to conduct church business. Our first and foremost reason for assembling as a church on the Lord's Day (Sunday) is to worship our great God and Redeemer.

d. Often, I blush and am appalled at the lack of homage and respect I see in churches. It's as if God is nowhere near and we've met just to visit with each other and go through a few rituals. *"God is greatly to be feared in the assembly of the saints, and to be had in reverence of all them that are about him,"* **Psalm 89:7**.

e. Ultimately every person will worship Him. **Philippians 2:9-11** is a prophecy about Jesus Christ: *"Wherefore God also hath highly exalted him, and given him a name which is above every name: That at the name of Jesus every knee should bow, of things in heaven, and things in earth, and things under the earth; And that every tongue should confess that Jesus Christ is Lord, to the glory of God the Father."*

WORSHIP MUST BE *"IN SPIRIT"*

A. Notice *"spirit"* not "Spirit."

1. It is true that no person is in a position to properly worship God who is not in the Holy Spirit; however, that is not what Jesus was explaining in this text.

2. Jesus was talking about the spirit of a person in the ordinary sense of the word. He was talking about the **pneuma**, the disposition or influence which fills and governs the soul of anyone.[3] He was talking about purity of heart: attitudes, motives and intentions. Having a right spirit means getting rid of unconfessed sins, pride, conceit, hatred, malice, hypocrisy, lustful thoughts and a corrupt, deceitful heart.

3. They who effectively worship God must be bowed in reverence in their minds, their hearts. There is no room for pride, self-exaltation, arrogance, starchiness, conceit or an un-bended heart. When those conditions are present, worship fails. That's true whether the worship is private or public; and a right condition in the spirit applies to preaching, praying, singing, giving and the Lord's Supper.

B. **One's approach to and behavior in worship reflects his heart.** Jesus said, *"Out of the abundance of the heart, the mouth speaketh,"* **Matthew 12:34**. Keep in mind that worship is to God. The worshipper is approaching the Almighty God of heaven and earth. There is no place for heartless, slipshod worship out of a spirit that is focused on and submitted to God. *"A son honoureth his father, and a servant his master: if then I be a father, where is mine honour? and if I be a master, where is my fear? saith the LORD of hosts unto you, O priests, that despise my name. And ye say, Wherein have we despised thy name? Ye offer polluted bread upon mine altar; and ye say, Wherein have we polluted thee? In that ye say, The table of the LORD is contemptible. And if ye offer the blind for sacrifice, is it not evil? and if ye offer the lame and sick, is it not evil? offer it now unto thy governor; will he be pleased with thee, or accept thy person? saith the LORD of hosts,"* **Malachi 1:6-8**.

1. **That's true in preaching/teaching.** The preacher must be prepared and ready; no leftovers or re-runs. He should always have (1) a prepared message, (2) a prepared heart and (3) be prepared to deliver God's message well without distortion.

2. **That's true in giving.** The worshipper must be ready to give the Lord's tithes and offerings with joy. God will not accept ritualistic giving. Giving should always be with gratitude, reverence and rejoicing. Giving should never be grudgingly. With God, the spirit matters.

---

[3] Ibid., ref. 4151.

3. **That's true in praying.** If the spirit isn't right, prayer fails. Prayer is talking to God. That's awesome! The focus must be on God. Prayer must never be offered to be seen and heard of men. Prayer must never be for show or to impress others. There's no place for vain repetitions. The spirit must be right; there's no room for ulterior motives.

4. **That's true in singing.** Singing blesses people, but it is unto the Lord. Every song from a solo to congregational number should be one's best, but singing is not one's best when the singer not prepared. In many churches, it is common for special music singers to come unprepared. Sometimes, they go through much distracting fanfare and talk before they start the song. Some music is performance oriented: emphasis on voices and instrument skills, audience entertainment and pious spirits.

   The focus of all worship should never be music styles; it should always be on what truth from the heart magnifies and exalts the God of heaven and earth. Any music that is merely a performance and not from the heart is not true worship. The spirit must be right and focused humbly on God.

5. **That's true in the Lord's Supper.** God forbid that the Lord's Supper ever be merely a pious ritual. It is a meeting with God to remember His enormous sacrifice on our behalf. When minds are wondering around and out of tune with the truths embodies in the ordinance, the Lord's Supper is not true worship. The spirit and focus must be right with God.

C. Public worship is not only for the one leading worship.

1. Everyone present should be in sync; prostrate and adoring God in his heart. Isaiah reflects the correct spirit and attitude of true worship: *"I saw also the Lord sitting upon a throne, high and lifted up,"* **Isaiah 6:1**. That's what ought to happen in worship every time

2. Compare this reality to what you see in most church worship services. Sadly, most people are not paying attention or engaged in worship. Children and some adults walk in and out indiscriminately, some sleep and many can't keep their eyes off their watch. There's so little reverence.

3. In corporate church worship, every person should be worshipping as one with the whole.

WORSHIP MUST BE OFFERED *"IN TRUTH"*

A. It's not enough to come to Him with a good *"spirit."* Worship must also be done in *"truth."* Both, not just one or the other. *"They that worship him must worship him in spirit and in truth,"* **John 4:24**.

1. Preachers must *"Preach the Word,"* **2 Timothy 4:2**.

a. Motivational stories do not honor God, and are not true worship.

b. Preachers must *"rightly divide"* the Word of God. Sermons full of Scriptures may seem impressive; but unless those Scriptures are used to correctly communicate the message of God which is in the Bible, the preacher fails. If a message fails to communicate the truth, a very authoritative approach doesn't mean a thing. Preachers must get the message straight. Sermons must be the Word of God, not the opinions of men. Truth matters everywhere, but especially in preaching.

c. For worship to occur, a preacher must present his sermon as an offering to the Lord. Second best will never be enough. God expects our best. That's especially obvious in worship.

2. With God giving is not measured by the size of the gift.

a. Most people judge true worship by the size of the gift. Not God. If given (1) in spirit and in (2) truth, a small gift worships God for more than a much larger gift which is not given (1) in the right spirit or (2) in truth. Jesus encountered a poor widow who gave a very small monetary gift; only a small fraction of the money given by rich people. Because she gave in truth, Jesus highly commended what she gave. *"And Jesus sat over against the treasury, and beheld how the people cast money into the treasury:*

and many that were rich cast in much. And there came a certain poor widow, and she threw in two mites, which make a farthing. And he called unto him his disciples, and saith unto them, Verily I say unto you, That this poor widow hath cast more in, than all they which have cast into the treasury: For all they did cast in of their abundance; but she of her want did cast in all that she had, even all her living.," **Mark 12:41-44**.

b. To be accepted by God, giving must be the right amount. The tithe is 10%. Offerings are open-ended. However sincere, a person has not worshiped God with his substance unless he gives the correct amount.

c. God is not honored with whelm giving: feelings, promptings, *whatever is on the heart.* The apostle Paul said, *"Upon the first day of the week let every one of you lay by him in store, as God hath prospered him, that there be no gatherings when I come,"* **1 Corinthians 16:2**. It is clear that the gift that is to be given on the first day of the week is systematic and proportional: *"As God hath prospered him."*

d. It's not the size of the gift that determine whether or not God accepts it as true worship. Giving will always be judged by God on the basis of (1) spirit and (2) truth.

3. For praying to be an act of true worship, the prayer must be according to the guidelines taught in the Bible.

a. Jesus gave us a model prayer, *"After this manner therefore pray ye: Our Father which art in heaven, Hallowed be thy name. Thy kingdom come. Thy will be done in earth, as it is in heaven. Give us this day our daily bread. And forgive us our debts, as we forgive our debtors. And lead us not into temptation, but deliver us from evil: For thine is the kingdom, and the power, and the glory, for ever. Amen,"* **Matthew 6:9-13**. Take a moment, and look at it. The focus is squarely on God, and how dependent we are on Him.

b. Prayer is not a free shopping place where we can gorge ourselves on the lusts of our flesh. It is not a place where we can get forgiveness while holding grudges and refusing to forgive those around us. It is not a place for vain, mindless repetitions; making selfish requests and making meaningless and senseless statements while the attention is really elsewhere.

c. Like all other worship prayer must be according to (1) truth in the (2) right spirit.

4. Singing must tell the truth and glorify God.

a. There are lovely melodies and other tunes with blasphemous words.

b. No true worshipful singing can make false statements and claims.

c. In the name of God, there are churches with music full of downright lies. Because it is highly stimulating and arousing to the emotions, it is thought to be great worship. Multitudes flock to it.

Thank God for wonderful, lively, stimulating church music. Far too many churches have a crying need for music that's alive and heart-touching.

Let it never be assumed that music is God-honoring and true worship because it is alive, sounds good and touches the emotions.

d. For music to be true worship, it must be done (1) in spirit and (2) in truth.

5. The Lord's Supper must be conducted according to the Bible method.

a. This deeply touching and meaningful ordinance of the church is an enormous reminder of Jesus Christ who gave His body and His blood to save lost, eternally damned sinners. It points squarely to God and His marvelous work. There's no place in the Lord's Supper for human glory and aggrandizement. The Lord's Supper worships God.

b. Yet, to many, it's merely a religious ritual. They can eat the bread and drink the wine while their minds are watching a football game or out shopping.

c. Jesus used unleavened Passover bread in the first Lord's Supper. He also used Passover wine. No pastor or church is at liberty to substitute other foods or drinks to represent His broken body and shed blood. The Lord's supper must be observed in truth as well as spirit. When it comes to worshiping God, substitutions will not work with God.

d. If the heart is not prone before God and focused on His great work, no worship occurs. In that case, the Lord's Supper is a vain ceremony.

e. For the Lord's Supper to be true worship, it too must be done (1) in spirit and (2) in truth.

B. No doubt, much modern worship is void of *"spirit"* and *"truth."*

1. So much is driven by emotions. It is more entertainment than worship. It appeals to the flesh, but fails to bring people bended and prostrate before God.

2. It has not been the intent of this chapter to attack or look deeply at false worship. Perhaps the best way to spot counterfeit money is to learn how to recognize legitimate money. Hopefully, all who read this chapter will know what true worship is, and thereby stay away from false worship.

Chapter 12

Voluntary Worship and Service to God

2 Corinthians 9:7

True Christians believe God's people should live holy and pure lives which are separate from the generally low standards of the world. They know God's people should give their lives unto God in worship and service. Sad to say, many Christians are watching other Christians to see how successfully they are separating themselves from the world, and performing the service of God. If they do not see a rigid performance, they judge weakness and worldliness on the part of the other Christian. If they see an exacting and orthodox lifestyle, they conclude true godliness and great spirituality in the performer.

As this chapter is designed to show, God's people should be extremely careful in forming conclusions (judgments) upon the strength of what they see in others. Though Jesus said, *"by their fruits ye shall know them,"* **Matthew 7:20**, He also said, *"Judge not, that ye be not judged. For with what judgment ye judge, ye shall be judged: and with what measure ye mete, it shall be measured to you again. And why beholdest thou the mote that is in thy brother's eye, but considerest not the beam that is in thine own eye? Or how wilt thou say to thy brother, Let me pull out the mote out of thine eye; and, behold, a beam is in thine own eye? Thou hypocrite, first cast out the beam out of thine own eye; and then shalt thou see clearly to cast out the mote out* *of thy brother's eye,"* **Matthew 7:1-5**. Using the standards of God as our source of judgment, we can judge words and actions as right or wrong; but before we do, we'd better be sure that (1) we are not judging the motives or heart of another person and (2) that our own lives are free of condemnation. A believer's maturity level cannot be fully ascertained by observing his external performances. Those who base their judgments on external factors are often deceived and guilty of very mistaken and evil judgments. Furthermore, since people act upon the judgments they make, terrible and unjust words and actions grow out of false judgments. Their words and actions are often met with equally evil words and actions, thus generating strife, divisions, injuries; and untold hurts to individuals, churches and the cause of Christ in general.

There's much more to what a believer is than what you can see on the surface. Since it is *"out of the abundance of the heart"* that *"the mouth speaketh,"* **Matthew 12:34**, there is also more to every word and deed than what other people hear and see. What a man says or does is not all that's important; the heart out of which he does so is also important. A believer with an exceedingly hard and evil heart may be putting on a big front, doing and saying all the right things to the letter of the law. One's external correctness does not avail with God, and make him a great, mature servant of God. On the other hand, a believer may be down and struggling. His performance level of words and deeds may be low; yet his heart may be convicted and tender. His lack of external correctness does not mean he has no spiritual maturity or he or she is a second rate, inferior Christian. David was a godlier person when he was down and poor in performance than King Saul was when he was up and offering sacrifices.

This is in no way intended to discredit godly words and deeds. What it is designed to do is cause God's people to realize that there is more to godly, holy living than mere external performance. May these words be used of God to put a damper on hasty judgments based on what one sees and hears. God's people should be very careful in making rash commendations or condemnations. Let none of God's people be *taken in* by external performances alone, be they good or bad. External performances are important, but they're not all that's importance. External performances alone, however exacting, correct and to the letter they be are not sufficient basis within themselves for anyone to decide on another's spiritual level. The heart out of which the performance was rendered is just as important as the performance itself. An evil heart renders the finest performance invalid and useless. Except when a person by words, actions and lifestyle shows his heart, we cannot know his heart. In **Matthew 7**, that is the nature of Jesus' warning against judging others.

THE IMPORTANCE OF THE HEART

Some individuals and churches tend to ignore and minimize the importance of the heart in worship and service to God.

A. Great spirituality and maturity are equated with zeal, passion, impressive activities and performances and careful adherence to the letter of the law.

   1. In many churches the insistence is on regular church attendance, never missing visitation, tithes to the penny, deep involvement and keeping the Lord's Supper *just right.* They're sticklers about doctrine. Every *"t"* must be crossed just right, and every *"i"* dotted correctly. They're sticklers about words and phrases which do not express views exactly as they see things.

   2. In many cases clothes and body appearance are extremely big. Heavy stress is laid on hair length and whether or not women wear pants.

B. In other circles there's a list of *"thou shalt not's."* They may be whether written, spoken or just understood. , If he adheres to the list, he is judged to be in good spiritual shape. If he does not adhere to the list, he's judged to be in bad spiritual shape; and that's a mild way to say it.

   1. Don't go to movies, don't let boys and girls touch in public, don't drink, don't smoke, don't let boys and girls swim together; and the list goes on and on. The prohibitions are not all bad.

   2. On the other hand, there's a *"thou shalt list."* One must go to church regularly, pay his tithes, go to visitation, be involved in church work, and follow *"the party line"* doctrinally. It's not a bad list.

3. With many individuals and churches, as long as these *"no-no"* and *"yes-yes"* requirements are being met, the good-performing person or another church is regarded as *okay*. Muster has been passed, and they're on the *approved* list. As long as the external is nice and pretty, everybody is satisfied and happy. With themselves and others. On the other hand, if enough of these surface performances are not being kept, the signs of disapproval and rejection show right up. External performance is obviously what matters most.

THE HEART THAT DRIVES THE PERSON

God is concerned about a person's external performance, but He is far more concerned about the heart that drives the person.

A. He thinks a person's external behavior and performances are important.

1. He's the one who invented the *"thou shalt"* list. He gave the Ten Commandments, and wrote the rest of the Bible which is full of dress codes, behavioral standards, moral *dos and don'ts* and plenty more. Committed Christians agree with God. They too think people should go to church regularly, tithe, visit, be involved in church work and follow *the party line* doctrinally.

2. God also has a *"thou shalt not"* list. According to His Word, He does not think Christians should have sex outside of marriage, steal, take His name in vain, get drunken, smoke or consume body-damaging substances, seduce others with immodest clothing or commit crimes. Committed Christians agree. They too are against pornography and viewing or reading ungodly materials which have the power to corrupt the mind. They think men should dress and look like men, and that women should dress and look like women. There are many worldly things they believe God's people should avoid; and they believe they ought to live holy, separate, pure lives and conduct themselves in ways which set them apart from unbelievers.

3. Furthermore, committed Christians think they should always do their best at whatever they do. Their creed is, *"Whether therefore ye eat, or drink, or whatsoever ye do, do all to the glory of God,"* **1 Corinthians 10:31**. Yes! With real, committed Christians it's *routine excellence.* Never second best, things half-done, leftovers, half-hearted or mediocre.

B. Committed Christians agree with God that things done legalistically, apart from a true, godly motivation in the heart do not count with God.

1. We believe people should do right because they're convicted in their hearts to do right; not because their church demands it, because it's the *in thing* to do as a member of a given church, or because they'll feel the scorn of the brethren, if they don't. God's way is expressed quite succinctly: *"Not with eyeservice, as menpleasers; but as the servants of Christ, doing the will of God from the heart,"* **Ephesians 6:6**.

2. We want people to serve God from the heart, and for no other reason. Therefore, our focus is not primarily on what another believer says or does; the main focus is on the kind of person he really is. Our emphasis is on principles more than on practices. We believe that if we can get godly principles of truth truly into a man's heart, then his practices will automatically change for the better. Conversely, if we get him to fit into a certain rigid mold without getting the *why and wherefore* into his heart, we've really done him no good. Worship and service to God from the heart is the kind applauded in the Bible. The apostle Paul wrote to the Romans, *"But God be thanked, that ye were the servants of sin, but ye have obeyed from the heart that form of doctrine which was delivered you,"* **Romans 6:17**.

3. In most circles, a passionate sermon full of scholarship and well-delivered is highly applauded, and the preacher is regarded in highest esteem. Likewise, a singer who *really gets into it* is a big hit, especially where there's a great voice. It's not difficult to see why many churches turn worship services into concerts and put on big shows. These activities draw crowds, and *turn people on.*

Praise God for passionate, well-prepared and well-delivered sermons, songs and prayers. All preaching, singing and preaching ought to be that way; never half-hearted, mundane and mediocre. Let every one of us be very careful about condemning highly moving worship and service.

4. The caution must ever be that we do not assume something is godly simply because it's big, glamorous, passionate and well-done. It's easy to do, but the Bible is clear that worship and service, however professional and emotionally appealing it may be, will never be acceptable to God apart from a heart that is right with God. Effect is important, but cause is more important.

C. The embracing of this position is not popular; and like natural growth, it takes time. It's the Bible way, and it's worth it.

1. Many, who insist on rigid standards and *going through the motions* whether or not the heart is right before God, are very critical of those who give people time to grow in the Lord. Just like natural children, spiritual children make lots of mistakes. It takes time to grow up to maturity in the Lord. Those who give new believers time to grow and worship and serve the Lord by choice out of the heart are sometimes accused of not taking a strong stand on separation.

2. Those, who are more concerned with the heart than the performance, do not apply scornful peer pressure on those who do not always dress or speak as they should. They do not spend the bulk of their teaching or pulpit time harping against T.V., movies, smoking, drinking, short skirts or slacks on women, or long hair on men. To the contrary they spend far more time teaching what modesty is and why it's right, what constitutes wholesome viewing for believer's eyes, what is wrong with body abuse and why it shouldn't be done, why a person should honor God with his substance, why a child of God should be faithful to and active in one of the Lord's churches, and other such core issues. These are concepts which will revolutionize a believer's conduct for the better. Jesus said, *"Ye shall know the truth, and the truth shall make you free,"* **John 8:32**.

3. As Christians, every one of us should do our best to cause people around us, especially other Christians to do right; but for the right reasons. We don't accomplish that by coming down in the pulpit on offenders like a sledgehammer, and with claws and fangs. Too often the pulpit has been used to shame and embarrass those who fail. Parents, pastors and older brothers and sisters in the Lord have too often used intimidation to force others to *walk the walk*. God forbid! All true worship, service and obedience to God must come out of a free heart; by choice, not intimidation.

4. This is not to say that disciplinary action is not sometimes in order. There are certain public acts which are so disgraceful to God that the church of which the offender is commanded by God to bring disciplinary action against un-repentant one who commit the offense. *"I wrote unto you in an epistle not to company with fornicators: Yet not altogether with the fornicators of this world, or with the covetous, or extortioners, or with idolaters; for then must ye needs go out of the world. But now I have written unto you not to keep company, if any man that is called a brother be a fornicator, or covetous, or an idolater, or a railer, or a drunkard, or an extortioner; with such an one no not to eat. For what have I to do to judge them also that are without? do not ye judge them that are within? But them that are without God judgeth. Therefore put away from among yourselves that wicked person,"* **1 Corinthians 5:9-13**.

AIM-FOR-THE-HEART APPROACH

This patient, *aim-for-the-heart* approach to Christian life and church practice is the proper biblical approach, and it is the approach which will best produce true and lasting results both in the individual and church.

A. It is difficult to see how anyone could spend very much time in the Bible, and fail to see the emphasis upon voluntary worship and service to God from the heart. It is clear that all acceptable worship and service must be rendered to God out of a free heart.

1. Whatever is done in worship or service must never be for show, to be seen and praised by others, or to gain status and popularity. Neither should it ever be out of duty, obligation

or coercion. That all worship and service to God must voluntarily flow out of a free will is a vintage Christian doctrine. *"What doth the Lord thy God require of thee, but to fear the Lord thy God, to walk in all his ways, and to love him, and to serve the Lord thy God with all thy heart and with all thy soul?"* **Deuteronomy 10:12**.

2. The heart is the wellhead from which our words and actions flow. Jesus said it this way, *"Out of the abundance of the heart the mouth speaketh,"* **Matthew 12:34**. He also said, *"Out of the heart proceed evil thoughts, murders, adulteries, fornications, thefts, false witness, blasphemies: these are the things which defile a man,"* **Matthew 15:19-20**.

3. Because the heart is the true seat of man from which his conduct springs, Jesus went right after the heart pointing out how vital it is that the heart be right. He said *"A good man out of the good treasure of the heart bringeth forth good things: and an evil man out of the evil treasure bringeth forth evil things,"* **Matthew 12:35**. He also said, *"Blessed are the pure in heart, for they shall see God,"* **Matthew 5:8**.

4. Paul called for sterling conduct, but not mechanically and without heart. He said, *"Servants, be obedient to them that are your masters according to the flesh, with fear and trembling, in singleness of your heart, as unto Christ; not with eyeservice, as menpleasers; but as the servants of Christ, doing the will of God from the heart; with good will doing service, as to the Lord, and not to men,"* **Ephesians 6:5-7**. Note well the emphasis on a pure heart, and that all that's done be ultimately to honor and glorify God.

5. Faith is a matter of hearing and believing what God said. Faith in action is acting upon what God said with confidence that the result will be exactly what He promised. No person is to act mechanically and cold-heartedly in faith. Paul said, it is *"Faith which worketh by love"* that avails with God, **Galatians 5:6**. Pleasing God is not a matter of going through the motions like a robot; what counts with Him is obeying in faith with a right heart; doing right for the right reasons. Again, I remind you of Paul's words to the believers in Rome. He commended the for obeying *"from the Heart that form of doctrine which was delivered you,"* **Romans 6:17**.

6. How can we approach God? *"Let us draw near with a true heart in full assurance of faith, having our hearts sprinkled from an evil conscience, and our bodies washed with pure water,"* **Hebrews 10:22**. Notice well: it is first a right heart, then right actions.

7. What anchors a believer? Not strict rules, impressive and passionate performances, being really busy in Christian work or coercion. Stability comes when the heart is established. *"Be not carried about with divers and strange doctrines: for it is a good thing that the heart be established with grace; not with meats, which have not profited them that have been occupied therein,"* **Hebrews 13:9**. What's a good thing? *"That the heart be established with grace."* That's what believers need, and they need someone who'll teach their hearts the great principles of Christian living.

8. God neither wants us to impose a rigid stand of conduct nor go to spiritual war with those who do not see this truth for themselves. To the contrary, He wants us to uphold the truth about worship and service to Him out of a free heart of love. He wants His children to *"walk circumspectly"* . . . *"as children of light,"* **Ephesians 5:15, 8**, be godly *examples* of holiness, **1 Timothy 4:12**, in a *"crooked and perverse"* world, **Philippians 2:15**. Listen to God say it in His book: *"Every man according as he purposeth in his heart, so let him give; not grudgingly, or of necessity: for God loveth a cheerful giver,"* **2 Corinthians 9:7**. We are not to impose legalistic requirements upon men; we're to teach them to freely worship and serve God by conviction from their own hearts.

B. God pronounces His woe and scorn upon those who go through the sham of worshipping and serving Him apart from true conviction in the heart.

1. King David said to God, *"Thou desirest not sacrifice; else would I give it: thou delightest not in burnt offering,"* **Psalms 51:16**. That is not to say that God was not interested in the very things He had personally previously commanded His people to do. It was God who had earlier commanded both sacrifices and burnt offerings. As the next verse explains, God does not want sacrifice and burnt offerings (worship and service) apart from true commitment in the heart. *"The sacrifices of God are a broken spirit: a broken and a contrite heart, 0 God, thou wilt not despise,"* **Psalm 51:17**.

God does not want church going, great performances, deep church involvement, tithing, correct hair lengths and styles, correct clothing or abstinence from liquor and tobacco apart from a pure free heart. Paul went so far as to say, *"Though I speak with the tongues men and of angels, and have not charity, I am become as sounding brass, or a tinkling cymbal. And though I have the gift of prophecy, and understand all mysteries, and all knowledge; and though I have all faith, so that I could remove mountains, and have not charity, I am nothing. And though I bestow all my goods to feed the poor, and though I give my body to be burned, and have not charity, it profiteth me nothing,"* **1 Corinthians 13:1-3**. At the Judgment Seat of Christ, all worship and service to God that was not from a pure heart will be no more than *"wood, hay, stubble,"* **1 Corinthians 3:12**.

2. In the days of Isaiah, the Israelis were keeping the law to the *"t:"* offerings, sacrifices and pious worship. They did it with a flair, yet God saw what they were doing as mockery, an abomination. *"To what purpose is the multitude of your sacrifices unto me? saith the Lord: I am full of the burnt offerings of rams, and the fat of fed beasts; and I delight not in the blood of bullocks, or of lambs, or of he goats. When ye come to appear before me, who hath required this at your hand, to tread my courts? Bring no more vain oblations; incense is an abomination unto me; the new moons and sabbaths, the calling of assemblies, I cannot away with; it is iniquity, even the solemn meeting. Your new moons and your appointed feasts my soul hateth: they are a trouble unto me; I am weary to bear them. And when ye spread forth your hands, I will hide mine eyes from you; yea, when ye make many prayers, I will not hear: your hands are full of blood,"* **Isaiah 1:11-15**. Yes. These people were going through all the right motions, but their hearts were far from God. The results? All of their worship and service to God was a stench in his nostrils.

3. The great prophet Hosea weighed in on this matter. *"For I desired mercy, and not sacrifice; and the knowledge of God more than burnt offerings. But they like men have transgressed the covenant: there have they dealt treacherously against me. Gilead is a city of them that work iniquity, and is polluted with blood,"* **Hosea 6:6-8**. Obviously, God wants holy worship and service; but only when it comes from a true heart.

An individual or church is practicing a rigid set of correct religious activities and restrictions may or may not be pleasing God at all. They may be or they may not be. It depends on whether or not these things are coming from the heart to the glory of God. If they are, then praise God for the successful effort; but if it's happening for any other reason, then write it off as vanity.

The same can be said of an individual or church with rip-roaring worship services: beautiful music, charismatic preaching, great performers, passion, excellence everywhere and plenty of emotions. If the worship and service are being done in spirit and truth from true hearts to the glory of God, then to God be the glory. If not, it has no eternal value.

Sadly, many of God's people are *taken-in* by flashy, emotional performances. Many others are impressed by separation standards and ritual activities. Many tend to believe that such behavior is a sure sign of spirituality. Conversely, they tend to view Christians who are not caught up in such behavior as unspiritual. Such thinking is judgmental and flawed. The truth is that one with a right heart, whose conduct has not yet matured to a high degree may well be far more spiritual than a cold-hearted or great performing Pharisee whose heart is not right with God.

C. May every one of us who names the blessed name of Jesus stand fast in Christian liberty while worshipping and serving our great God from our hearts!

1. Paul, our great father in the faith taught us: *"Stand fast therefore in the liberty wherewith Christ hath made us free, and be not entangled again with the yoke of bondage,"* **Galatians 5:1**.

2. Let us teach believers that *"all things are lawful . . . but all things are not expedient,"* **1 Corinthians 10:23**.

3. Let us teach believers that, *"Where the Spirit of the Lord is, there is liberty,"* **2 Corinthians 3:17**. Let us also teach them that *"as free,"* we are never to use our *"liberty for a cloak of maliciousness, but as the servants of God,"* **1 Peter 2:16**.

4. Let our biblical mindset ever be that it's the love of Christ which is to constrain us and be our motivation in the heart to worship and serve our God, **2 Corinthians 5:14**. This verse sums up the correct approach to worship and service: *"Whether therefore ye eat, or drink, or whatsoever ye do, do all to the glory of God,"* **1 Corinthians 10:31**.

5. May all of God's people worship and serve God to the absolute maximum of their capacities in true holiness and separation; and may they do so only out of a free voluntary heart of love and devotion to God!

Chapter 13

Distractions

Ecclesiastes 5:1

"Keep thy foot when thou goest to the house of God, and be more ready to hear, than to give the sacrifice of fools: for they consider not that they do evil," **Ecclesiastes 5:1**.

Many years ago, a pastor friend of mine told me about a lady who visited a church. After her first visit she said to the pastor, *"You're a great preacher."* After the worship service on the following Sunday, she said to the pastor, *"That was a great message."* When she spoke to the pastor after her third visit, she said, *"In this Church, you serve a great God."* She got it! Time in church is not about the preacher, the music, the facilities or the programs; it's all about the one who *"loved the church, and gave himself for it,"* **Ephesians 5:25**.

WORSHIP IS ALL ABOUT JESUS

The hope of all believers is in Jesus Christ who did the work necessary to redeem them, and worship is all about Him.

Sunday Worship Is an On-Going Acknowledgment That Jesus Is the Living Savior

He rose from the dead, and *"ever liveth to make intercession for them,"* **Hebrews 7:25**. On the first Sunday after Jesus was crucified to death and buried in a tomb in Jerusalem, Israel, some of His closest followers went to the tomb fully expecting to find His body. Instead of finding a dead body, they found the tomb empty. *"Now upon the first day of the week, very early in the morning, they came unto the sepulchre, bringing the spices which they had prepared, and certain others with them. And they found the stone rolled away from the sepulchre. And they entered in, and found not the body of the Lord Jesus,"* **Luke 24:1-3**.

It was a Sunday morning. Within minutes the risen Jesus began to make bodily appearances to His awestricken followers. Right there in the Garden where He was buried, He appeared to Mary Magdalene who mistakably thought His body had been stolen, **John 20:11-18**.

"And after eight days again his disciples were within, and Thomas with them: then came Jesus, the doors being shut, and stood in the midst, and said, Peace be unto you," **John 20:26**. That was the next Sunday following Jesus' resurrection. His closest followers were assembled. The practice of routine Sunday assembly continued in the ancient city of Troas. *"And upon the first day of the week, when the disciples came together to break bread, Paul preached unto them,"* **Acts 20:7**. The believers in the church at Corinth assembled every Sunday to worship the risen Christ. *"Upon the first day of the week let every one of you lay by him in store, as God hath prospered him, that there be no gatherings when I come,"* **1 Corinthians 16:2**. The Apostle John referred to Sunday as *"The Lord's day,"* **Revelation 1:10**. The practice of assembling to remember the risen Savior has continued through the centuries to this present hour.[1]

By their actions, each Sunday when believers assemble to worship in churches, they testify that their redeemer lives. One of the things the followers of Christ are exhorted to do in their church worship is observe communion (The Lord's Supper) in memory of His broken body and shed blood. Jesus personally said, *"This do in remembrance of me,"* **Luke 22:19**. This memorial ordinance is vivid testimony that He's alive. Followers do not go to church to meet with a dead Savior, one whose decomposed body is in a tomb. The chief foundational doctrine of Christianity is the resurrection of Jesus Christ, and on Sundays His followers go to one of His churches to meet with and worship Him.

---

[1] For more extensive information on Sunday worship, see *What We Believe and Why* by Lester Hutson, volume 2, chapters 20 and 21.

True Church Worship is Always About Jesus Christ

The Bible puts that reality in unmistakable terms. In view of Christ's death, burial and resurrection, *"God also hath highly exalted him, and given him a name which is above every name: That at the name of Jesus every knee should bow, of things in heaven, and things in earth, and things under the earth; And that every tongue should confess that Jesus Christ is Lord, to the glory of God the Father,"* **Philippians 2:9-11**. Jesus Christ is the Lamb of God who gave Himself to be slain in the place of guilty sinners. He took their punishment and paid their death penalty. All who come to Him in faith will ultimately sing His praises in worship: *"Worthy is the Lamb that was slain to receive power, and riches, and wisdom, and strength, and honour, and glory, and blessing,"* **Revelation 5:12**. Jesus is God, and only God is to be worshipped. God emphatically declared, *"I am the LORD: that is my name: and my glory will I not give to another,"* **Isaiah 42:8**.

Every Sunday in God's churches around the world, His people praise and worship God the Father, the Son and the Holy Spirit, the triune God of the Bible. They acknowledge who He is, and publicly affirm that all of their hope is in Him. They know Christ is *"the blessed and only Potentate, the King of kings, and Lord of lords; Who only hath immortality, dwelling in the light which no man can approach unto; whom no man hath seen, nor can see: to whom be honour and power everlasting. Amen,"* **1 Timothy 6:15-16**. They praise Him for who He is and for His goodness.

Five formal acts by one of the Lord's churches constitute *worship*: preaching, praying, singing, giving and The Lord's Supper.[2] *Preaching* delivers God's messages, His Word. *Praying* allows His people to speak to Him. *Singing* enables God's people to extol and praise Him with both words and emotions. *Giving* acknowledges God is owner and Master, and enables us to praise Him as Lord of all, including our substance. *The Lord's Supper* is intended to bring God's people face-to-face with their exclusive deliverance through the redemptive work of Christ whose sinless body was broken and His perfect blood was shed for them. When God's people come together in church to worship Him, they are not at liberty to do whatever they please; they are to follow the pattern or example seen in the Bible. He's the one who determined what true worship is. The focus of all five acts is solely on Him.

---

[2] For more extensive information on the five formal acts of worship, see *What We Believe and Why* by Lester Hutson, volume 1, chapter 39.

Worship may be somber or very upbeat and joyous. That reality is made very clear in the **Psalms** which is a book of worship, especially musical worship. The whole Bible is the subject material for preaching, and it is extremely broad with a huge variety of subjects and moods. Jesus personally gave rules about praying; and forbade vain repetitions, empty rhetoric and prayer for show. Jesus also put bridles on giving. He said giving should never be for show, self-aggrandizement or the praise of men. He made sure that The Lord's Supper always be authentic and from the heart; never ritualistic.

In a blanket statement about all worship, Jesus said, *"God is a Spirit: and they that worship him must worship him in spirit and in truth,"* **John 4:24**. Obviously, two requirements are essential to worship which God will accept: (1) it must be offered in the right *"spirit,"* and it must (2) always conform to the *"truth"* as set forth in the Bible. This erases all sermons, songs and prayers that are not true. Preachers must *"Preach the word,"* **2 Timothy 4:2**. All music must be Scriptural. Praying must be after the models given in the Bible. Giving can't be merely what a person *feels led to give.* God has taught His people how to give. Jesus statement about *spirit* and *truth* excludes trans-substantiation, any food or drink containing leavening and communion without self-examination and confession. It eliminates all music where the spotlight is on the performer, all giving to be seen of men, all praying to be heard of men and all preaching which takes the spotlight off the Lord and His Word.

The prophet Isaiah gave an example of how a meeting with God should look. He said, *"In the year that king Uzziah died I saw also the Lord sitting upon a throne, high and lifted up, and his train filled the temple. Above it stood the seraphims: each one had six wings; with twain he covered his face, and with twain he covered his feet, and with twain he did fly. And one cried unto another, and said, Holy, holy, holy, is the LORD of hosts: the whole earth is full of his glory. And the posts of the door moved at the voice of him that cried, and the house was filled with smoke. Then said I, Woe is me! for I am undone; because I am a man of unclean lips, and I dwell in the midst of a people of unclean lips: for mine eyes have seen the King, the LORD of hosts. Then flew one of the seraphims unto me, having a live coal in his hand, which he had taken with the tongs from off the altar: And he laid it upon my mouth, and said, Lo, this hath touched thy lips; and thine iniquity is taken away, and thy sin purged. Also I heard the voice of the Lord, saying, Whom shall I send, and who will go for us? Then said I, Here am I; send me,"* **Isaiah 6:1-8**. What an occasion! A meeting with the God of the Universe. The meeting was all about Him. That's the way worship should always be. It's never about worshippers and how great they are. Its purpose is to bring people face-to-face with God, and to do so in a way that changes the heart of the worshipper for the better. Isaiah went away a changed man who was willing to do whatever God wanted.

All of God's Creatures Should Routinely Worship Him, Especially His People

The Bible says, *"Let every thing that hath breath praise the LORD.* Praise *ye the LORD,"* **Psalm 150:6**. Of all of God's creatures who should praise and worship Him, it should be those whom He has redeemed with His own blood! The Bible puts it this way, *"Let the redeemed of the LORD say so, whom he hath redeemed from the hand of the enemy,"* **Psalm 107:2**.

God wants and expects every believer who is not providentially hindered to meet together in His assembly (*"church"*) every Sunday to worship Him. He put it this way, *"And let us consider one another to provoke unto love and to good works: Not forsaking the assembling of ourselves together, as the manner of some is; but exhorting one another: and so much the more, as ye see the day approaching,"* **Hebrews 10:24-25**.

There Are Three Primary Reasons Why God's People Should Regularly Assemble on Sundays

They should assemble (1) to worship Him. Clear, regular, systematic, dynamic, undistracted worship; not hit-and-miss, spasmatic, only when *it doesn't interfere with my life*. *"Give unto the LORD the glory due unto his name: bring an offering, and come before him: worship the LORD in the beauty of holiness,"* **1 Chronicles 16:29**.

They should assemble (2) to hear from God. God has churches; they're His idea. He places men in His churches to act as *"overseers." "Remember them which have the rule over you, who have spoken unto you the word of God: whose faith follow, considering the end of their conversation,"* **Hebrews 13:7**. These *"overseers"* are also called *"pastors and teachers,"* **Ephesians 4:11**. The first and chief job of a pastor is to *"Preach the word,"* **2 Timothy 4:2**. God's primary method of getting His messages to His people is through His preachers. Every time you are in church, you should expect to receive a message from God. Pastors are men called by God to lead His churches and feed His flocks. In order for these men to spend the majority of their time in prayer and study of God's Word, they're to be financially supported by the church. These men should become scholars of the Bible. They are commanded to use much of their time to *"Study to shew thyself approved unto God, a workman that needeth not to be ashamed, rightly dividing the word of truth,"* **2 Timothy 2:15**. They should routinely give worshippers messages from God. Their job is to *"Feed the flock of God which is among you, taking the oversight thereof, not by constraint, but willingly; not for filthy lucre, but of a ready mind,"* **1 Peter 5:2**. Faithful attendance in a good church with a faithful pastor should result in growth to spiritual maturity.

God's people should assemble (3) to fellowship with their church body. They need the mutual support that comes with a strong church family. The need of Christian fellowship is clearly seen in the world's first church. That church in Jerusalem is the model church for all of us. *"And they continued stedfastly in the apostles' doctrine and fellowship, and in breaking of bread, and in prayers,"* **Acts 2:42**. Under divine inspiration, King Solomon said, *"Iron sharpeneth iron; so a man sharpeneth the countenance of his friend,"* **Proverbs 27:17**. A good church is a tremendous showcase of how *"Iron sharpeneth iron."* God knows our need for the right kind of influences in our lives. He insists that we faithfully meet with Christian people in one of His churches.

EVERY WORSHIP SERVICE SHOULD BRING PEOPLE TO A FACE-TO-FACE MEETING WITH GOD

A meeting with the God of the Universe is an awesome thought. What a privilege! *"Enter into his gates with thanksgiving, and into his courts with praise: be thankful unto him, and bless his name. For the LORD is good; his mercy is everlasting; and his truth endureth to all generations,"* **Psalm 100:4-5**. Surely, every person who would enter the presence of God should do so with awe, reverence and joy!

When we go to church to worship, we're meeting with God. That's so easy to forget. We become so accustomed to going to church that we trivialize it. We treat it like we're going home, to work, to school or to the grocery store. If invited to meet with the owner and CEO of General Motors or the King of England, most of us would view the meeting as something extremely special. We'd dress for the occasion, be on our best behavior and find our pulse up a bit. How is it that we so often go to church as though it's just another mundane chore? Isaiah *"saw also the Lord,"* **Isaiah 6:1**. That ought to happen every time we go to church to worship *"the blessed and only Potentate, the King of kings, and Lord of lords,"* **1 Timothy 6:15**. Worship of the living God should never, never be frivolous, trite, paltry, trivial or insignificant.

Let those of us who personally know Jesus Christ, especially those of us who lead in one of His churches, never forget why we meet to worship. Our job is to get worshippers into the presence of God. Whether they are lost or saved, people in a church worship service need to both (1) *"see the LORD"* and (2) hear from Him. If we fail here, it matters not how flashy and impressive our sermons and music are. We're not in the entertainment business, and our objective is not to make celebrities out of people. We're in the business of glorifying God. The 3rd chapter of **Ephesians** places the spotlight on Jesus Christ, and calls on His people to know and show His character in their daily lives. The last verse makes it clear that the focus of every church should be on Jesus Christ, *"Unto him be glory in the church by Christ Jesus throughout all ages, world without end. Amen,"* **Ephesians 3:21**.

DISTRACTIONS ARE A CHIEF MEANS OF SATAN FOR DEFEATING TRUE WORSHIP

Satan is the chief enemy of God; and every day, he works cunningly and feverishly against God and truth. His objective is to frustrate the work of God. He works against all Christians, especially preachers. He doesn't want people to *"see the LORD."* He wants people to see hypocrites, corrupt people and activity, shortcomings and those who are false prophets. In every imaginable way, Satan seeks to hinder, disrupt, distract and discourage. He's always there to ruin.

There are many people who are searching for a place where (1) they can meet with and worship God, see Him without distractions; and (2) hear from Him without distractions. There are still Christians who see worship as about God; not entertainment, personalities, performances or pats-on-the-back. They're looking for truth presented in love, and in a routinely excellent way. There are still preachers, teachers and singers who in their hearts say to God, *"Hide me behind the cross. Let Jesus Christ have the pre-eminence, the limelight."*

Yet, in far too many churches there are distractions, lots of distractions. They come in a kaleidoscope of forms and fashions. Most can be prevented; some can't. Too many are the direct byproduct of slothfulness and downright neglect.

It's hard to keep your focus on the Lord when there's a big distraction right there in your face. One Sunday, I was in a church when a man stood for prayer, then suddenly collapsed. Right there on the scene, he died of a heart attack. The episode stole the attention of everyone. People walking in and out of the building during the sermon, a siren screaming in the street in front of a church, a child allowed to scream or misbehave in church, a blaring cell phone and a squawking sound system keep people from *seeing the Lord* in worship or hearing His message from God's messenger. The list of distractions seems to have no end.

Distractions tend to fall into two main categories: unpreventable and preventable. Rest assured that most distractions are preventable. Obviously, heart attacks, sudden weather events, power outages, noises from outside the church building and unexpected words or behavior from visiting strangers (sometimes members) cannot be prevented.

Preventable distractions generally fall into categories.

Negligence

Church facilities can be neglected: the parking lot, the flower beds and hedges and the building(s). Unkept and unclean church buildings are a reproach and keep worshippers from *seeing the Lord* and *hearing His Word.* The same dead roach in a restroom two weeks in a row is a distraction to people who came to meet with God. Six weeks in a row shouts *neglect.* Church restrooms and nurseries are hot-spots; neglect of either turns people off.

Neglect can show up in many places in church facilities. Obvious places are carpets, lighting, song book holders on the backs of pews, bulletin boards, lawns, grass that needs cutting and flower beds.

Paint and ceiling tiles speak pretty loud about routine maintenance and neglect of church facilities. So do roofs and parking lots.

Support Personnel

Very few people in a church generate a more immediate impact than church ushers. Most of the time, they are the first to meet people, particularly guests. Someone has wisely said, *"You never get a second chance to make a first impression."* Within the first 5-10 minutes, most people make up their minds as to whether they will come back to the church. The ushers and members who either show them a warm welcome or neglect them make a tremendous difference in whether or not they will connect with God and get His message.

For several years, I represented the Christian Law Association in hundreds of churches across America. From the time I arrived on the parking lot until the church service started, most of the time I was able to get a very good idea of the spirit and health of the church. In a few cases, I sensed an upbeat, vibrant spirit. The facilities were attractive and well-kept. The greeters were friendly, warm, happy and accommodating. The men's restroom was clean, discreet and smelled good. The people were smiling, positive and upbeat. They started on time. The service was obviously well planned and executed. Those involved in conducting the service were prepared. Ushers, those on the instruments, the music leader, the singers and the pastor were ready. I was not constantly bombarded with distractions.

It was not always that way. In so many cases, the situation was altogether different. There was nobody around to greet or welcome anybody. Once inside church buildings, it was not uncommon to find little groups here and there, obviously into themselves. There was no vibrant, contagious atmosphere. It was easy to see that there was not much planning or organization. The service seemed to be thrown together, the music leader often flipping through the hymnal to decide on the next song.

Bad, unfriendly attitudes in support personnel are distractions. They take the attention of worshipers off the Lord.

That's especially true in the worship leader. It's hard for a worshipper to *see the Lord* when the leader is making goof after goof: announcing the wrong song, leading the wrong verse, losing his place in the order of worship, making cracks or needless statements, rebuking the sound room people and from the public stage privately communicating with the instrument people. Some worship leaders use the time between songs to preach little messages or to put the spotlight on themselves. They do very little to help worshippers *see the Lord;* there are too many distractions.

Sound room personnel have an inordinate ability to distract. Sound systems are notorious for squeals and other bad sounds, usually at the worst possible times. They're not always avoidable. Things that are avoidable are turning on and off microphones at the right times, controlling volume and getting the right information on and off the screen at the proper time. These take planning and the cooperation of other support personnel, but with time they should be solved. Lapses in these areas distract and keep people from true worship.

The person in a church with the most power to be a distraction is the preacher. His #1 job is to deliver the message of God to the audience which came to worship God and receive His message. Poor preparation and poor delivery will distract every time. People will see the pastor, not God. No man who fails to adequately study God's Word, prepare true Bible messages with good structure and flow and deliver them without pathologies will enable his audience to *see the Lord* and hear His Word. Filler words like *and uh, Amen, you-know, Listen, You see, You hear me* (there are lots of them, and most preachers have many) are distractions which keep people from true worship. Yelling, stuttering, monotones, unnecessary pauses, poor gestures, cracks that depart from the message from God (especially those that draw attention to self and family), humor that has no bearing on the message, disjointed and poorly organized material that has little or no flow and lack of passion and heart all distract.

Any person in church who either intentionally or unintentionally takes the spotlight off Jesus Christ is a distraction. Every effort should be made to avoid it. Let us always exalt the Lord, and draw men and women to Him!

Leadership

Another area of distraction involves leadership. Lee Robertson is famous for his saying that *"Everything rises or falls on leadership."* Almost always, change for the better in any organization is from the top down, not the bottom up. The pastor with his deacons and other chief leadership determines the priorities and direction of a church.

As important, necessary and good as they are, emphasis on outreach, facilities, missionary work, youth ministry, landscaping and budgeting have the power to put eliminating distractions on the back burner. Putting together a worship service free of distractions in the pastor's sermons, the sound room and worship activities take a back seat to facility improvements, missionary projects and youth programs like summer camp and Vacation Bible School.

Leadership makes the decision about worship style; where the spotlight will be. There is a popular style where the emphasis is on performance and performers. There's lots of talk about God; but in a concert style approach, worshipers see performances and very animated performers. Smoke and lighting often prevail, and worshippers become emotionally charged; but not much is said *"of sin, and of righteousness, and of judgment,"* **John 16:8**. With this approach, Bible doctrine is not popular and preaching is kept shallow and to a minimum. The very approach of this kind of "worship" makes *"seeing the Lord"* and hearing His Word very difficult. The approach itself is a big distraction, and that's a leadership choice. Though worship should deeply touch the emotions, the primary purpose of worship is not to excite and arouse emotions. Its purpose is to bring worshippers face to face with God and His truth: sin, righteousness, judgment, holiness, separation, humility, godliness, love and the person and work of Jesus Christ.

Unkept facilities, continuously unaddressed distractions in worship services, unaddressed financial issues, lack of vision, misplaced emphasis and other such weaknesses are traceable directly to leadership.

One indisputable fact is that *"the hour cometh, and now is, when the true worshippers shall worship the Father in spirit and in truth: for the Father seeketh such to worship him. God is a Spirit: and they that worship him must worship him in spirit and in truth,"* **John 4:23-24**. The goal of every one of us who serves the Master should be that those who worship Him in church do so without distractions.

Chapter 14

The Past and Present Work of Christ

Hebrews 8:1-2

Every person who has committed his or her all in faith to Jesus Christ for forgiveness of sins and eternal life knows what Christ has already done for sinners. The great gospel work of Christ's death, burial and resurrection is *finished.* Knowing what He was about to do for lost mankind, Jesus said to the Father, *"I have glorified thee on the earth: I have finished the work which thou gavest me to do,"* **John 17:4**. (Jesus was God, and God is the only one who can use the past tense when speaking of a future event. He knows all things both past and future, and can thus speak of a coming event as though it was already done.) As Jesus was giving His life on the cross, He said, *"It is finished,"* **John 19:30**.

The redemptive work of Jesus Christ is finished. It's a *done-deal.* Nothing more needs to be done to deliver a lost, hell-bound sinner from sin's penalty, and give that sinner forgiveness and eternal life. That's right! *"Nothing!"* The sin debt (eternal death) has been paid in full. Jesus paid the debt with His own blood. In view of Christ's death, burial and resurrection, the Apostle Paul said, *"Moreover, brethren, I declare unto you the gospel which I preached unto you, which also ye have received, and wherein ye stand,"* **1 Corinthians 15:1**. Our eternity with Him was secured once and for all by what He has already done for us.

Is that it? Is Christ now sitting idly at the right hand of the Father in Heaven with no thought or care for where we are now? Is He done until His Second Coming? After that moment when we're saved though faith in Him, does He do any current work on our behalf?

The writer of Hebrews concluded that Jesus Christ *"was counted worthy of more glory than Moses,"* **Hebrews 3:3**. Moses built an earthly tabernacle; Jesus *"built all things,"* **Hebrews 3:4**. That's a huge claim. Jesus built the universe, but His prize is those whom He redeemed with His own blood by His death in their place on the cross. In view of His one-time sacrifice of Himself on the cross, He now acts as the High Priest of all who come to Him in faith. *"Wherefore, holy brethren, partakers of the heavenly calling, consider the Apostle and High Priest of our profession, Christ Jesus,"* **Hebrews 3:1**.

The main text verses for this study makes clear that in addition to what He has already done for us, Jesus Christ is now acting on our behalf in His role as High Priest. *"Now of the things which we have spoken this is the sum: We have such an high priest, who is set on the right hand of the throne of the Majesty in the heavens; A minister of the sanctuary, and of the true tabernacle, which the Lord pitched, and not man,"* **Hebrews 8:1-2**. A high priest has an on-going job. He works for the good and welfare of all those under his jurisdiction. In the case of believers (those who truly know Jesus Christ as Savior), Christ works continually for them on the basis of His past work on their behalf.

How does He *"continually work for them?"* What does He do? Once a person is saved, he expects certain help from God above that which a lost person gets. Is this a legitimate expectation? Do all saved persons receive unlimited blessings from God merely as a result of being saved? Are certain blessings limited to only saved people? Furthermore, can saved people who are not actively engaged members of one of the Lord's churches expect the same favor and blessings from God which He gives to saved people who are faithful, serving members of one of His churches? The Word of God answers these questions.

THE UMBRELLA OF GOD'S SPIRITUAL BLESSINGS

A. The high priestly work of Christ is not the only work of Christ on behalf of those who believe.

1. By His work on the cross, He is the means of their eternal salvation. Simply by faith which results in the New Birth, all believers *"are dead, and your life is hid with Christ in God,"* **Colossians 3:3**. All of these are sealed with the Holy Spirit, **Ephesians 1:13**, on the eternal foundation which is Jesus Christ, **1 Corinthians 3:11**, and are new creatures in Christ, **2 Corinthians 5:17**. Each of these has *"passed from death unto life"* and *"shall not come into condemnation,"* **John 5:24**. These all have Jesus as *"the captain of their salvation,"* **Hebrews 2:10**, and they are all *"kept by the power of God,"* **1 Peter 1:5**.

2. All who are saved enjoy these great blessings, plus many more, whether or not they're ever baptized; and regardless of their church membership.

3. This they enjoy because of the finished work of Christ on the cross. Of Jesus **Hebrews 10:12** says, *"But this man, after he had offered one sacrifice for sins forever, sat down on the right hand of God."* The work by which God saves men from sin's penalty is done: finished: completed: past tense. In short, it is called the *"gospel"* of Christ, **Romans 1:16**, and consists of the fact that Jesus died, was buried, and rose again, **1 Corinthians 15:1-4**. Upon the strength of that finished work, all who believe have the forgiveness of sins and life eternal, whether or not they are baptized, church members or do any good thing.

B. Yet, God wants to give those who believe spiritual blessings beyond their deliverance from sin's penalty. As the great High Priest of believers, he wants to bless his people in a unique spiritual way on a day-to-day basis.

1. He gave himself on the cross as *"that prophet"* for whom the people looked, **John 1:21**. Today he lives as our great *"high priest,"* **Hebrews 3:1**. One day when this age ends and the millennium of glory shall arrive, Jesus will rule and reign as *"King of Kings, and Lord of Lords,"* **Revelation 19:16**.

2. On the cross as our great Savior from sin's penalty, He completed the work by which believers have life. Now, as our living High Priest, He does the work by which we have *abundant life*, **John 10:10**. The work and blessings of the

cross, were accomplished by His death. The work and blessings of the High Priest, He accomplishes by His life.

3. In His current role of High Priest is referred to as, *"a great high priest that is passed into the heavens, Jesus the Son of God,"* **Hebrews 4:14**. The key passage for this study says, *"We have such an high priest, who is set on the right hand of the throne of the Majesty in the heavens,"* **Hebrews 8:1**. Jesus is not an ordinary priest, He is an *"High Priest,"* and there is only one *"High Priest."* All other priests fail and sin; but not Jesus. He is an High Priest *"Who is holy, harmless, undefiled, separate from sinners, and made higher than the heavens,"* **Hebrews 7:26**. All other priests fail, and fade with the years; but not Jesus. He was *"Made an high priest forever after the order of Melchisedec,"* **Hebrews 6:20**.

C. Every believer is a priest, but Jesus is the High Priest who intercedes for all the priests.

1. In the days of the Old Testament priesthood, there were many priests; but only one high priest. In this, the Old Testament foreshadows Jesus Christ and those who trust in Him. Every believer is a priest unto God. Christ *"loved us and washed us from our sins in his own blood,"* He *"made us kings and priests unto God and his Father,"* **Revelation 1:5-6**. Thus, **1 Peter 2:5** refers to us as *"an holy priesthood."* Although every believer is a priest, no believer is a *high priest*. Jesus is our High Priest, and there is only one high priest. He is Jesus.

2. Under that Old Testament Levitical priesthood, only the high priest could go in before God to the Holy of Holies. *"Now when these things were thus ordained, the priests went always into the first tabernacle, accomplishing the service of God. But into the second went the high priest alone once every year, not without blood, which he offered for himself, and for the errors of his people,"* **Hebrews 9:6-7**. The typical teaching of this Old Testament priestly order is that every believer is a priest, whose job it is to offer up acceptable worship to God; however, that can only be done through the intercessory work of a high priest. He alone can go into the direct presence of God. Jesus is our High Priest, and we who offer praise unto God can do so only through him. Our access to the Father is only through Jesus Christ, our High Priest.

Jesus is the fulfillment of the Old Testament high priest typology. Believers are the fulfillment of the other Levitical priests. Do not miss the obvious in the following verses. Jesus Christ is the ever-living High Priest who shall never die. On the strength of His one-time sacrifice of Himself, He ever lives to make intercession for those who are His. *"And they truly were many priests, because they were not suffered to continue by reason of death: But this man, because he continueth ever, hath an unchangeable priesthood. Wherefore he is able also to save them to the uttermost that come unto God by him, seeing he ever liveth to make intercession for them. For such an high priest became us, who is holy, harmless, undefiled, separate from sinners, and made higher than the heavens; Who needeth not daily, as those high priests, to offer up sacrifice, first for his own sins, and then for the people's for this he did once, when he offered up himself. For the law maketh men high priests which have infirmity; but the word of the oath, which was since the law, maketh the Son, who is consecrated for evermore. Now of the things which we have spoken this is the sum: We have such an high priest, who is set on the right hand of the throne of the Majesty in the heavens,"* **Hebrews 7:23-8:1**. Note well **Verse 25**, *"He ever liveth to make intercession."*

3. As believers we are priests, but Jesus is our high priest. In that role, he intercedes before the Father for us. What a blessing and privilege to have him interceding for us! Were it not for his intercessory work as our high priest, we would have no way of presenting our offerings to the Father or of beseeching him for the daily help we need.

D. What glorious news for the children of God! Jesus is our high priest, and He instructs us to come to him in praise and worship that he might bless us with unique and rich spiritual blessings which we can only receive through him as our high priest.

1. Peter wrote, *"Ye also, as lively stones, are built up a spiritual house, an holy priesthood, to offer us spiritual sacrifices, acceptable to God by Jesus Christ,"* **1 Peter 2:5**.

2. Paul instructed, *"I beseech you therefore, brethren, by the mercies of God, that ye present your bodies a living sacrifice, holy, acceptable unto God, which is your reasonable service. And be not conformed to this world: but be ye transformed by the renewing of your mind, that ye may prove what is that good, and acceptable, and perfect, will of God,"* **Romans 12:1-2**.

3. It is the writer of Hebrews who says, *"By him therefore let us offer the sacrifice of praise to God continually, that is, the fruit of our lips giving thanks to his name. But to do good and to communicate forget not: for with such sacrifices God is well pleased,"* **Hebrews 13:15-16**. Note well that the offering of these is only *"by him."* To be successful in our praise and in the offering of our lives to God, we must have the current intercessory work of the living Christ, who is high priest. We are no more capable of offering our lives in praise and usefulness to Him apart from His living intercessory work as our High Priest than we were capable of receiving the forgiveness of sins apart from His dying sacrificial work on the cross. All of our offerings of worship and service to God, the walk by which He can bless us with the fruit of the Spirit, **Galatians 5:22-23**, can only succeed because of the intercessory work of Christ. Nothing we offer to God from our praises to our life is acceptable to God upon the strength of who we are. In our own right we have no approach or access to God. Our daily access to God is because we have a High Priest who intercedes for us.

4. It is not difficult to see that the daily high priestly work of Christ closely relates to our offering of praise, worship and service to Him. His spiritual blessings upon us such as peace and contentment in the heart, spiritual strength, the power of God in our lives, patience and joy are directly related to our submission to Him as our High Priest.

THE KEY TO ACCEPTABLY SERVING AND WORSHIPING GOD

Consider now these divinely inspired words: *"Wherefore Jesus also, that he might sanctify the people with his own blood, suffered without the gate. Let us go forth therefore unto him without the camp, bearing his reproach. For here have we no continuing city, but we seek one to come. By him therefore let us offer the sacrifice of praise to God continually, that is, the fruit of our lips giving thanks to his name,"* **Hebrews 13:12-15**. Note well, *"… let us offer the sacrifice of praise to God continually, that is, the fruit of our lips giving thanks to his name,"*

A. In view of the fallen, sinful people we are, how is this possible? How can we continually offer *"the sacrifice of praise to God continually?"*

1. Worship consists of our offering of praise to God. Formally in a church setting, we do it through praying, singing, giving, preaching and the Lord's Supper. Also, we should engage in some of these privately and informally. (The Lord's Supper we do not do informally since it is a collective church ordinance to be done when the whole church be "come together into one place," **1 Corinthians 11:20-26**; however, praying, singing, giving and preaching are not limited to a church setting).

   Service is the giving of ourselves unto the Lord, even as did the Macedonians. They "First gave their own selves unto the Lord," **2 Corinthians 8:5**. Every day, in the home, on the job, as a citizen, in the church, as a parent, and in so many other ways, every believer has opportunity to serve or give himself unto the Lord. The Bible puts it this way, *"Whether ye eat or drink or whatsoever ye do, do all to the glory of God,"* **1 Corinthians 10:31**. Our life, with all its thoughts, words and actions really should be one big, giant offering to the Lord.

2. However, even though we are saved by grace, we are still nothing of ourselves. *"So then neither is he that planteth any thing, neither he that watereth; but God that giveth the increase,"* **1 Corinthians 3:7**. There is no way our offerings of worship or service will be accepted by the Father apart from the intercessory work of Jesus Christ, our High Priest. Apart from the priestly intercessory work of Christ on our behalf no singing, praying, preaching, giving, observance of the Lord's Supper would be acceptable to God and honor Him. The same is true of our daily praise and service to God. What we offer counts only because we have a High Priest. Our daily help is all because of him, and any rewards we receive here or hereafter will be because of him.

   How thankful we ought to be that we have Him. In view of how vital He is to our successful worship and service, and all subsequent spiritual blessings; we ought to make doubly sure we place ourselves into that realm or sphere over which he works. There is substantial evidence that the place where God is most honored with our lives, and where is blessings are the greatest is the church. Therefore, it cannot be stressed too strongly that every believer promptly follow his Lord in baptism and thereby become a member of one of the Lord's churches over which he acts as High Priest. As a member of that church, he should submit himself to God in all things. Our plans and actions should be of God *"both to will and to do of his good pleasure"* in and through us, **Philippians 2:13**.

Submission is the key. Thinking, talking, behaving, walking daily in the power of God, and not in our strength is the sphere in which God is glorified most in a person's life. It is the place where His protection and blessings are greatest.

Stubbornness, self-will, an unyielded spirit, unaddressed and unconfessed sins in the life of a believer will withhold the blessings of God in the life of a believer. God said to Israel, and to us, *"Behold, the LORD'S hand is not shortened, that it cannot save; neither his ear heavy, that it cannot hear: But your iniquities have separated between you and your God, and your sins have hid his face from you, that he will not hear,"* **Isaiah 59:1-2**.

3. This is especially evident when it comes to prayer. **Hebrews 4:14-16** speaks of Christ, our high priest. In prayer we are exhorted to come to him to receive certain benefits. It is stated this way, *"Let us therefore come boldly unto the throne of grace, that we may obtain mercy, and find grace to help in time of need,"* **Hebrews 4:16**. Note the two things one can expect when he comes to the high priest in prayer. One is *"mercy"* and the other is *"grace."* Mercy is what God's children need when they sin, which they will often do. They need forgiveness and mercy. Because they have an interceding High Priest, they can get it. Such ones who have particular weaknesses to repeated sins also need the grace of God to help them conquer those weaknesses. And, this too they can get When they come in prayer to Jesus the high priest, they can also *"find grace to help in time of need."* How blessed and wonderful it is to worship and serve the Lord the right way, when what we do is in His strength, and not our own!

The resulting mercy and grace are only possible because such ones have an interceding High Priest. Note well the goodness of God to those who avail themselves of the privilege offered here. The High Priest *"ever liveth to make intercession"* for them, **Hebrews 7:25**. Red-handed offenders get mercy plus the unmerited help of God in overcoming their infirmities all because of Jesus, their High Priest. What gracious help for current living! Why should any child of God fail to avail himself of it by refusing baptism and church membership?

4. Do not forget that with our lives, we're to offer *"the sacrifice of praise to God continually,"* **Hebrews 13:15**. This verse predicates that command by saying that it can only be done *"by him."* That's right. Acceptable worship and service to God is only possible because of the intercessory work of our High Priest, and the place where He offers His greatest approval and watch-care is over his church. *"Having therefore, brethren, boldness to enter into the holiest by the blood of Jesus, By a new and living way, which he hath consecrated for us, through the veil, that is to say, his flesh; And having an high priest over the house of God; Let us draw near with a true heart in full assurance of faith, having our hearts sprinkled from an evil conscience, and our bodies washed with pure water. Let us hold fast the profession of our faith without wavering; (for he is faithful that promised;) And let us consider one another to provoke unto love and to good works: Not forsaking the assembling of ourselves together, as the manner of some is; but exhorting one another: and so much the more, as ye see the day approaching,"* **Hebrews 10:19-25**. Be reminded that Jesus Christ is *"an high priest over the house of God,"* and *"the house of God"* is the church.

B. Does the intercessory work of the High Priest extend to any worship or service offered outside a formal church setting?

1. The answer is a most assured "Yes." The building is not the church; the people constitute the church. There are appointed times when the church as a whole is to come together to worship God. One of those times is the first day of the week (**Acts 20:7, 1 Corinthians 16:2**, etc.). When the church comes together, the members are commanded to be present, **Hebrews 10:25**. On such occasions, no member is to be off somewhere else conducting his own private worship service. If he is, his worship will not avail before God.

2. Yet, this is not to say that no private worship or service avails before God. In fact, the vast majority of our worship

and service to God is to be private. Only a small percentage will be rendered in a public worship service when the whole church comes together. That's when the tithe is to be paid. That's only 10% of the 100% which God gives us. All He gives is to be used to glorify Him. Every facet of a believer's life is to be a living tribute to God. In a formal church worship service, only a few minutes of singing or prayer will occur. Most of the believer's praise to God should go on day by day. *"Let the word of Christ dwell in you richly in all wisdom; teaching and admonishing one another in psalms and hymns and spiritual songs, singing with grace in your hearts to the Lord. And whatsoever ye do in word or deed, do all in the name of the Lord Jesus, giving thanks to God and the Father by him,"* **Colossians 3:16-17**.

3. All giving is not to be done in a church service. We're to privately give to the poor, **Matthew 6:1-4**. Believers are to privately pray, **Matthew 6:5-6**. The daily service of every child of God should be caring for the domestic needs of our families, **1 Timothy 5:8**, and helping people in need, **Matthew 25:34-40**. These are a part of our offering of our lives to God. In no sense is our offering of worship and service to God to be only occasional as we attend a church service. To the contrary, it is to be continual, day-by-day every day. True Christianity is not a little praise and worship rendered to God in a public church service; it's a 24-hours every day proposition. We do not need a high priest only for public church services; we need an high priest all of the time. Our high priest is not merely interceding for the worship and service we offer at church; He is interceding for all of the worship and service we offer, both public and private.

4. Our great high priest, Jesus Christ cares for and helps all believers. Every day, He showers even the unsaved with many blessings. *"He maketh his sun to rise on the evil and on the good, and sendeth rain on the just and on the unjust,"* **Matthew 5:45**. All people, lost and saved, those who are living right and those who are not enjoy enormous blessings from God. However, those who come to Him as personal Savior, identify with Him in believer's baptism and humbly serve Him with a right heart in one of His churches are the ones who will benefit most from His intercessory work as high priest. He is honored and glorified by their worship and service to Him both in church worship services and in their day-to-day giving of themselves to Him.

5. A member of one of the Lord's churches is not only a member when the church is in public assembly. He is just as much a member when the church is not in assembly. Thus, the worship and service he renders to God on Monday or Friday while he's home or at work is just as acceptable as that which he offers during the Sunday morning worship service. Furthermore, it is acceptable on the same basis as his public worship. In both the public case and the private case, the believer offers to God as a member of one of the Lord's churches over which Jesus acts as High Priest. And, it is solely upon the strength of his intercessory work that the offering of worship or service in either case avails with God.

6. No one can offer up acceptable worship and service unto God except he does so through the proper channel, and we believe that channel is the Lord's church. No one can by-pass the church, and yet experience the full extent of the intercessory work of Christ. We believe that a person must be saved and baptized, and thus be a member of some local church, in order for his prayers, singing, giving, participation in the Lord's Supper, or any act of service to be truly blessed of and honored by the Lord. When a saved person attempts to worship and serve God apart from membership in one of the Lord's churches, his worship and service simply will not honor God and draw His spiritual blessings as will worship and service by yielded members of a church. The worship and service may sound and look good, and be offered with deepest sincerity; yet at the judgment seat of Christ such efforts will constitute *"wood, hay, and stubble,"* **1 Corinthians 3:12**.

Chapter 15

An Overview of the Work of the Holy Spirit

1 John 5:7

Talk about misconceptions, they truly abound with regard to the Holy Spirit of God, especially in His current role. All sorts of weird thinking and behavior are accredited to Him.

In spite of how inconsistent or out of harmony with the Bible it may be, some claim that He prompts most of their behavior. They accredit most of what they do to the leadership of God through His Holy Spirit.

Others are reluctant to admit that the Holy Spirit is involved in any of their daily affairs. To them it's as though the Holy Spirit authored the Bible, made it alive and then vanished into a passive, uninvolved role. They acknowledge that He lives in believers, but they don't think He does anything except quietly ride around in their hearts.

These extremes briefly express the two ends of a spectrum of misunderstandings about the Holy Spirit. Sadly, most of those who call themselves *Christians* are very good at civil war. Refusal to embrace what another *Christian* believes about the Holy Spirit often prompts a quick knee-jerk reaction: *"You don't believe in the Holy Spirit."* The truth is rarely at one extreme or the other. The truth is that some well-meaning people have blamed the Holy Spirit for radical behavior which is not grounded in Scripture. Others have made the Holy Spirit little more than a retired author. He gets little or no credit for what He is currently doing on earth. In many believers, He is *"quenched"* in their daily lives and boxed-up in the Bible.

Foundational to a correct understanding of the Holy Spirit is a realization that He is a very real person. The Holy Spirit is just as much God as Jesus Christ is God or the Father is God. The apostle John said, *"There are three that bear record in heaven, the Father, The Word* (which John declared to be Jesus, the Son, **John 1:14**), *and the Holy Ghost: and these three are one,"* **1 John 5:7**. Do not allow yourself to think that the Father and the Son are real persons; but that the Holy Spirit is nothing more than an influence or mystical force, and not a real person. Every distinguishing quality of God can be ascribed to the Holy Spirit just as readily as it can be ascribed to the Father or the Son. Just as they are eternal, omniscient, omnipresent, omnipotent, good and perfect; even so is the Holy Spirit.

THE PAST MINISTRY OF THE HOLY SPIRIT

A. His work in creation.

1. As were the Father and the Son, the Holy Spirit was involved in creation. *"In the beginning God created the heaven and the earth. And the earth was without form, and void; and darkness was upon the face of the deep. And the Spirit of God moved upon the face of the waters,"* **Genesis 1:1-2**. The Holy Spirit of God was there.

2. The statement that *"God created the heaven and the earth"* includes Father, Son and Holy Spirit, **Genesis 1:1**. *"God"* is translated from the masculine Hebrew noun **Elohim**. The *im* ending is the Hebrew plural. Thus, Elohim is a plural noun; however, it is clearly used here in the singular. This is the first of over two thousand times where the mighty name of God the creator is used in this way.[1] *"Created"* is translated from the Hebrew verb **bara**. This verb has only God as its

[1] Henry M. Morris, *The Genesis Record: A Scientific and Devotional Commentary on the Book of Beginnings,* (San Diego, California: Creation-Life Publishers, 1976), 39.

subject. Only God can create (bring into existence that which had no prior existence) in the sense of **Genesis 1:1**.[2]

3. The plural noun used with a singular verb speaks of the triune God of the Bible: Father, Son and Holy Spirit. Though each is identified by specific roles, they always function as one in perfect unison. They acted as one in creation.

B. Periodically, in Old Testament times, the Holy Spirit embodied specific people causing them to prophesy.

1. The Spirit of God was upon Moses. At one point *"the LORD came down in a cloud, and spake unto him, and took of the spirit that was upon him, and gave it unto the seventy elders: and it came to pass, that, when the spirit rested upon them, they prophesied, and did not cease,"* **Numbers 11:25**.

2. Saul is another case in point. In Samuel's search for a man to lead Israel he said to Saul, *"And the Spirit of the LORD will come upon thee, and thou shalt prophesy with them, and shalt be turned into another man,"* **1 Samuel 10:6**. Shortly thereafter it happened. *"And when they came thither to the hill, behold, a company of prophets met him; and the Spirit of God came upon him, and he prophesied among them,"* **1 Samuel 10:10**. On several later occasions, the Spirit came upon Saul, and he prophesied. See **1 Samuel 19:24**.

3. This phenomenon by the Holy Spirit occurred on several occasions in Old Testament days.

C. On numerous occasions in the Old Testament era, the Holy Spirit gave people knowledge which was far beyond their human abilities.

1. A notable example is Joseph, the son of Jacob. It was God the Spirit who enabled him to interpret Pharaoh's dreams of a prolonged famine in Egypt and surrounding countries. Joseph took no credit for this knowledge which was above human ability. Joseph said to Pharaoh and his officers, *"God hath shewed Pharaoh what he is about to do,"* **Genesis 41:25**. Pharaoh didn't miss the obvious: *"Pharaoh said unto his*

---

[2] W.E. Vine, Merrill F. Unger, William White, Jr., *Vine's Expository Dictionary of Biblical Words*, (Nashville, Tennessee: Thomas Nelson Publishers, 1985), 51.

servants, Can we find such a one as this is, a man in whom the Spirit of God is?" **Genesis 41:38**.

2. Daniel unrelentingly credited the Spirit of God for his ability to interpret dreams. When the Babylonian king, Nebuchadnezzar had a powerful prophetic dream which none of his wise men could interpret, Daniel said to Nebuchadnezzar, *"There is a God in heaven that revealeth secrets, and maketh known to the king Nebuchadnezzar what shall be in the latter days,"* **Daniel 2:28**. He adamantly insisted that the special knowledge he had was not of himself; instead, it came to him through the Spirit of God. *"As for me, this secret is not revealed to me for any wisdom that I have more than any living,"* **Daniel 2:30**.

D. In Old Testament days, frequently the Spirit of God came with miraculous power upon a person for a specific purpose.

1. Israel was invaded and placed in servitude by the king of Mesopotamia. When the children of Israel *"cried unto the LORD"* the LORD raised up *"Othniel the son of Kenas, Caleb's younger brother,"* **Judges 3:9**. *"The Spirit of the LORD came upon him, and he judged Israel, and went out to war: and the LORD delivered Chushanrishathaim king of Mesopotamia into his hand; and his hand prevailed against Chushanrishathaim,"* **Judges 3:10**.

2. The mighty exploits of Samson are well known. What is not so well known is that they were only possible because the Spirit of God came upon him. The Bible says of Sampson's encounter with a lion, *"The Spirit of the LORD came mightily upon him, and he rent him as he would have rent a kid, and he had nothing in his hand,"* **Judges 14:6**. On another occasion, Samson was captured and bound by a large, well-trained and armed Philistine military force. As they preceded to kill him, *"the Spirit of the LORD came mightily upon him, and the cords that were upon his arms became as flax that was burnt with fire, and his bands loosed from off his hands. And he found a new jawbone of an ass, and put forth his hand, and took it, and slew a thousand men therewith,"* **Judges 15:14-15**.

3. There are numerous other Old Testament examples of the Holy Spirit empowering people for specific purposes.

E. At the end of the Old Testament era, as God initiated His long-standing plan of redemption the Holy Spirit impregnated Mary who would give birth to the body of Jesus Christ, the eternal God and Redeemer.

1. Hundreds of years before the birth of Jesus Christ, the Old Testament prophet Isaiah predicted, *"Therefore the Lord himself shall give you a sign; Behold, a virgin shall conceive, and bear a son, and shall call his name Immanuel,"* **Isaiah 7:14**. What a sign! The birth of Jesus the Messiah was and is nothing short of a God thing. When the predicted moment arrived, the Lord appeared unto Joseph who was engaged and preparing to marry Mary. In summary, here is what He said: *The woman you are about to marry is pregnant. She is pure and was not impregnated by a man. This is the fulfillment of Isaiah's prophesy which said, "Behold, a virgin shall be with child, and shall bring forth a son, and they shall call his name Emmanuel, which being interpreted is, God with us,"* **Matthew 1:23**. *Joseph, you're a special man. God has selected you to marry a virgin girl who has been impregnated by the Holy Spirit.* Thus come these words: *"Now the birth of Jesus Christ was on this wise: When as his mother Mary was espoused to Joseph, before they came together, she was found with child of the Holy Ghost,"* **Matthew 1:18**.

2. What a miraculous thing! It was and is a one-time occurrence. In the entire history of humanity, this is the only virgin birth to have ever occurred. It was the doing of the Holy Spirit.

F. Many miss the work of the Holy Spirit in the earthly ministry of Jesus Christ.

1. The issue at hand in **Matthew 12:22-32** is the sin against the Holy Ghost, generally known as *the unpardonable sin*. By the power of the Holy Ghost, Jesus healed a man who was possessed by a devil. The people who saw it were amazed. When the Pharisees heard of it, they accused Jesus of casting out the devil *"by Beelzebub the prince of the devils,"* **Matthew 12:23**. Jesus made it clear to them that He *"cast out devils by the Spirit of God,"* **Matthew 12:28**. Jesus went farther, erasing any doubt that He was casting out devils by His own power. By

accrediting His miracles to Beelzebub, they were sinning against the Holy Spirit by whose power the miracle was done; and to do that was an unpardonable sin. *"Wherefore I say unto you, All manner of sin and blasphemy shall be forgiven unto men: but the blasphemy against the Holy Ghost shall not be forgiven unto men. And whosoever speaketh a word against the Son of man, it shall be forgiven him: but whosoever speaketh against the Holy Ghost, it shall not be forgiven him, neither in this world, neither in the world to come,"* **Matthew 12:31-32**. The sin against the Holy Spirit or unpardonable sin occurred when a person saw Jesus Christ perform a miracle by the power of the Holy Spirit, and then accredit that miracle to Satan. Obviously, the divine powers demonstrated by Jesus during His earthly ministry were through the Holy Spirit, not His own power.

2. When Jesus took upon Himself a mortal, human body, He temporarily surrendered some of His powers to the Holy Spirit. He was still God and had the power; but didn't exercise the power by His own authority. Instead, He performed miracles by the power of the Holy Spirit. *"Who, being in the form of God, thought it not robbery to be equal with God: But made himself of no reputation,* (emptied himself) *and took upon him the form of a servant, and was made in the likeness of men: And being found in fashion as a man, he humbled himself, and became obedient unto death, even the death of the cross,"* **Philippians 2:6-8**. Jesus pointed to this reality when He said, *"I can of mine own self do nothing: as I hear, I judge: and my judgment is just; because I seek not mine own will, but the will of the Father which hath sent me,"* **John 5:30**.

G. Furthermore, it was the Holy Spirit who empowered the apostles to work the miraculous signs and wonders which characterized their lives.

1. Before Jesus ascended into heaven, He made this promise to the apostles: *"Ye shall receive power, after that the Holy Ghost is come upon you,"* **Acts 1:8**

2. Mark thus recorded what followed: *"They went forth, and preached every where, the Lord working with them, and confirming the word with signs following,"* **Mark 16:20**.

H. It must be noted that a chief role of the Holy Spirit was His inspiring men to write the holy books which are known as the Bible.

1. The apostle Peter explained, *"For the prophecy came not in old time by the will of man: but holy men of God spake as they were moved by the Holy Ghost,"* **2 Peter 1:21**. All of the Old Testament from the great Pentateuch to Malachi was given by the Holy Spirit of God. The Spirit used Moses, David, Daniel, Isaiah, Jeremiah, Ezekiel and a host of others to give humanity the Old Testament Scriptures.

2. The Holy Spirit did not stop inspiring men with the completion of the Old Testament books; He continued and inspired 27 New Testament books.

a. Jesus Christ promised it would happen. To the apostles He said, *"I have yet many things to say unto you, but ye cannot bear them now. Howbeit when he, the Spirit of truth, is come, he will guide you into all truth: for he shall not speak of himself; but whatsoever he shall hear, that shall he speak: and he will shew you things to come. He shall glorify me: for he shall receive of mine, and shall shew it unto you. All things that the Father hath are mine: therefore said I, that he shall take of mine, and shall shew it unto you,"* **John 16:12-15**. He promised more divine revelation.

b. Thus, Paul who was an apostle said to the Corinthian church, *"And I, brethren, when I came to you, came not with excellency of speech or of wisdom, declaring unto you the testimony of God. For I determined not to know any thing among you, save Jesus Christ, and him crucified. And I was with you in weakness, and in fear, and in much trembling. And my speech and my preaching was not with enticing words of man's wisdom, but in demonstration of the Spirit and of power:"* **1 Corinthians 2:1-4**. What a candid acknowledgment that the information he gave them was divine, not of human reasoning including his own intelligence. By miracles, He further credentialed and fortified his claim that his messages which include his writings were divine: *"My preaching was not with enticing words of man's wisdom, but in demonstration of the Spirit and of power."* (Because some preachers get loud, animated and sweaty, they think they're preaching in demonstration of the Spirit and of power. What a glaring misapplication of Scripture. Paul was speaking of the miraculous power of the Holy Spirit in confirming to be divine what he and the other apostles were inspired to teach and write.)

Paul continued in this address to the Corinthians: *"But we speak the wisdom of God in a mystery, even the hidden wisdom, which God ordained before the world unto our glory: Which none of the princes of this world knew:* (It is clear that Paul was speaking of information above the knowledge of humans) *for had they known it, they would not have crucified the Lord of glory. But as it is written, Eye hath not seen, nor ear heard, neither have entered into the heart of man, the things which God hath prepared for them that love him.* (The divine information of which Paul spoke could not be ascertained by observation, much study or deep introspection) *But God hath revealed them unto us by his Spirit:* (divine revelation) *for the Spirit* (the Holy Spirit) *searcheth all things, yea, the deep things of God. For what man knoweth the things of a man, save the spirit of man which is in him? even so the things of God knoweth no man, but the Spirit of God. Now we* (the apostles, not everybody) *have received, not the spirit of the world, but the spirit which is of God;* (the Holy Spirit) *that we might know the things that are freely given to us* (the apostles) *of God. Which things also we speak,* (the books of the New Testament) *not in the words which man's wisdom teacheth, but which the Holy Ghost teacheth;* (divine revelation) *comparing spiritual things with spiritual,"* **1 Corinthians 2:7-13**.

c. Luke was not an apostle but was with Paul from the beginning. As he began the book of Luke, here is how he justified its reliability: *"Forasmuch as many have taken in hand to set forth in order a declaration of those things which are most surely believed among us, Even as they delivered them unto us, which from the beginning were eyewitnesses, and ministers of the word; It seemed good to me also, having had perfect understanding of all things from the very first, to write unto thee in order, most excellent Theophilus, That thou mightest know the certainty of those things, wherein thou hast been instructed,"* **Luke 1:1-4**.

d. Here is the apostle Peter's claim of divine revelation and infallibility: *"For we have not followed cunningly devised fables, when we made known unto you the power and coming of our Lord Jesus Christ, but were eyewitnesses of his majesty. For he received from God the Father honour and glory, when there came such a voice to him from the excellent glory, This is my beloved Son, in whom I am well pleased. And this voice which came from heaven we heard, when we were with him in the holy mount. We have also a more sure word of prophecy; whereunto ye do well that ye take heed, as unto a light that shineth in a dark place, until the day dawn, and the day star arise in your hearts: Knowing this first, that no prophecy of the scripture is of any private interpretation. For the prophecy came not in old time by the will of man: but holy men of God spake as they were moved by the Holy Ghost,"* **2 Peter 1:16-21**.

3. *"Eyewitnesses." "Chosen before of God." "A more sure word of prophecy." "The prophecy came not . . . by the will of man." "Holy men of God spake as they were moved by the Holy Ghost."* The books they wrote are not the products of their own intelligence. Every Bible book (Old Testament and New Testament) came by divine revelation. *"Eye hath not seen, nor ear heard, neither have entered into the heart of man, the things which God hath prepared for them that love him. But God hath revealed them unto us by his Spirit,"* **1 Corinthians 2:9-10**. Note well: *"God hath revealed them unto us by his Spirit."* The divine revelation came by the Holy Spirit of God!

4. Thus, you hear the divine conclusion of Almighty God through His inspired apostle Paul, *"All scripture is given by inspiration of God, and is profitable for doctrine, for reproof, for correction, for instruction in righteousness: That the man of God may be perfect, throughly furnished unto all good works,"* **2 Timothy 3:16-17**. *"All scripture,"* not just some of it, is the work of God the Holy Spirit!

THE CURRENT MINISTRY OF THE HOLY SPIRIT

A. Every minute of every day, the Holy Spirit is at work sustaining the world in which we live.

1. As God, in concert with the Father and the Son, the Holy Spirit holds the natural universe together in stasis (balance). *"For by him were all things created, that are in heaven, and that are in earth, visible and invisible, whether they be thrones, or dominions, or principalities, or powers: all things were created by him, and for him: He is before all things, and by him all things consist,"* **Colossians 1:16-17**. The Greek word for *"consist"* is **sunistano** from which we get the English word *sustain.* It is God as the Holy Spirit whose current role is to lead in sustaining or holding together the universe; and He does it to the glory of the Son.

2. Dr. Henry Morris said, *"The most basic of all scientific principles is implied in these two verses (Colossians 1:16, 17). The principle of conservation of mass-energy or 'all things.' According to this principle, nothing is now being either created or annihilated – only conserved, as far as quantity is concerned."* Dr. Morris goes on to say that existing things can change from one state to another, *"but the total quantity of mass-energy is always conserved. This law – also called the First Law of Thermodynamics – is the best-proved law of science, but science cannot tell us why it's true."* Nothing new is being created, and *"the reason why nothing is now being annihilated is because all things are now being sustained by Him. If it were not so, the binding energy of the atom, which holds its structure together, would collapse, and the whole universe would disintegrate into chaos."* [3]

3. Because our great triune God controls all things that exist (of which our universe is a part), Paul said, *"In him we live, and move, and have our being,"* **Acts 17:28**. We call it the Providence of God. We know that nothing can happen without His permission, and He has the ultimate, final word in all things. Daniel wrote, *"Blessed be the name of God for ever and ever: for wisdom and might are his: And he changeth the times and the seasons: he removeth kings, and setteth up kings: he giveth wisdom unto the wise, and knowledge to them that know understanding: He revealeth the deep and secret things: he knoweth what is in the darkness, and the light dwelleth with him,"* **Daniel 2:20-21**. Here is God's own rhetorical question: *"Am I a God at hand, saith the LORD, and not a God afar off?"* **Jeremiah 23:23**.

---

[3] Dr. Henry Morris, *The Defender's Study Bible,* (Grand Rapids, Michigan: World Publishing, 1995), study notes on Colossians 1:17.

4. Never allow yourself to think that God is far away and disengaged from the world and its operations. He is not. Though we are usually blind to it, His Holy Spirit is active in our world and lives every minute of every day.

B. His most specific assignment from heaven is to be a Comforter in the hearts and lives of believers.

1. Jesus specifically said, *"I will pray the Father, and He shall give you another Comforter, that He may abide with you for ever; Even the Spirit of truth; whom the world cannot receive, because it seeth Him not, neither knoweth Him: but ye know Him; for He dwelleth with you, and shall be in you,"* **John 14:16-17**. The Holy Spirit was sent first as a Comforter to the apostles. He inspired them to write the Holy Scriptures, to heal and to perform miracles, **John 16:7-15**. Let it be clearly understood that the Holy Spirit's work as a Comforter was not limited to the apostles. It is true that only they and a few of their hand-picked co-workers were His tools in divine revelation, Scripture-writing and miracles; but He was sent as a Comforter to all believers. Believer, let that glorious truth soak into the core of your being; the God of heaven and earth lives in you in the person of His Holy Spirit. Getting hold of that truth can revolutionize your life. Don't treat Him as a stranger. Treat Him as your most intimate friend. Get to know Him, and learn to lean on Him to direct your life every day. He will produce good in your life that you could never experience in your own strength.

2. By the Holy Spirit, divine messages or letters were written to churches mentioned in the Bible. Those messages were specific to those churches, but the truths in those letters are timeless. They speak truth that transcends the ages, and the messages are applicable to believers and churches wherever they are regardless of the period of time in which they exist. Keep that in mind as you hear Paul say to the Corinthian believers, *"Know ye not that ye are the temple of God, and that the Spirit of God dwelleth in you?"* **1 Corinthians 3:16**. The Holy Spirit of God indwells or lives in every believer. Paul put it this way, *"Ye are not in the flesh, but in the Spirit, if so be that the Spirit of God dwell in you. Now if any man have not the Spirit of*

Christ, he is none of his," **Romans 8:9**. Paul wrote of God to the church that was at Thessalonica. He said God *"hath also given unto us his holy Spirit,"* **1 Thessalonians 4:8**.

3. It is truly a comfort to know that the Holy Spirit of God lives within. He is able to help and sustain us through whatever life has to offer. Praise God! *"Ye are of God, little children, and have overcome them: because greater is he that is in you, than he that is in the world,"* **1 John 4:4**. Because He's there living within us, we have the comforting assurance that *"There hath no temptation taken you but such as is common to man: but God is faithful, who will not suffer you to be tempted above that ye are able; but will with the temptation also make a way to escape, that ye may be able to bear it,"* **1 Corinthians 10:13**. Because of Him, we can know *"the peace of God, which passeth all understanding"* which *"shall keep your hearts and minds through Christ Jesus,"* **Philippians 4:7**.

4. Yes, the Comforter has come. He is the Holy Spirit of God. What an amazing thought! God lives in those who are born into the family of God by faith in the Lord Jesus Christ, and He's there to look out for our welfare. He helps us with our prayers, even when we don't know how to ask for what we need. *"Likewise the Spirit also helpeth our infirmities: for we know not what we should pray for as we ought: but the Spirit itself maketh intercession for us with groanings which cannot be uttered. And he that searcheth the hearts knoweth what is the mind of the Spirit, because he maketh intercession for the saints according to the will of God. And we know that all things work together for good to them that love God, to them who are the called according to his purpose,"* **Romans 8:26-28**. What a comfort to know that the Holy Spirit living within us has everything covered! Paul who knew the presence of God in him by the Holy Spirit said, *"For to me to live is Christ, and to die is gain,"* **Philippians 1:21**. There is no greater comfort.

C. It is the Holy Spirit who regenerates the hearts of all who believe in Christ as personal Savior.

1. *"For we ourselves also were sometimes foolish, disobedient, deceived, serving divers lusts and pleasures, living in malice and envy, hateful, and hating one another. But after that the kindness and love of God our Saviour toward man appeared, Not by works of righteousness*

which we have done, but according to his mercy he saved us, by the washing of regeneration, and renewing of the Holy Ghost; Which he shed on us abundantly through Jesus Christ our Saviour; That being justified by his grace, we should be made heirs according to the hope of eternal life," **Titus 3:3-7**.

2. It is not within the realm of human possibilities for any of us to change our sinful states; but at the point of true faith in Christ alone, the Holy Spirit does for us what we could never do for ourselves. He transforms us into the family of God, and clothes us with the righteousness of God in Christ. Paul described the divine transition this way: *"Yea doubtless, and I count all things but loss for the excellency of the knowledge of Christ Jesus my Lord: for whom I have suffered the loss of all things, and do count them but dung, that I may win Christ, And be found in him, not having mine own righteousness, which is of the law, but that which is through the faith of Christ, the righteousness which is of God by faith,"* **Philippians 3:8-9**.

3. Talk about a glorious current work of the Holy Spirit, He changes the life of every person who comes in faith to Christ!

D. The Holy Spirit is not a person in retirement or on a leave of absence.

1. Many of God's sincere people have denied much of the power of the Holy Spirit. They've pretty well shoved Him out of their real everyday life. To them, He's just a *"used to be"* force which is now basically pent-up in the Word and in the hearts of believers. As many people see it, the Holy Spirit is almost a non-person doing very little today. Oh, they think He did great back there in Bible days. He worked in men to perform miracles, to cast out demons, and to write the Bible; but then He seemed to vanish off the scene. It's as if He's a retired author quietly sitting in the hearts of believers doing very little.

2. That is not the case. The Holy Spirit is a real person with plenty to do today. He is not boxed up in the Word or in the hearts of men. He always works consistent with His Word, the Bible; but He is not the Word. The Holy Spirit is not the same as the Word of God. He is a person and the Word is His product. He works in and through His Word; but He also does works such as run the universe. His works of this

sort are not through His Word; however, those works are always consistent to the Word.

3. The Holy Spirit is a very real, living, viable person. He didn't just *"used to be"* a real person; He *"is"* a real person. He didn't just *"used to have"* a job to do; He *"has"* a job to do right now. And, it should be noted that He is doing it! It is painfully obvious that many people do not realize or see what He is currently doing; but He's doing it anyway. Thank God, His great work is not dependent upon our recognition of what He's doing; however, we would be wise to pay attention to what He's doing.

Chapter 16

The High Priestly Work of Christ

Hebrews 4:14-16

Pride is an ever-present danger for all humans, both those who know Jesus Christ as personal Savior and those who don't. Self-reliance and self-exaltation are always close by, if not in control. Our innate nature to want to be in control, and our desires for self-sufficiency ever seek to exert themselves.

Old Testament prophet Habakkuk said to God, *"Thou art of purer eyes than to behold evil, and canst not look on iniquity . . ."* **Habakkuk 1:13**. God is of such awesome majesty and power that no man apart from an intercessor can approach Him and survive. Moses is one of history's greatest men, with man and with God. He said to God, *"I beseech thee, shew me thy glory."* God answered, *"I will make all my goodness pass before thee, and I will proclaim the name of the LORD before thee; and will be gracious to whom I will be gracious, and will shew mercy on whom I will shew mercy. And he said, Thou canst not see my face: for there shall no man see me, and live"* **Exodus 33:18-20**. *"And the LORD said"* to Moses, *"Behold, there is a place by me, and thou shalt stand upon a rock: And it shall come to pass, while my glory passeth by, that I will put thee in a clift of the rock, and will cover thee with my hand while I pass by: And I will take away mine hand, and thou shalt see my back parts: but my face shall not be seen,"* **Exodus 33:21-23**. In an unparalleled display of God to a human, *"The LORD descended in the* *cloud, and stood with him there, and proclaimed the name of the LORD. And the LORD passed by before him, and proclaimed, The LORD, The LORD God, merciful and gracious, longsuffering, and abundant in goodness and truth, Keeping mercy for thousands, forgiving iniquity and transgression and sin, and that will by no means clear the guilty; visiting the iniquity of the fathers upon the children, and upon the children's children, unto the third and to the fourth generation,"* **Exodus 34:5-7**. Even in this veiled appearance, Moses was overwhelmed. *"Moses made haste, and bowed his head toward the earth, and worshipped,"* **Exodus 34:8**.

Hundreds of years later a similar event occurred. Jesus Christ was God; but during His earthly ministry, to prevent the deaths of all who saw Him, His glory as God was veiled.[1] At one point while He was here, He took three of His apostles up onto a high mountain where He *"was transfigured [2] before them: and his face did shine as the sun, and his raiment was white as the light. And, behold, there appeared unto them Moses and Elias talking with him,"* **Matthew 17:2-3**. For that brief moment, Jesus took on some of the unveiled appearance He had prior to His incarnation. His apostles (Peter, James and John) were so stunned that they really didn't know what to say. As they struggled to grasp the sense of the moment, *"a bright cloud overshadowed them: and behold a voice out of the cloud, which said, This is my beloved Son, in whom I am well pleased; hear ye him,"* **Matthew 17:5**. At even this brief glimpse of God in His unveiled glory, *"when the disciples heard it, they fell on their face, and were sore afraid,"* **Matthew 17:6**.

In spite of the holiness, majesty and refusal of God to allow any mortal to approach Him apart from a qualified mediator, many people have little grasp or appreciation of what it takes for a person to enter into the presence of God. Pride and self-sufficiency cause people to think they can come right into the presence of the holy God who created the heavens and the earth as if they are worthy because of their own merits and abilities.

The truth is that for any man to enter into the presence of God, it takes a mediator, someone to act as an intercessor. The fact is that *"there is one God, and one mediator between God and men, the man Christ*

---

[1] See Chapter 3 of this book.

[2] The Greek word for *"transfigured"* is **metamorphoō**. It means to change to another form. See James Strong, *Greek Dictionary of the New Testament,* (Nashville, Tennessee: Abingdon Press, 1958), reference 3339.

Jesus," **1 Timothy 2:5**. Old Testament Job agonized in his heart about how he could get an audience with God. He said to God, *"If I wash myself with snow water, and make my hands never so clean; Yet shalt thou plunge me in the ditch, and mine own clothes shall abhor me,"* **Job 9:30-31**. He realized that God *"is not a man, as I am, that I should answer him, and we should come together in judgment,"* **Job 9:32**. He rightfully concluded that he could never approach God apart from a mediator: *"Neither is there any daysman betwixt us, that might lay his hand upon us both,"* **Job 9:33**.

It's still that way. Every man that comes to the Father must come through the Son who is Jesus Christ. Jesus left no doubt about that reality when He said, *"No man cometh unto the Father, but by me,"* **John 14:6**.

This chapter is therefore given to the High Priestly work of Jesus Christ. It is in this role that He acts as mediator between God and man. Apart from Jesus in this role, no person would ever be able to reach God. No man can bypass Jesus Christ, and reach God.

THE ROLE OF A BIBLICAL HIGH PRIEST

A. Because of their sins, the people could not come before God.

1. In view of his sin, the first man to ever live was driven from the presence of God. *"So he drove out the man; and he placed at the east of the garden of Eden Cherubims, and a flaming sword which turned every way, to keep the way of the tree of life,"* **Genesis 3:24**.
2. Isaiah later stated what is true of every man: *"Your iniquities have separated between you and your God, and your sins have hid his face from you, that he will not hear"* **Isaiah 59:2**.
3. Mankind is universally sinful. *"There is not a just man upon earth, that doeth good, and sinneth not,"* **Ecclesiastes 7:20**. In his sinful condition and merits, no man can ever expect to come into the presence of God.

B. In order to appease God and come into his presence, from the start man began to offer sacrifices to God.

1. Both Cain and Abel, the first two sons of Adam and Eve offered *sacrifices,* and *"By faith Abel offered unto God a more excellent sacrifice than Cain,"* **Hebrews 11:4**.

2. By the time of Abraham, his neighbors had *priests* who existed for the purpose of appeasing the gods. By his time idolatry had infected the people of the earth. There were many false gods, and pagan priests were abundant throughout the Middle East, especially in Egypt. They came out in force to oppose Moses.[3]

C. In His goodness, and to remedy man's hopeless condition, God established a legitimate priesthood to intercede with Him for the people.

1. The word *"priest"* is from the Hebrew primary root verb **kahan**. It means *"to mediate."*[4]

2. From the Israeli tribe of Levi, God chose Aaron and his sons to be the family of Hebrew *priests* or mediators between Him and the people. God said to Moses, *"Take thou unto thee Aaron thy brother, and his sons with him, from among the children of Israel, that he may minister unto me in the priest's office, even Aaron, Nadab and Abihu, Eleazar and Ithamar, Aaron's sons,"* **Exodus 28:1**.

3. From this family of priests, God chose one *"High Priest."* Aaron was the first *High Priest,* **Exodus 28:2-42**. At his death, one of his sons became the next *High Priest.* The office passed down from generation to generation, **Exodus 28:43**.

4. Ordinary priests offered for individuals. The High Priest offered for all the people once a year, on the Day of Atonement, **Leviticus 16**. In a most elaborate ceremony, the High Priest took a bullock and two kid goats. He sacrificed the bullock and one of the goats. He offered the blood of the bullock and one of the goats in the holy place before God. *"And he shall take of the blood of the bullock, and sprinkle it with his finger upon the mercy seat eastward; and before the mercy seat shall he sprinkle of the blood with his finger seven times. Then shall he kill the goat of the sin offering, that is for the people, and bring his blood within the vail, and do with that blood as he did with the blood of the bullock, and sprinkle it upon the mercy seat, and before the mercy*

---

[3] See the Bible book Exodus.

[4] James Strong, *Hebrew and Chaldee Dictionary,* (Nashville, Tennessee: Abingdon Press, 1958), ref. 3547.

seat: And he shall make an atonement for the holy place, because of the uncleanness of the children of Israel, and because of their transgressions in all their sins: and so shall he do for the tabernacle of the congregation, that remaineth among them in the midst of their uncleanness," **Leviticus 16:14-16**. With blood on the goat's head, Aaron released him into the wilderness as a *scapegoat.* This Day of Atonement is observed annually by Jews on the 10th day of the lunar month of Tishri. Jews know this day as Yom Kippur. It falls in September or October of the Gregorian Calendar used by most of the world.[5]

5. All mortal *priests* had sin problems of their own. Hebrews therefore says they had *"to offer up sacrifice, first for his own sins, and then for the people's,"* **Hebrews 7:27**.

D. Four key points were vital to the work of a high priest.

1. He existed for the specific purpose of offering or mediating on behalf of sinners. *"For every high priest taken from among men is ordained for men in things pertaining to God, that he may offer both gifts and sacrifices for sins,"* **Hebrews 5:1**.
2. The offering of the High Priest must have a basis. *"Every high priest is ordained to offer gifts and sacrifices: wherefore it is of necessity that this man have somewhat also to offer,"* **Hebrews 8:3**.
3. The High Priest offered alone, and the basis of his offering was blood. *"Now when these things were thus ordained, the priests went always into the first tabernacle, accomplishing the service of God. But into the second went the high priest alone once every year, not without blood, which he offered for himself, and for the errors of the people,"* **Hebrews 9:6-7**.
4. The High Priest had to offer the offering once every year. *"The high priest entereth into the holy place every year with blood of others,"* **Hebrews 9:25**. The process had to be repeated by the Levitical priests and Aaron because what they did could never address the sin problem. They only moved the problem forward (*kicked the can down the road*). *"And every priest standeth daily ministering and offering oftentimes the same sacrifices, which can never take away sins,"* **Hebrews 10:11**.

---

[5] https://www.britannica.com/topic/Yom-Kippur

E. The work of the High Priest was a work of intercession.

1. The people had no access to God except through the work of the High Priest.

2. Upon the basis of a blood sacrifice, the High Priest interceded for the people.

JESUS IS THE ONE AND ONLY HIGH PRIEST

A. The Old Testament High Priest pointed forward to Christ.

1. The purpose of the Levitical Priesthood was to point sinners to Jesus Christ. Note well the divine reasoning of the Apostle Paul. He asked why God gave the Law (which included the Levitical Priesthood), and answered that it was given because of the sin problem. *"Wherefore then serveth the law? It was added because of transgressions,"* For how long would the Law continue and be in effect? *"Till the seed should come to whom the promise was made."* Read the context. Jesus Christ is the seed to whom the promise was made. *"It was ordained by angels in the hand of a mediator."* The purpose of the Priesthood was and is *mediation. "Now a mediator is not a mediator of one, but God is one."* In mediation, there are at least two parties. *"Is the law then against the promises of God?"* Was the Law intended to be a means to access God on the basis of good human behavior? *"God forbid!"* No way! *"For if there had been a law given which could have given life, verily righteousness should have been by the law."* If a legal system could forgive sins and give eternal life, then the Levitical system of laws and priests would have solved the sin problem. *"But the scripture hath concluded all under sin,* (The sin problem continued in spite of the Levitical system) *that the promise by faith of Jesus Christ might be given to them that believe."* Forgiveness of sins and eternal life come through a Savior, not living by the Law. *"But before faith came, we were kept under the law, shut up unto the faith which should afterwards be revealed."* The Law was there, but it was never the salvation of anyone. *"Wherefore the law was our schoolmaster to bring us unto Christ."* The Law was to teach sinners that salvation is found in *"Christ,"* the Messiah. *"That we might be*

justified by faith." Sinners must trust the Savior to mediate for them upon the basis of what He has done, not their merits. *"But after that faith is come, we are no longer under a schoolmaster."* In view of the coming of Jesus Christ and His redemptive work for sinners, it is futile and foolish to seek salvation in a system of laws. Salvation (access to God) is exclusively in Christ, the one mediator between God and man.

2. The Law with its priesthood was never intended to be the way to address the sin problem. That it didn't solve the problem is evidenced by the fact that they had to keep offering sacrifices over and over. *"Every priest standeth daily ministering and offering oftentimes the same sacrifices, which can never take away sins,"* **Hebrews 10:11**. The Levitical Day of Atonement had to be repeated annually. *"This shall be an everlasting statute unto you, to make an atonement for the children of Israel for all their sins once a year,"* **Leviticus 16:34**.

3. The Bible calls the Old Testament Levitical Priesthood only a foreshadow or preview of the better way which was to come in Christ. *"For the law having a shadow of good things to come, and not the very image of the things, can never with those sacrifices which they offered year by year continually make the comers thereunto perfect,"* **Hebrews 10:1**. The Law could not *"make the comers thereunto perfect"* because it was not the means of justification before God. It was *"a shadow,"* not the real thing. It was *"the figures of the true,"* the counterpoint to reality, **Hebrews 9:24**. In speaking of the Old Testament priests Hebrews says, *"There are priests that offer gifts according to the law,"* **Hebrews 8:4**. Included in this group is *"every high priest"* who was *"ordained to offer gifts and sacrifices,"* **Hebrews 8:3**. This encompasses the entire Levitical Priesthood *"who serve unto the example and shadow of heavenly things,"* **Hebrews 8:5**.

   Sadly, generation after generation of Jews missed the point. They thought salvation results from keeping the *Levitical law*. They couldn't get hold of the fact that salvation and access to God comes by faith in Jesus Christ who is the fulfillment of the Law, not by strict adherence to a good legal system. They couldn't see the Law as a foreshadow of God's provision for access to Him and eternal life; they saw it as the means itself.

B. Jesus Christ is what no other priest ever was or will be.

1. Christ alone paid the full price of eternal redemption. *"And every priest standeth daily ministering and offering oftentimes the same sacrifices, which can never take away sins: But this man, after he had offered one sacrifice for sins for ever, sat down on the right hand of God,"* **Hebrews 10:11-12**. Note well, *"one sacrifice for sins for ever."* How glorious! Jesus Christ did what all priests before Him could never do. By the sacrifice of Himself, He solved the sin problem once and for all. *"Forever"* is from the Greek adverb **diēnekes** meaning continuous and perpetual.[6] He will never again repeat His offering for sin; it will never again be needed. If His sacrifice of Himself had not been fully sufficient, He would have had to repeat it for every generation;[7] but that will never be needed. *"For Christ is not entered into the holy places made with hands, which are the figures of the true; but into heaven itself, now to appear in the presence of God for us: Nor yet that he should offer himself often, as the high priest entereth into the holy place every year with blood of others; For then must he often have suffered since the foundation of the world: but now once in the end of the world hath he appeared to put away sin by the sacrifice of himself,"* **Hebrews 9:24-26**. Note well the word *"once."* He offered *one "sacrifice of himself."* The Greek word for *"once"* is **hapax** meaning *one time with perpetual validity. Not requiring repetition.*[8] Thus come the words, *"From henceforth expecting till his enemies be made his footstool. For by one offering he hath perfected for ever them that are sanctified"* **Hebrews 10:14**.

2. Be reminded that the High Priest must have a basis for his intercession. *"Every high priest is ordained to offer gifts and sacrifices: wherefore it is of necessity that this man have somewhat also to offer,"* **Hebrews 8:3**.

---

[6] James Strong, *Greek Dictionary of the New Testament,* (Nashville, Tennessee: Abingdon Press, 1958), ref. 1336.

[7] Kenneth S. Wuest, *Wuest's Word Studies From the Greek New Testament,* vol.2, *Hebrews in the Greek New Testament,* (Grand Rapids, Michigan: Wm. B. Eerdmans Publishing Company, 1971), 169-171.

[8] W.E. Vine, Merrill F. Unger, William White, Jr., *Vine's Expository Dictionary of Biblical Words,* (Nashville, Tennessee: Thomas Nelson Publishers, 1985), 445.

In view of His fulfillment of all prophetic typologies by the sacrifice of Himself, Christ alone now intercedes for us (sinners); and He does so upon the strength of His own shed blood. His blood is the basis of His intercession for us. *"But Christ being come an high priest of good things to come, by a greater and more perfect tabernacle, not made with hands, that is to say, not of this building; Neither by the blood of goats and calves, but by his own blood he entered in once into the holy place, having obtained eternal redemption for us. For if the blood of bulls and of goats, and the ashes of an heifer sprinkling the unclean, sanctifieth to the purifying of the flesh: How much more shall the blood of Christ, who through the eternal Spirit offered himself without spot to God, purge your conscience from dead works to serve the living God? And for this cause he is the mediator of the new testament, that by means of death, for the redemption of the transgressions that were under the first testament, they which are called might receive the promise of eternal inheritance,"* **Hebrews 9:11-15**.

3. Unlike all other priests, including Aaron and all other High Priests, by His death, burial and resurrection, Jesus Christ fully address the sin problem forever. Upon His death, He offered His own blood as the one-time offering to God for the sins of the world. *"Neither by the blood of goats and calves, but by his own blood he entered in once into the holy place, having obtained eternal redemption for us,"* **Hebrews 9:12**. *"By his own blood."* Furthermore, He didn't offer his own blood on some earthly, man-made altar. He offered His blood in heaven before God. *"Christ is not entered into the holy places made with hands, which are the figures of the true; but into heaven itself, now to appear in the presence of God for us,"* **Hebrews 9:24**. Note well: *"in the presence of God for us."* Sins paid! Once and for all! By the blood of Jesus Christ!

4. Jesus Christ alone is uniquely qualified to intercede for sinners as High Priest. *"And they truly were many priests, because they were not suffered to continue by reason of death: But this man, because he continueth ever, hath an unchangeable priesthood. Wherefore he is able also to save them to the uttermost that come unto God by him, seeing he ever liveth to make intercession for them. For such an high priest became us, who is holy, harmless, undefiled, separate from sinners, and made higher than the heavens; Who needeth not daily, as those high priests, to* *offer up sacrifice, first for his own sins, and then for the people's: for this he did once, when he offered up himself,"* **Hebrews 7:23-27**.

C. In view of Jesus Christ the High Priest, sinners are invited to come to God.

1. Jesus is there. He can connect any person to God. Here are the words of God in the Bible: *"Seeing then that we have a great high priest, that is passed into the heavens, Jesus the Son of God, let us hold fast our profession. For we have not an high priest which cannot be touched with the feeling of our infirmities; but was in all points tempted like as we are, yet without sin. Let us therefore come boldly unto the throne of grace, that we may obtain mercy, and find grace to help in time of need,"* **Hebrews 4:14-16**.

2. This High Priest has addressed the sin problem once and for all and is capable of bringing even the vilest sinner into the presence of the holy God of the Universe.

   When will He bring *even the vilest sinner* into the presence of the holy God of the Universe? When that sinner comes to Him in the heart, trusting Him and Him alone to forgive his sin and give eternal life. *"For God so loved the world, that he gave his only begotten Son, that whosoever believeth in him should not perish, but have everlasting life. For God sent not his Son into the world to condemn the world; but that the world through him might be saved. He that believeth on him is not condemned: but he that believeth not is condemned already, because he hath not believed in the name of the only begotten Son of God,"* **John 3:16-18**.

3. That's as straightforward as it gets. Whether or not a sinner can approach God does not depend on the condition of the sinner be it good or bad. No. It depends upon the intercession of the High Priest in view of what the High Priest has done for the sinner. If the sinner tries to come to God on his own, then he will never see God. If the sinner is willing to give up on all he is and claim in trust/faith the finished work of the High Priest on his behalf, then he will receive forgiveness of sins and eternal life. Old Testament Job looked forward in faith/trust to the redemptive work of Jesus Christ the great High Priest. He spoke for every believer in the finished work of Jesus Christ when he said,

> *"For I know that my redeemer liveth, and that he shall stand at the latter day upon the earth: And though after my skin worms destroy this body, yet in my flesh shall I see God: Whom I shall see for myself, and mine eyes shall behold, and not another; though my reins be consumed within me,"* **Job 19:25-27**.

Do not imagine that the High Priestly work of Christ is some small, insignificant matter. Ever person's eternal destination turns on Christ's work as a mediator. Without Christ as High Priest, no person can see God.

JESUS CHRIST IS FOREVERMORE THE ONE AND ONLY HIGH PRIEST

A. No person can come to God apart from Jesus Christ.

1. Jesus personally said no one can come to the Father apart from Him. *"I am the way, the truth, and the life: no man cometh unto the Father, but by me,"* **John 14:6**.

2. In speaking of Himself Jesus said, *"If ye believe not that I am he, ye shall die in your sins,"* **John 8:24**.

3. If it is possible for people to come to God apart from Jesus Christ, then Jesus left heaven, took on Himself a human body, lived a perfect sinless life, went to the cross, offered Himself a sacrifice for sins and presented His own blood before God on man's behalf all in vain. It wasn't necessary.

4. The truth is, what Jesus Christ did was necessary. There was and is no other way. *"Neither is there salvation in any other: for there is none other name under heaven given among men, whereby we must be saved"* **Acts 4:12**.

5. Sinners must have a mediator, and Jesus Christ is the only mediator there is. *"There is one God, and one mediator between God and men, the man Christ Jesus,"* **1 Timothy 2:5**.

B. No person can by-pass God's plan for reconciliation and still receive the benefits of Christ including salvation and prayer.

1. *"He that believeth on the Son hath everlasting life: and he that believeth not the Son shall not see life; but the wrath of God abideth on him,"* **John 3:36**. Salvation comes only by the work of a mediator, and the only one who can mediate for sinners is *"the Son,"* the Lord Jesus Christ.

2. In view of the depth and clarity of the Bible on Christ being the only way of reaching God, the number of people think it is possible to reach God while leaving Jesus Christ out of the loop is amazing.

    a. Multitudes feel that just believing there is *a god* is enough, especially if that god is the God of the Bible. Some years ago, an American president indicated that men cannot go to heaven apart from faith in Jesus Christ. For several months, there was a firestorm in the Jewish community.

    b. An increasing number of people say things like, *"I'm okay with God. I don't need this church and Jesus business."*

    c. Through the years, millions of people have united with some church with little thought to sin, Jesus Christ and a personal relationship to Him. They felt that was all they needed to spend eternity with God

    d. The grasp of true Christianity has become extremely shallow with the vast majority of people who claim to embrace it. It is getting more and more difficult to find professing Christians with a clear, strong testimony of meeting with Christ in their hearts. Chapters like this about the High Priestly work of Christ have a distant and somewhat shallow ring.

3. Even in the ranks of those who staunchly believe and be guided by the Bible, the need for a mediator in getting people to Christ is left out of the picture. Lost people are not first told to believe on Christ in view of His finished redemptive work. They're first told to pray a prayer. The Bible verse that is commonly used is, *"For whosoever shall call upon the name of the Lord shall be saved,"* **Romans 10:13**. They're not told who Christ is, and of the great sin sacrifice He

offered on the cross for them. The same passage that talks about *"calling on the name of the Lord"* also says that *"faith cometh by hearing, and hearing by the word of God,"* **Romans 10:17**. The verse immediately following the statement about *"calling"* asks, *"How then shall they call on him in whom they have not believed? and how shall they believe in him of whom they have not heard? and how shall they hear without a preacher?"* **Romans 10:14**. It is unmistakably obvious that a person with no knowledge or poor knowledge of sin, of Jesus Christ, of what He has done about sin and of what belief in Him (faith) is cannot *call on the Lord.*

Look at the scenario. Here's a lost person who has no mediator being asked to *call on the Lord.* They can't do it until they have a mediator, and the only mediator is Jesus Christ. What the lost sinner must first do is *"Believe on the Lord Jesus Christ."* That will result in salvation: *"and thou shalt be saved,"* **Acts 16:31**. When the sinner believes in Jesus Christ in view of His sacrifice for sins, Christ will become his mediator, his intercessor. The person will then be in a position to *call upon the Lord.* However, asking a person without a mediator to have an audience with God violates the entire concept that no person can come to God except through Jesus Christ.

The High Priestly work of Christ is a profound and precious truth. The Scriptures are saturated with the teaching. Never let us take it for granted, or in our zeal suggest that men can somehow get to God apart from Jesus Christ our High Priest.

Chapter 17

The Transitional Era and Gifts of the Holy Spirit

John 16:5-16

The gifts of the Holy Spirit are highly controversial. What are they? What was their purpose? Does every believer receive a gift? Do all of the promises of the Bible apply to all believers? Did Jesus' promise to the thief on the cross apply to every believer? Who do you know that can raise a dead person? If you have a gift, how do you know what it is?

What God can do or enable a person to do is not in question. The Bible is clear that *"with God nothing shall be impossible,"* **Luke 1:37**. *"Our God is in the heavens: he hath done whatsoever he hath pleased,"* **Psalm 115:3**. The question is what He will or will not do. The Bible says God, *"cannot lie,"* **Titus 1:2**. He is always *good. "O give thanks unto the LORD; for he is good; for his mercy endureth for ever,"* **1 Chronicles 16:34**. God never does evil. The fact that He gives eternal life to those who trust Christ, and eternal death to those who reject Christ does not make Him evil or inconsistent. He consistently offers life to all who believe on the Son, and damnation to all who don't. God always speaks and acts consistently with Himself. With God there *"is no variableness, neither shadow of turning,"* **James 1:17**. The fact that Jesus raised Lazarus from the dead, **John 11:43-44**, but did not raise all other dead persons didn't make Him inconsistent or a respecter of persons. *"God is no respecter of persons,"* **Acts 10:34**. God is equitable and just with all people, but He doesn't treat everybody the same. Some are born males, and some are born females. Some are born in America; some are born in China. Yet, who God is remains the same. His love, mercy, justice, omnipotence and essential goodness remain the same.

He gave divine revelation directly to some people such as Moses, David, Isaiah, Daniel, John, Matthew and Paul. The rest of us get divine revelation from His Word (the Bible) which He gave directly to those prophets and apostles. That in no way makes God inconsistent. He gave the power to heal a lame man to Peter and John. See **Acts 3:1-8**. He could give you or me the power to miraculously heal someone, but He doesn't. He's still just and impartial. It is not necessary for Him to treat everybody the same in order to remain just and changeless. There are those who claim they can do everything anyone in the Bible did. Surely, if that was true, we would need no doctors, other medical people and medicines; those with special healing powers would be out there healing all the sick people and those with birth defects. If Jesus' promise of infallibility was for all believers, we wouldn't need to rely on the Bible as our final authority for truth; every believer would be full of new revelation.

THE ERA SURROUNDING THE EARTHLY LIFE OF CHRIST WAS A TIME OF TRANSITION

A. During Jesus' earthly ministry and immediately following, a many-faceted transition was in progress.

   1. The new covenant of grace was replacing the old covenant of law. *"Behold, the days come, saith the Lord, when I will make a new covenant with the house of Israel and with the house of Judah,"* **Hebrews 8:8**. Jesus Christ is *"Christ is the end of the law for righteousness to every one that believeth,"* **Romans 10:4**. Salvation is exclusively in the one to whom the Levitical law pointed; not in keeping the law. Jesus became the new High Priest replacing the Levitical priesthood. *"Seeing then that we have a great high priest, that is passed into the heavens, Jesus the Son of God, let us hold fast our profession. For we have not an high priest which cannot be touched with the feeling of our infirmities; but was in all points tempted like as we are, yet without sin,"* **Hebrews 4:14-15**.

2. The temple was being replaced by the church. God would recognize no more animal sacrifices; henceforth, only the blood sacrifice of His Son would count. *"Neither by the blood of goats and calves, but by his own blood he entered in once into the holy place, having obtained eternal redemption for us,"* **Hebrews 9:12**. As divine testimony that animal sacrifices were to end, when Jesus offered Himself on the cross as the one-time eternal sacrifice for the world, *"The veil of the temple was rent in twain from the top to the bottom; and the earth did quake, and the rocks rent,"* **Matthew 27:51**.

3. This is the time when the Holy Spirit ceased to come upon people for special purposes, but instead came to dwell in the heart of every believer. *"Know ye not that ye are the temple of God, and that the Spirit of God dwelleth in you?"* **1 Corinthians 3:16**. Jesus said, *"The Comforter, which is the Holy Ghost, whom the Father will send in my name, he shall teach you all things, and bring all things to your remembrance, whatsoever I have said unto you,"* **John 14:26**.

4. This brief mention is not intended to be a full explanation of things which were in transition during this era. It is adequate to establish the fact that a transitional era existed, and that many things were in transition. It was a special era in which God was doing some things in different ways.

B. Jesus spoke specifically of one major aspect of the transition which was in process.

1. Here are His words describing one major aspect of the transition: *"But now I go my way to him that sent me; and none of you asketh me, Whither goest thou? But because I have said these things unto you, sorrow hath filled your heart. Nevertheless I tell you the truth; It is expedient for you that I go away: for if I go not away, the Comforter will not come unto you; but if I depart, I will send him unto you. And when he is come, he will reprove the world of sin, and of righteousness, and of judgment: Of sin, because they believe not on me; Of righteousness, because I go to my Father, and ye see me no more; Of judgment, because the prince of this world is judged. I have yet many things to say unto you, but ye cannot bear them now. Howbeit when he, the Spirit of truth, is come, he will guide you into all truth: for he shall not speak of himself; but whatsoever he shall hear, that shall he speak: and he will shew you*

things to come. He shall glorify me: for he shall receive of mine, and shall shew it unto you. All things that the Father hath are mine: therefore said I, that he shall take of mine, and shall shew it unto you. A little while, and ye shall not see me: and again, a little while, and ye shall see me, because I go to the Father," **John 16:5-16**.

2. For more than three years, Jesus had been with His apostles teaching, training and mentoring. In this text, He told them that He was about to leave them. *"Now I go my way to him that sent me . . . It is expedient for you that I go away . . . A little while, and ye shall not see me."*

3. For 400 years the Holy Spirit had been silent, and no new revelation had come from God. During the time of Christ and immediately following His return to Heaven, new divine revelation would be given. It would be called the New Testament. Although some of His leaders missed it (and many have missed it in the generations which have followed), Jesus made this truth very clear. He said to His apostles to whom He would give this new revelation, the 27 books of the New Testament, *"I have yet many things to say unto you, but ye cannot bear them now. Howbeit when he, the Spirit of truth, is come, he will guide you into all truth: for he shall not speak of himself; but whatsoever he shall hear, that shall he speak: and he will shew you things to come. He shall glorify me: for he shall receive of mine, and shall shew it unto you. All things that the Father hath are mine: therefore said I, that he shall take of mine, and shall shew it unto you,"* **John 16:12-15**.

   It's hard to imagine anything being made clearer. Jesus was talking to His apostles, not everybody. He told them that there was more revelation to come, and that they would be infallible in receiving this new revelation. (*"He will guide you into all truth"* is a promise of infallibility.) He also told them that this special revelation would be shown to them. There's zero hint that the promise was for all believers. As clear as it is, large numbers of good, earnest people have completely missed it. They think this promise is to them too. The fact is that the best of them is very fallible is solid proof that the promise was not for them. The truth is that only the divinely inspired Bible (Old and New Testaments) is infallible.

C. Lest you fall into grave error, it is extremely important to know that the purpose of the Holy Spirit empowered miraculous signs and wonders was to confirm that the apostles were messengers from God, and that their writings were authentic.

1. Since only the apostles could confer these special powers to a third person, bystanders realized that the giving of new revelation was inseparably tied to the apostles. The revelation came from one of the apostles or from one under their immediate and direct authority. Be reminded that Philip, who was not an apostle, did miracles. He received that ability (power) from the apostles, but had no ability to give the power to a third person. In Samaria, Simon-the-sorcerer *"Saw that through laying on of the apostles' hands the Holy Ghost was given,"* **Acts 8:18**. It isn't the person of the Holy Ghost that is under consideration in this passage; it's the *"power."* It was the *"power"* that got Simon's attention. He saw that Philip couldn't give the *"power"* to a third person, but Peter and John (apostles) could. He promptly *"he offered them money,"* **Acts 8:18**. He also quickly recognized how this *"power"* was given to a third person. It was *"through laying on of the apostles' hands."*

2. Jesus promised the apostles: *"Ye shall receive power, after that the Holy Ghost is come upon you,"* **Acts 1:8**. To *"the eleven"* Jesus said, *"And these signs shall follow them that believe; In my name shall they cast out devils; they shall speak with new tongues; They shall take up serpents; and if they drink any deadly thing, it shall not hurt them; they shall lay hands on the sick, and they shall recover,"* **Mark 16:17-18**.The apostles could speak a language and hearers who didn't know the local language could hear in their own language, **Acts 2:6**. The apostles could instantly heal people with birth defects, **Acts 3:1-8**, raise the dead, **Acts 9:36-41**, remain unharmed by the bite of a lethal snake, **Acts 28:1-5**, and write infallible truth which we call the New Testament. Mark put it this way: *"They* (the apostles) *went forth, and preached every where, the Lord working with them, and confirming the word with signs following,"* **Mark 16:20**. Note well, this is a statement about *"the eleven,"* and nobody else, **Mark 16:14**. The apostles had *"the power."*

3. Note well Mark's words: *"Confirming the word with signs following,"* **Mark 16:20**. The miraculous works *confirmed "the word." "Confirming"* is translated from the Greek verb **bebaioo**. It means to establish, make firm and sure; *"To prove its truth; divinity."*[1]

4. The apostles were not the only men claiming to be of God. Many others were teaching and writing materials which they claimed to be inspired of God. There were Gnostics, Jews who rejected Christ and sought to subvert true believers. In his letter to the Galatians, the apostle Paul mentioned *"False brethren unawares brought in, who came in privily to spy out our liberty which we have in Christ Jesus, that they might bring us into bondage,"* **Galatians 2:4**. The apostle Peter reported that *"there were false prophets also among the people, even as there shall be false teachers among you, who privily shall bring in damnable heresies, even denying the Lord that bought them, and bring upon themselves swift destruction"* **2 Peter 2:1**.

5. Knowing who and what to believe could be confusing to people: There were so many voices, all claiming to be of God and have the truth. *Who is telling the truth, and who is not? How do we know?* The apostles were God's men with His truth, and they could prove it. The others had no proof. All they could do was argue and contend with passion. The apostles and those upon whom they laid their hands could do miracles; nobody else could.

6. The apostles were divinely confirming the words of the New Testament to be in truth God's Words. They had His divine stamp of approval and confirmation. The miraculous abilities were not to glorify and exalt the apostles; they were God's way of confirming His Word. They enabled the people to tell the true from the counterfeit. God did it in one era of time, the transitional era. The Bible says it was *"once delivered unto the saints,"* **Jude 3**. God confirmed His Word as He gave it. He does not need to reconfirm it. It's done. It's proven! The Bible will stand inspection. No further proof or confirmation is necessary.

---

[1] James Strong, *Greek Dictionary of the New Testament,* (Nashville, Tennessee: Abingdon Press, 1958), ref. 950.

7. Once the task of finalizing the New Testament was completed, there was no further need for the miraculous *"power."* It had served its purpose. There remains a need for the power of God whereby we may serve Him acceptably. That need will never go away. That *power* is not the same as the miracle-working *"power"* the apostles had for the purpose of confirming God's Word as it was given. The apostle Paul explained that *"Charity never faileth: but whether there be prophecies, they shall fail; whether there be tongues, they shall cease; whether there be knowledge, it shall vanish away. For we know in part, and we prophesy in part. But when that which is perfect is come, then that which is in part shall be done away,"* **1 Corinthians 13:8-10**. *"Chairty"* is true, godly *love.* It never goes away; however, that's not true of *"prophecies," "tongues"* and the divine *"knowledge"* (revelation) Jesus gave the apostles. That's what Jesus meant when He said, *"Ye shall receive power, after that the Holy Ghost is come upon you,"* **Acts 1:8**. Paul said these special powers would end: *"whether there be prophecies, they shall fail; whether there be tongues, they shall cease; whether there be knowledge, it shall vanish away."* When was that to happen? *"When that which is perfect is come."* When Paul was writing these words, the revelation was *"in part."* Once the revelation was complete, it was and is no longer *"in part;"* instead it is *"that which is perfect."* Paul was not talking about the Second Coming of Christ or the death and eternal home of the believer. He was talking about the completed Word of God, the Bible.

8. Obviously, during the transitional era, God gave special miraculous gifts to the men He used to finalize His Word, the Bible. When God made it clear that the gospel of Christ is for all people, not only Jews; the apostle Peter spoke of *"How God anointed Jesus of Nazareth with the Holy Ghost and with power: who went about doing good, and healing all that were oppressed of the devil; for God was with him. And we are witnesses of all things which he did both in the land of the Jews, and in Jerusalem; whom they slew and hanged on a tree: Him God raised up the third day, and shewed him openly; Not to all the people, but unto witnesses chosen before of God, even to us, who did eat and drink with him after he rose from the dead. And he commanded us to preach unto the people, and to testify that it is he which was ordained of God to be the Judge of quick and dead. To* *him give all the prophets witness, that through his name whosoever believeth in him shall receive remission of sins,"* **Acts 10:38-43**. It is important to note that after His resurrection Jesus was seen of many people, His main focus was on His apostles. *"Him God raised up the third day, and shewed him openly; Not to all the people, but unto witnesses chosen before of God, even to us, who did eat and drink with him after he rose from the dead."* These are the ones who were *"chosen before of God"* to receive His divine inspiration, and to receive His special miraculous gives.

THE GIFTS OF THE HOLY SPIRIT

A. A correct understanding of *"gifts"* necessitates knowledge of what a *gift from God* is.

1. James said, *"Every good gift and every perfect gift is from above, and cometh down from the Father of lights, with whom is no variableness, neither shadow of turning,"* **James 1:17**. In this passage, the word *"gift"* is from the Greek word **dosis**.[2] It speaks of something given to another. It can be tangible such as *"gold, frankincense and myrrh,"* **Matthew 2:11**. The gift can be intangible such as restored ability to walk. That's the *gift* Peter gave to a lame man: *"Silver and gold have I none; but such as I have give I thee,"* **Acts 3:6**. James established the fact that the ultimate source of all *gifts* is God. *"Every good gift and every perfect gift is from above, and cometh down from the Father of lights."*

2. Several Greek words in common use at the time the New Testament was written can be translated into English as gift. The most commonly translated word is charisma which speaks of a gratuity or endowment. Inherent in charisma is the idea of granting a favor. From it the Greeks got **charis** meaning graciousness of manner or act. We call it grace. We speak of charming or graceful people as charismatic. We know that no person can give natural abilities to another person. Only God can do that. We thus know that natural abilities are gifts from God. They are never merited; God simply gives or endows different people in different areas. It's

[2] Ibid., ref. 1394.

a matter of grace. The Greeks saw charisma as a divine gratuity. It is noteworthy that in the Bible, the word talent always refers to money, never to excelling natural ability. Every time natural abilities are under consideration in the Bible, a Greek word meaning gift is used. When we refer to one's talent or natural ability, we merely speak of what one has. These words talent or natural ability say nothing of where their source. The word gift says instantly that the natural ability came from an outside source; it is not native to the person who possesses it. By God's use of *"gift"* He reminds everyone that He is the source and the glory goes to Him.[3]

B. There are two kinds or types of gifts.

1. There are natural gifts.

a. Natural gifts from God come at birth, not when a person is saved. These natural gifts from God are obvious and observable. Some people are naturally athletic. Others are musical and still others are handsome or beautiful. Some are mechanical. There are natural scholars, natural organizers, natural entrepreneurs and the list could go on for a very long time. The propensities and abilities often begin to show in children at very young ages.

b. These are natural birthrights, gifts from God. They do not suddenly start when a person is saved; they are already there. The person who is a good singer or musician at church had the ability (and was usually practicing it) before he/she was saved and became a part of a church. Likewise, the person who has great church administrative skills, the person with a winning personality and the person with business and financial wisdom.

c. In a very literal sense, in one way or another all people have been naturally gifted by God. The Apostle Paul stated the obvious when he said, *"But every man hath his proper gift of God, one after this manner, and another after that,"* **1 Corinthians 7:7**. In society in general it is not difficult

---

[3] Lester Hutson, *Great Bible Truths Revisited,* (Amazon: ISBN: 978-1-7324282-0-1, 2011), 386.

to observe different abilities and strengths in different people. It is common practice for educators and employers to give aptitude tests and seek by other means to identify natural abilities and use people in the areas of their strengths.[4]

d. Once a person is saved, he/she should use his/her natural gift to the fullest extent in his church to the glory of God. If he does not know what his gift is, he should indeed identify it. If his gift has not been cultivated, he should cultivate it. God gave it and it should be used to glorify God. The apostle Paul wrote a letter to the Church at Rome. He spoke to them of their intimate connection as members of the same church. He made it clear that every member had a gift from God: *"Having then gifts differing according to the grace that is given to us."* There is no indication that any of these Romans received their *"gifts"* from God only when they became Christians. What is clear is that every one of them was to use his *"gift"* to build and strengthen the church to the glory of God. It is also obvious that the many differing *"gifts"* could beautifully mesh together to enhance the work of the church. *"For I say, through the grace given unto me, to every man that is among you, not to think of himself more highly than he ought to think; but to think soberly, according as God hath dealt to every man the measure of faith. For as we have many members in one body, and all members have not the same office: So we, being many, are one body in Christ, and every one members one of another. Having then gifts differing according to the grace that is given to us, whether prophecy, let us prophesy according to the proportion of faith; Or ministry, let us wait on our ministering: or he that teacheth, on teaching; Or he that exhorteth, on exhortation: he that giveth, let him do it with simplicity; he that ruleth, with diligence; he that sheweth mercy, with cheerfulness,"* **Romans 12:3-8**. Natural gifts are not given without responsibility. Every man, especially those who have been born again into the family of God, is accountable to use his gift to honor God. *"As every man hath received*

---

[4] Ibid.

the gift, even so minister the same gift one to another, as good stewards of the manifold grace of God," **1 Peter 4:10.**[5]

e. Sadly, many in the current Christian community claim that these natural of gifts are given by the Holy Spirit only at the point of one's salvation. That really disillusions bystanders who know that the great church pianist was a great pianist long before he/she was saved. The same can be said of the great teachers, those with extraordinary insight, the financial wizards, the good organizers, those with an eye for decoration, those with deep warmth and compassion and those who have the gift of exhortation.

Natural gifts should not be equated with or called spiritual gifts. Natural gifts and spiritual gifts are not one and the same. They are in different categories; one is natural, the other is supernatural. A natural gift should not be called a spiritual gift. No one with a natural gift should claim or imply that the gift was received from God only at the point of salvation. The honest thing to do is admit the obvious: the natural gift was given by God at birth. Bystanders already know that. The right thing to do is give God the glory for your abilities (gifts). Once you are saved, commit your gifts to Him to be used in His church to the fullest of your capacity.[6]

2. There are spiritual gifts.

a. The Bible is precise as to what the spiritual gifts are. In total there were nine spiritual gifts; they are listed in **1 Corinthians 12:8-10**.

1) *"The word of wisdom,"* **verse 8.**

2) *"The word of knowledge,"* **verse 8.**

3) *"Faith,"* **verse 9.**

4) *"The gifts of healing,"* **verse 9.**

---

[5] Ibid., 387.
[6] Ibid., 388.

5) *"The working of miracles,"* **verse 10**.

6) *"Prophecy,"* **verse 10**.

7) *"The discerning of spirits,"* **verse 10**.

8) *"Divers kinds of tongues,"* **verse 10**.

9) *"The interpretation of tongues,"* **verse 10**.

b. Each of these spiritual gifts was supernatural, not natural. Each was miraculous in nature; it could neither be performed nor explained by natural means of any sort. Each was beyond all natural abilities. Those who had these powers were not born with them; these powers or abilities were special divine powers given and performed directly through the Holy Spirit. *"Now there are diversities of gifts, but the same Spirit. And there are differences in administrations, but the same Lord"* **1 Corinthians 12:4-5**. *"But all these worketh that one and the selfsame Spirit, dividing to every man severally as he will"* **1 Corinthians 12:11**.

1) *"The word of wisdom"* was divine power to reason. It was perception and ability to make decisions and judgments above and beyond what any human could do through natural reasoning processes. This special power was embodied in Jesus Christ who had power to perceive what others were thinking. *"And Jesus, perceiving the thoughts of their heart,"* **Luke 9:47**. Peter had this special divine wisdom. He immediately perceived the deception in the heart of Ananias and in his wife Sapphira. *"But a certain man named Ananias, with Sapphira his wife, sold a possession, And kept back part of the price, his wife also being privy to it, and brought a certain part, and laid it at the apostles' feet. But Peter said, Ananias, why hath Satan filled thine heart to lie to the Holy Ghost, and to keep back part of the price of the land? Whiles it remained, was it not thine own? and after it was sold, was it not in thine own power? why hast thou conceived this thing in thine heart? thou hast not lied unto men, but unto God,"* **Acts 5:1-4**. Paul demonstrated this spiritual gift. *"And there sat a certain man at Lystra, impotent in his feet,* *being a cripple from his mother's womb, who never had walked: The same heard Paul speak: who stedfastly beholding him, and perceiving that he had faith to be healed, Said with a loud voice, Stand upright on thy feet. And he leaped and walked,"* **Acts 14:8-10**. Notice that Paul *"perceiving that he had faith to be healed."* This is power from God that no man has naturally. The spiritual gift of wisdom was not merely extraordinary human wisdom. It was wisdom beyond natural human ability.

2) *"The word of knowledge"* was the ability to know without any possible human way of knowing. People with this gift had divine illumination apart from study or human methods of gaining knowledge. This was knowledge by special divine revelation. It was by this knowledge that the Scriptures were given. *"All scripture is given by inspiration of God,"* **2 Timothy 3:16**. *"For the prophecy came not in old time by the will of man: but holy men of God spake as they were moved by the Holy Ghost,"* **2 Peter 1:21**. God gave this spiritual gift to the Apostles. Jesus thus said to them, *"I have yet many things to say unto you, but ye cannot bear them now. Howbeit when he, the Spirit of truth, is come, he will guide you into all truth: for he shall not speak of himself; but whatsoever he shall hear, that shall he speak: and he will shew you things to come,"* **John 16:12-13**. There are many brilliant people with high intelligence quotas. No human naturally has the *"the word of knowledge."* This kind of knowledge was a spiritual gift by the Holy Spirit of God.

3) *"Faith"* was faith by which one could perform miracles, not extraordinarily strong trust in God. Jesus demonstrated this faith when He raised Lazarus from the dead. *"He cried with a loud voice, Lazarus, come forth,"* **John 11:43**. This special divine faith is seen by Peter's healing of the lame man. See **Acts 3:1-8**.

4) *"The gifts of healing"* were divine ability to restore one instantly to health regardless of the physical infirmity and regardless of lack of faith on the part of the person with the disease, affliction or other infirmity. Peter demonstrated this spiritual gift when he raised the lame man. *"Silver and gold have I none; but such as I have give I thee: In the name of Jesus Christ of Nazareth rise up and walk. And he took him by the right hand, and lifted him up: and immediately his feet and ankle bones received strength. And he leaping up stood, and walked, and entered with them into the temple, walking, and leaping, and praising God,"* **Acts 3:6-8**.

5) *"The working of miracles"* was divine power by which a human could perform the humanly impossible. This spiritual gift was demonstrated when Peter raised Dorcas from the dead. See **Acts 9:36-41**.

6) *"Prophecy"* was the ability to tell forth the mind of God prior to it being set forth in any other way and prior to its fulfillment. It was more than merely heralding forth or preaching a previously declared portion of the Word of God. Paul exhibited this ability when the ship upon which he was a passenger encountered a great storm. He stood before the other passengers and announced, *"And now I exhort you to be of good cheer: for there shall be no loss of any man's life among you, but of the ship. For there stood by me this night the angel of God, whose I am, and whom I serve, Saying, Fear not, Paul; thou must be brought before Caesar: and, lo, God hath given thee all them that sail with thee. Wherefore, sirs, be of good cheer: for I believe God, that it shall be even as it was told me,"* **Acts 27:22-25**. The outcome was just as Paul predicted. *"And so it came to pass, that they escaped all to land,"* **Acts 27:44**.

7) *"The discerning of spirits"* was the ability to discern at once whether or not the spirit prompting any speech or action was of God. This is the spiritual gift that enabled Peter to say to Simon the Sorcerer, *"For I perceive that thou art in the gall of bitterness, and in the bond of iniquity,"* **Acts 8:23**. No man by natural human ability can know another person's motives. Only God looks on the heart, **1 Samuel 16:7**, and only He can reveal to a man the condition of another man's heart. It takes a special spiritual gift for one to discern spirits in this sense.

8) *"Divers kinds of tongues"* was the ability to speak a foreign language never previously known by the speaker. *"Tongues"* is from the Greek word **glossa** simply meaning a *"language, specially one naturally unacquired."*[7] From either a biblical or linguistic standpoint, there is no reason to believe that tongues have anything to do with ecstatic languages or unintelligible utterances. Since *"unknown"* did not appear in the original manuscripts, the King James translators included *"unknown"* in italics simply to communicate the idea that the speaker spoke fluently a language that was unknown to him because he did not previously know that language. The language was not unknown to the world; it was unknown to the speaker. For example, Hebrew and Greek were both well-established languages of that day; however, there were many Greek-speaking Romans who did not know Hebrew. The spiritual gift of tongues would allow one whose native tongue was Greek to fluently speak Hebrew without learning Hebrew.

9) *"The interpretation of tongues"* was the divine ability to interpret to a native audience the unknown language spoken by the man with the spiritual gift of tongues. Obviously, the interpreter, who never before knew the new language, had to understand the new language in order to interpret it into his native tongue. That ability is not natural to anyone; the ability was possible only as a divine spiritual gift.[8]

3. There are natural gifts and there are spiritual gifts. In both cases, they come from God. He gives all men various natural gifts. He gave spiritual gifts only to the apostles and those upon whom they laid their hands. Only the apostles had

---

[7] Strong, ref. 1100.
[8] Hutson, 388-392.

power to convey a spiritual gift to a third person. Thus, when the apostles and those upon whom they had laid their hands died, the spiritual gifts ceased. No person today has a spiritual gift.[9]

[9] For more information on whether or not spiritual gifts are currently operable, Unknown Tongues and Miracle Healing, see *Great Bible Truths revisited* by Lester Hutson. The book is available from Amazon.com.

Chapter 18

The Leadership of the Holy Spirit

Romans 8:14

Keep clearly in mind that the Holy Spirit is a real person; not merely a strong, compelling force or influence. He is the third person in the Godhead, in all ways one with the Father and the Son. At all times, the Holy Spirit sees, knows and understands all things including who and where we are in our hearts. *"The Spirit searcheth all things, yea, the deep things of God,"* **1 Corinthians 2:10**.

According to Dictionary.com, a ghost is *"the soul of a dead person, a disembodied spirit imagined, usually as a vague, shadowy or evanescent form, as wandering among or haunting living persons."*[1] That definition neither defines nor identifies the Holy Spirit. The word *"Spirit"* is translated into English from the Greek word **pneuma** which means *a breath or current of air.*[2] *"Holy"* is translated from the Greek adjective **agios** meaning *"sacred (physically, pure, morally blameless or religious, ceremonially, consecrated):—(most) holy (one, thing), saint."*[3]

---

[1] https://www.dictionary.com/browse/ghost

[2] James Strong, *Greek Dictionary of the New Testament,* (Nashville, Tennessee: Abingdon Press, 1958), ref. 4151.

[3] Ibid., ref. 40.

"Spirit" is often used in the Bible to speak of the Holy Spirit; however, *"Ghost"* is also used. *"Spirit"* and *"Ghost"* are both translated from the same word **pneuma**. When *"Ghost"* is translated in reference to the third person of the Godhead, the modifier *"Holy"* is always required.[4] Thus, the words *"Holy Ghost"* in the Scriptures without exception denote the third person in the Godhead; however, the word *"Spirit"* without the modifier also can refer to the Holy Spirit. In the **Textus Receptus** Greek text, **pneuma** appears 385 times in 350 verses.[5] Not all refer to the Holy Spirit, but most do; and a knowledge of Paul's theology and the context make clear which ones do and which ones don't. The King James translators translated **pneuma** with **agios** (*"Holy"*) 183 times in the New Testament.[6]

Many people who have not bothered to research what *"Holy Ghost"* means have falsely assumed that the Holy Ghost is much like the imaginary *Casper the Ghost.* They think He flits around haunting and producing weird conduct in people. Talk about **eisegesis** (reading preconceived notions into the Scriptures), this is truly a case in point. The Holy Spirit is never to be viewed with contempt as an imaginary comic strip character.

THE HOLY SPIRIT IS ALWAYS CONSISTENT WITH HIMSELF

The Holy Spirit is *"the Spirit of the living God,"* **2 Corinthians 3:3**. God is always consistent. *"For I am the LORD, I change not; therefore ye sons of Jacob are not consumed,"* **Malichi 3:6**. God is *"The Father of lights, with whom is no variableness, neither shadow of turning,"* **James 1:17**. *"And, Thou, Lord, in the beginning hast laid the foundation of the earth; and the heavens are the works of thine hands: They shall perish; but thou remainest; and they all shall wax old as doth a garment; And as a vesture shalt thou fold them up, and they shall be changed: but thou art the same, and thy years shall not fail,"* **Hebrews 1:10-12**.

---

[4] W.E. Vine, Merrill F. Unger, William White, Jr., *Vine's Expository Dictionary of Biblical Words,* (Nashville, Tennessee: Thomas Nelson Publishers, 1985), 593.
[5] The Blue Letter Bible, *Strong's Greek Dictionary of the New Testament*, ref. 4151.
[6] Ibid.

With the passing of time, all things including people, change. Not God. He never gets old. He never comes up with a better idea. As He was at the beginning of creation and before the foundations of the world, so is He now. The Holy Spirit never says or does anything that is not in complete harmony with Himself, and with the Father and Son. They are one God. *"Hear, O Israel: The LORD our God is one LORD,"* **Deuteronomy 6:4**. From time to time for various reasons, God may do things in different ways, but He never contradicts Himself. He's never inconsistent. *"God is not the author of confusion,"* **1 Corinthians 14:33**.

The Bible is the book of the Holy Spirit. He is the author. *"For the prophecy came not in old time by the will of man: but holy men of God spake as they were moved by the Holy Ghost,"* **2 Peter 1:21**. Never in **The Revelation** did He say something out of 100% harmony and agreement with something He said in **Genesis** or any other book of the Bible. Never! Listen to His words about Himself: *"I have not spoken in secret, in a dark place of the earth: I said not unto the seed of Jacob, Seek ye me in vain: I the LORD speak righteousness, I declare things that are right,"* **Isaiah 45:19**.

THE BIBLE IS CLEAR ABOUT HOLY SPIRIT LEADERSHIP

A. The Holy Spirit does lead people; not everybody, but some.

1. The Bible plainly states that the Holy Spirit leads certain people: *"For as many as are led by the Spirit of God, they are the sons of God,"* **Romans 8:14**. From this verse note (1) that He leads and (2) that He leads saved people, those who have been born again into the family of God.

2. Just how does He lead saved people; that's the big question. Through the centuries this question has truly been a fountain of confusion. Multitudes with no biblical basis and whose words and actions are inconsistent with their own selves, and contradictory to the Bible, have claimed the leadership of the Holy Spirit.

B. The Holy Spirit leads people through His Word, the Bible.

1. *"Thy word is a lamp unto my feet, and a light unto my path,"* **Psalm 119:105**. Leadership and guidance are in clear view, and it's the *"word"* of God that provides both. *"Wherewithal shall a young man cleanse his way? by taking heed thereto according to thy word,"* **Psalm 119:9**. *"Thy word have I hid in mine heart, that I might not sin against thee,"* **Psalm 119:11**. God extols the merits of letting His Word be our guide: *"The law of the LORD is perfect, converting the soul: the testimony of the LORD is sure, making wise the simple. The statutes of the LORD are right, rejoicing the heart: the commandment of the LORD is pure, enlightening the eyes. The fear of the LORD is clean, enduring for ever: the judgments of the LORD are true and righteous altogether. More to be desired are they than gold, yea, than much fine gold: sweeter also than honey and the honeycomb. Moreover by them is thy servant warned: and in keeping of them there is great reward. Who can understand his errors? cleanse thou me from secret faults. Keep back thy servant also from presumptuous sins; let them not have dominion over me: then shall I be upright, and I shall be innocent from the great transgression. Let the words of my mouth, and the meditation of my heart, be acceptable in thy sight, O LORD, my strength, and my redeemer,"* **Psalm 19:7-14**.

2. The apostle Paul spent much time with his young protégé, Timothy. He repeatedly emphasized staying in God's Word for leadership and guidance. (Paul was giving him God's Word.) *"Consider what I say; and the Lord give thee understanding in all things,"* **2 Timothy 2:7**. *"Meditate upon these things; give thyself wholly to them; that thy profiting may appear to all,"* **1 Timothy 4:15**. *"Study to shew thyself approved unto God, a workman that needeth not to be ashamed, rightly dividing the word of truth,"* **2 Timothy 2:15**.

3. Here is both the advice and warning of God for all of His people: *"Trust in the LORD with all thine heart; and lean not unto thine own understanding. In all thy ways acknowledge him, and he shall direct thy paths,"* **Proverbs 3:5-6**.

4. God has revealed Himself in the Holy Bible. There is where we learn who He is, how He thinks and what He wants from and for us. Those things are not up for speculation. Years ago, God told us in writing how to walk with Him and be what He wants us to be. How does God lead us by His Holy Spirit? Through His written Word, the Bible.

C. The Holy Spirit no longer talks to people in the way He did before the completion of the Bible.

1. Though Moses was not allowed a direct look at God *"the LORD spake unto Moses face to face, as a man speaketh unto his friend,"* **Exodus 33:11**. God gave His Word to most of the Bible writers in dreams and visions. For example, *"In Gibeon the LORD appeared to Solomon in a dream by night: and God said, Ask what I shall give thee,"* **1 Kings 3:5**. Ezekiel said, *"The spirit took me up, and brought me in a vision by the Spirit of God into Chaldea, to them of the captivity. So the vision that I had seen went up from me,"* **Ezekiel 11:24**. Of the New Testament writers (not everybody) before His ascension Jesus promised, *"I have yet many things to say unto you, but ye cannot bear them now. Howbeit when he, the Spirit of truth, is come, he will guide you into all truth: for he shall not speak of himself; but whatsoever he shall hear, that shall he speak: and he will shew you things to come. He shall glorify me: for he shall receive of mine, and shall shew it unto you. All things that the Father hath are mine: therefore said I, that he shall take of mine, and shall shew it unto you,"* **John 16:12-15**. (It is alarming to see so many pastors and preachers today misapply this passage to themselves.) Paul, who was one of the apostles confessed, *"I have received of the Lord that which also I delivered unto you,"* **1 Corinthians 11:23**. In this case, he was speaking of the Lord's Supper; however, the statement applies to all he wrote. Furthermore, the statement applies to all Bible writers, both to Old Testament and to New Testament.

2. Since the completion of the Scriptures, God has spoken to men through His Word; not in strange and mystical ways. With the completion of divine revelation in mind, God inspired Jude to refer to the Bible as *"The faith which was once delivered unto the saints,"* **Jude 3**. In this reference *"faith"* is used with the definite article. It is thus a noun, and not a verb. *"The faith"* refers to the body of divine revelation which we call the Bible. It was *"once delivered."* The Greek word for *"once"* is **hapax** conveying the idea of *one time with perpetual validity.*[7] As the Bible was being written, it was a work *"in part"* or unfinished. When God completed the project of giving mankind His revelation, it was

[7] Strong, ref. 530.

no longer *"in part."* It was complete, whole or *"perfect."* In anticipation of that day, God inspired Paul to write, *"Charity never faileth: but whether there be prophecies, they shall fail; whether there be tongues, they shall cease; whether there be knowledge, it shall vanish away. For we know in part, and we prophesy in part. But when that which is perfect is come, then that which is in part shall be done away,"* **1 Corinthians 13:8-10**. *"Charity"* is love, and it never ends; however, with the completion of the Bible, continued tongues and divine revelation ended. God doesn't speak directly to people today as He did before the Bible was completed. Today He speaks to men through His completed revelation, His Word, the Bible.

D. In spite of the clarity of the Bible on the subject, there are earnest, sincere people who believe the Holy Spirit talks to and leads people today other than through the Bible.

1. It is not uncommon to hear sincere, conscientious believers say, "The Lord told me." They then go on to state what He said. One televangelist affirmed the Lord appeared to him, and told him about a hospital he was to build. Radio and T.V. "evangelists" are prone to tell their audiences that the Lord told them that some people in the listening audience are to send $1,000.00, $500.00 or some other sum of money. They are known to share their prayer and "time with God" experiences which consist of conversations they had with the Lord. The beautiful hymn, "In the Garden" says, "I come to the garden alone, while the dew is still on the roses. And the voice I hear, is the voice of cheer." The refrain continues, "And He walks with me, and He talks with me; and He tells me I am His own. And the voice I hear falling on mine ear, none other has ever known." If that song is interpreted to mean that the Spirit of God brings to attention biblical truths upon which the believer meditates with joy and comfort, then well and good. Conversely, if the song is interpreted to mean God carries on some sort of extra-scriptural conversation as would two people walking through a park, then there is a major misconception of the Holy Spirit. As a young boy, I recall the evening that a certain Baptist man came to my parent's home. The man said that for many days he had been wrestling with the call to preach. He told my dad that about 2:00 A.M. the night before, the Lord came to him and called him by name. He said the Lord stood there in bodily form and told him he was to be a preacher. He affirmed the Lord stood there and spoke clearly and audibly to him just as one person would speak to another. Even as a naïve young boy, that sounded a little spooky to me.

2. The Holy Spirit of God speaks to and leads the saved, but He doesn't do so through some *"still small voice,"* face-to-face or in a dream or vision. There is no question as to whether or not the Lord can speak to a man in an audible voice or through a direct statement in the heart. He has done so; but as previously addressed, since He completed His written revelation to mankind, He speaks to men exclusively through His written revelation, The Holy Bible. *"All scripture is given by inspiration of God, and is profitable for doctrine, for reproof, for correction, for instruction in righteousness: That the man of God may be perfect, throughly furnished unto all good works,"* **2 Timothy 3:16-17**. The revealed Scriptures are complete and provide us with all of the revelation we need to serve God acceptably. There is no need for a new word or revelation from God. What we do need is for the truths and principles of the Bible to be brought to our attention. Once we fill our hearts with God's revealed Word, the Holy Spirit will bring it to our attention. *"It is God which worketh in you both to will and to do of his good pleasure,"* **Philippians 2:13**. Obviously, if we do not *"hide"* His *"word . . . in our heart,"* He will not bring it to our attention in the time of need.

3. The idea that God talks to men today through some audible or inner voice is a concept that opens *"Pandora's box"*. Every mystic around can seize upon it as a basis for his new ideas. He can also say, *"God told me this"* or *"God led me to do this."* The stance of continuing divine revelation gives people a way to justify virtually every word they speak or action they take; they can blame God for whatever they say or do by claiming He told them to do it.

Even if the Holy Spirit did speak to men today in some *"still small voice"* or other way, it would be virtually impossible to say for sure which inner conversation was generated by the Holy Spirit. The counterfeiting Devil also works in the heart to tempt and influence men to evil. Our hearts are deceitful and untrustworthy. Every honest man knows that *"the heart is deceitful above all things, and desperately wicked: who can know it?"* **Jeremiah 17:9**. Men can and do talk and reason with themselves. The Bible is therefore careful to remind us that *"There is a way which seemeth right unto a man, but the end thereof are the ways of death,"* **Proverbs 14:12** and **Proverbs 16:25**. Men today do not need a new revelation; all they need is to apply the revelation we already have.

E. It is harmful to the cause of Christ to portray the Holy Spirit in such confusing and inconsistent ways.

1. Imagine the message to young people in churches and to unchurched bystanders who hear a trusted preacher make a statement such as, *"A few days ago, God gave me a message for today, but on the way to church, He changed it. So, this morning I shall preach on this subject."* Is the Holy Spirit that fickle and inconsistent? Isn't the Holy Spirit of God who knows all things able a week or month in advance to direct a preacher on the sermon to preach? Is the Holy Spirit so dumb or near-sighted that He must reverse Himself just before a worship service? Being God, He knows the end from the beginning. *"Remember the former things of old: for I am God, and there is none else; I am God, and there is none like me, Declaring the end from the beginning, and from ancient times the things that are not yet done, saying, My counsel shall stand, and I will do all my pleasure,"* **Isaiah 46:9-10**. Every true preacher seeks God's leadership in the message he preaches in any given service. Sometimes he thinks he has just the message God would have him preach only to decide later that another message is in order. There is no reason for a preacher to be embarrassed about that. Just admit human frailty, but don't blame such inconsistent, short-sighted behavior on the Holy Spirit. Preachers are just mortal men trying to determine the Lord's will and leading in matters, including message selection. As preachers pray, study the Word, and consider the circumstances and needs of a given audience, they sometimes come up with the wrong message, only to have that fact become clear as the service approaches. What should the preacher who must change messages do? Just be honest about it. Admit that he made a mistake, but don't blame the mistake on the Holy Spirit. Before the foundations of the world, the Holy Spirit of God knew exactly the message that every preacher should preach at any given service until the end of time. He doesn't ever lead a preacher to preach a message at a given service then change it before that service arrives. We who preach God's Word should admit the fact that we are mortals who sometimes mistake what the Lord is leading us to do. Our messages change not because the Holy Spirit reverses Himself (because He never does); but because we're often slow to perceive what He is leading us to do. The blame for change must rest on us; not the Holy Spirit. Sometimes, we never perceive what He's leading us to preach, and thus end up preaching the wrong message.

2. This same line of biblical reasoning could be applied to a multitude of other lofty decisions made by preachers as well as Christians who are not preachers. Preachers are famous for saying such things as, *"God is leading me to another church," "The Lord is leading us to build this new building,"* and *"God led me to make these changes."* Bystanders hear those lofty claims and watch what happens down the road. Often, they see civil wars in churches which grind up good people and often wound or kill churches. They see people quitting church and families ripped apart. *"The Lord led me to do it!"* Really? Believe me when I tell you that the preacher's kids get the message as do lots of others. It's hard for people in a good church to watch it bleed to death by degrees, and believe those *glorious changes* were the leading of God.

What about the good Christian who says, *"God is moving me to a new job in another city?"* How about the couple who say God is leading them to move to or build a bigger house? Couples about to marry claim this relationship was made in heaven. Sometime, a move or a new home or a marriage is of God. Every child of God should seek God's will in decisions of this sort. Many times, God is not in these lofty decisions. Let every child of God be very cautious about blaming his decision on God. Every decision demands homework from the believer. Go to the Word of God to be sure no biblical command or principle is being violated. Wait upon the providence of God. (That issue is addressed in another chapter in this book.)

3. It is extremely easy to *"Blame it on God." "If He led me to do it; and it didn't work out, it must be His fault."* Yes! It is easy to excuse ourselves and blame God. It is doubtful that most of those who piously make lofty claims about the leadership of the Holy Spirit realize what they're doing. The fact is that often the Holy Spirit is made to look really fickle, inconsistent and short-sighted. To many who are watching, the credibility of Christianity is seriously undermined. The integrity of God is compromised. Sadly, the lives of countless preachers and other believers are a continuing saga of un-ending inconsistencies and reversals all accredited to the leadership of God through the Holy Spirit. Why blame it on God? Why not honestly admit that the mistakes, inconsistencies and reversals of our lives are our own doings through selfishness, short-sightedness and our mistaking of the Lord's will? Why make the Holy Spirit our scapegoat? God forbid that His Spirit be blamed for our human blunderings!

King David made lots of mistakes, but he didn't want God blamed for his failings. The impact of his sin with Bathsheba was of prime concern to him. He wanted God to look good, and not take the fall for his sin. Listen to his words to God: *"Have mercy upon me, O God, according to thy lovingkindness: according unto the multitude of thy tender mercies blot out my transgressions. Wash me throughly from mine iniquity, and cleanse me from my sin. For I acknowledge my transgressions: and my sin is ever before me. Against thee, thee only, have I sinned, and done this evil in thy sight: that thou mightest be justified when thou speakest, and be clear when thou judgest,"* **Psalm 51:1-4**. Note well his words, *"That thou mightest be justified when thou speakest, and be clear when thou judgest."* People know we are mortals and that we are going to fail. Most will understand when we admit our errors in judgment and inconsistencies in life; but when we piously act as though it happened because the Holy Spirit led us to it, we not only bring reproach upon the Spirit of God, we also make ourselves stink with hypocrisy. What a hurtful shame it is to the cause of Christ that so many well intending people blame so many of their whelms, inconsistent words and deeds and anti-scriptural activities on the leadership of the Holy Spirit!

4. Never doubt the fact that the Holy Spirit will always be absolutely consistent with Himself. *"God is not the author of confusion,"* **1 Corinthians 14:33**. Abraham asked, *"Shall not the judge of all the earth do right?"* **Genesis 18:25**. He surely will. Every time! No man can in truth lay inconsistencies in word or deed on the leadership of the Holy Spirit.

5. I will close this chapter with a brief word to you who have been watching. You may very well have been disillusioned by some of the inconsistencies and blunderings you've seen in the name of Holy Spirit leadership. I plead with you to not allow the mistakes and misconceptions you see in people cause you to turn against God. They're just people, and people make mistakes. Please don't blame God for what people do. It's not His fault that some accuse Him of things He doesn't do. He is a great God and always works in consistent and sensible ways. You can see that in His Word, the Bible. Don't let the failures of people turn you from the God of the Bible who is your only eternal hope.

Chapter 19

Submission to the Holy Spirit

1 Thessalonians 5:19

The Holy Spirit of God is a real person living in the heart of every born-again person. Of believers, the Bible says, *"Ye are the temple of the living God; as God hath said, I will dwell in them, and walk in them; and I will be their God, and they shall be my people,"* **2 Corinthians 6:16**. The truth of the Holy Spirit indwelling every saved person was confirmed by Paul: *"Ye are not in the flesh, but in the Spirit, if so be that the Spirit of God dwell in you. Now if any man have not the Spirit of Christ, he is none of his,"* **Romans 8:9**. *"Know ye not that ye are the temple of God, and that the Spirit of God dwelleth in you?"* **1 Corinthians 3:16**. He should rule in every church.

He is not there because He needs a place of residence; He is there to marvelously enrich the life of the believer in whom He dwells.

THE DESIRE OF THE HOLY SPIRIT FOR THOSE IN WHOM HE DWELLS

A. God wants spiritual success and joy for all His spiritual children.

1. Keep in mind that God the Father, God the Son and God the Holy Spirit are one God in three persons. What one wants is what the others want. God is always in perfect unity.

2. God expressed **His heart toward His people** when He said to Old Testament Israel, *"For I know the thoughts that I think toward you, saith the LORD, thoughts of peace, and not of evil, to give you an expected end,"* **Jeremiah 29:11**. Christian brother or sister, do not be intimidated by the presence of the Holy Spirit in you. He is not there to make you timid and up-tight, constantly afraid that you are going to make a mistake. Absolutely not! The Holy Spirit is there to help you, keep you out of trouble and fill your heart and life with joy.

3. God desires **abundant life** for His children. Jesus said, *"I am come that they might have life, and that they might have it more abundantly,"* **John 10:10**. He wants your life to be full, rich and satisfied. His control and leadership of your life will enrich it in a multitude of ways.

4. God desires **abundant grace** for His children. *"God is able to make all grace abound toward you; that ye, always having all sufficiency in all things, may abound to every good work,"* **2 Corinthians 9:8**. *Grace!* What a blessed concept! The Greek word is **charis**. The word speaks not only of *unmerited favor*, but with it comes the idea of pleasure, delight and favorable regard. It is applied to beauty and gracefulness of the person. It produces gracious words. In Bible times, it was a common greeting: *"Grace"* meaning *to rejoice.*[1] The Holy Spirit is there to give you a gracious life on every front.

5. God desires abundant joy for His children. *"These things have I spoken unto you, that my joy might remain in you, and that your joy might be full,"* **John 15:11**. *"These things write we unto you, that your joy may be full,"* **1 John 1:4**. The Holy Spirit in control of you will increasingly turn your attention to the blessings in your life, especially your glorious win-win position in Christ as your Redeemer. His love will flood your heart with thanksgiving and joy and take your focus off this fleshly veil of tears.

6. God desires **to meet all our needs**. Paul said, *"My God shall supply all your need according to his riches in glory by Christ Jesus,"*

---

[1] W.E. Vine, Merrill F. Unger, William White, Jr., *Vine's Expository Dictionary of Biblical Words,* (Nashville, Tennessee: Thomas Nelson Publishers, 1985), 277.

Philippians 4:19. What comfort! The knowledge that you will never find yourself in a place where He can't help you! Even in the valley of the shadow of death!

7. God desires to give us **peace of heart regardless of the severity of the storms** of life. *"Rejoice in the Lord alway: and again I say, Rejoice. Let your moderation be known unto all men. The Lord is at hand. Be careful for nothing; but in every thing by prayer and supplication with thanksgiving let your requests be made known unto God. And the peace of God, which passeth all understanding, shall keep your hearts and minds through Christ Jesus,"* **Philippians 4:4-7**. Peace, even in life's worst circumstances.

8. Paul enumerated **the fruit of the Spirit**: *"The fruit of the Spirit is love, joy, peace, longsuffering, gentleness, goodness, faith, meekness, temperance: against such there is no law,"* **Galatians 5:22-23**. There is no legitimate reason for a child of God to be negative, pessimistic, bent-out-of-shape, sour and defeated. When He's in control, that sort of thinking and behavior go away.

9. Listen to this **general expression of God's desire** for His people: *"For this cause I bow my knees unto the Father of our Lord Jesus Christ, Of whom the whole family in heaven and earth is named, That he would grant you, according to the riches of his glory, to be strengthened with might by his Spirit in the inner man; That Christ may dwell in your hearts by faith; that ye, being rooted and grounded in love, May be able to comprehend with all saints what is the breadth, and length, and depth, and height; And to know the love of Christ, which passeth knowledge, that ye might be filled with all the fulness of God. Now unto him that is able to do exceeding abundantly above all that we ask or think, according to the power that worketh in us, Unto him be glory in the church by Christ Jesus throughout all ages, world without end. Amen,"* **Ephesians 3:14-21**. Did you hear that: *"The power that worketh in us?"* That *"power"* is the Holy Spirit of God who has permanent residency in us, every believer.

B. The Holy Spirit within us is able to do in and through us things impossible through our own strength and power.

1. The Holy Spirit is God who has all power within us. *"Greater is he that is in you, than he that is in the world,"* **1 John 4:4**. Imagine that! Why should we be discouraged and afraid?

2. The Holy Spirit within us provides all the power we will ever need for spiritual success, victory and fruitfulness. He works in us *"both to will and to do of his good pleasure,"* **Philippians 2:13**. Working in and through us, He makes us *"perfect"* or *complete.* Through Him we can be all we need to be to the glory of God. *"Now the God of peace, that brought again from the dead our Lord Jesus, that great shepherd of the sheep, through the blood of the everlasting covenant, Make you perfect in every good work to do his will, working in you that which is well-pleasing in his sight, through Jesus Christ; to whom be glory for ever and ever. Amen,"* **Hebrews 13:20-21**.

   Why should your life be dull and boring? Why should you ever be discouraged and defeated? If you're saved, the Spirit of the living God lives in you for the specific purpose of comforting and strengthening you.

   Why should worship in one of the Lord's churches be dry, cold and boring? The Holy Spirit of God is present in every true worship service. In view of the work of God which has been done for people who know Christ, how can there ever be anything short of thanksgiving, awe and reverence? Why shouldn't there be genuine joy and rejoicing? How can church members service after service, week after week sit there like wax figures behaving like ritualistic robots just going through dry, lifeless, gloomy motions?

   One thing is sure, no individual or church can approach like Zombies the worship and praise of our great God who gave His all and say they are filled with the Holy Spirit and under His control.

GOD'S CHILDREN MUST SUBMIT TO THE HOLY SPIRIT

A. Self-will is one of the greatest enemies of spiritual success in saved people.

1. Three great enemies are always out to wreck and ruin us: the flesh, the world and the Devil. Satan continually uses the world to exploit our flesh. On the night before His crucifixion Jesus said to His apostles, *"Watch and pray, that ye*

enter not into temptation: the spirit indeed is willing, but the flesh is weak," **Matthew 26:41**. What a timeless warning and admonition! Jesus described *"the flesh"* in a moral sense. It is morally *"weak,"* but do not imagine that the flesh has no appetites and desires that are capable of wrecking both soul and body. Paul warned, *"He that soweth to his flesh shall of the flesh reap corruption,"* **Galatians 6:8**. Fleshly, self-will is always around; and most of the time, it rules us. In fact, many (if not most) of God's people are so good at keeping self in full control that they are hardly aware that it's happening.

2. Let every one of us get hold of the truth that the power in believers for spiritual success is not within ourselves. The Bible consistently shouts that message to us. It warns against pride and self-will and tells us that any spiritual power we have comes from the Lord. Paul wrote, *"Not that we are sufficient of ourselves to think any thing as of ourselves; but our sufficiency is of God,"* **2 Corinthians 3:5**. Zechariah the prophet wrote, *"Not by might, nor by power, but by my spirit, saith the Lord of hosts,"* **Zechariah 4:6**. It is only when God works in and through us that our efforts are of any spiritual value. This is a major point of Solomon: *"Trust in the Lord with all thine heart; and lean not unto thine own understanding. In all thy ways acknowledge him, and he shall direct thy paths,"* **Proverbs 3:5-6**. The entire concept of *trusting the Lord* and *leaning on His strength* assumes intimacy of the closest sort. It speaks of knowing someone, being close to and in sync with that person. It is doubtful that most Christians would be aware that another person called the Holy Spirit lives in them, if they had not stumbled across it in the Bible or heard about it in a sermon. They have no personal awareness that He's there. Who do you know who could give you one single example of a time when he was actually aware that the Holy Spirit was doing anything in or through him?

3. God forbid that any one of us should ever think that any spiritual success, victory or fruitfulness we enjoy is ours because of our own strength or ability! Of ourselves, we are nothing. Paul made that point crystal clear when he said, *"So then neither is he that planteth anything, neither he that watereth; but God that giveth the increase,"* **1 Corinthians 3:7**. Were it not for

His Holy Spirit living within us, we'd be as impotent for spiritual success as every lost man. We might put on a good, human-generated performance which might look good and impressive to those around us; but God would count it as *"wood, hay, and stubble,"* **1 Corinthians 3:12**. It is only that which God works in us by His Holy Spirit that constitutes true, eternal success as God sees it. It's only as we yield self and let Him work in our lives that we become mature, victorious, fruitful, and spiritually successful.

Oh boy, that's high and lofty talk. It's heartbreaking to say that we've reached a day of two extremes, particularly in church worship. On the one extreme, there are some who put on shows which really exalt themselves: their voices, showmanship, musical abilities and oratorical skills. There's a whole lot of chest-beating and no obvious humility; attention-getters. There's sometimes talk about God; but it's hard to spot Him in all the fanfare and glamor. Furthermore, much of what is said, not to mention the implications, is downright contrary to the written teachings, principles and spirit of the Bible.

On the other extreme, there are some who are reluctant to show any emotion: joy, passion, enthusiasm or feelings; none of the fruit of the Spirit. Many of them are quick to squelch and criticize those who do. They sit almost emotionless in a worship service, rarely express approval, show almost no joy and generally behave like they have no feelings. Churches made up of these people are cold, dry, lifeless, boring and unmotivated. In such churches, you rarely see anything that would make you think the Holy Spirit is anywhere near: no joy, no tears, no shouting, no emotions; just stoicism in the name of God. Cold, dry, emotionless Christianity had become the norm, especially in many super-orthodox churches some of which seem to think they're the only ones who know much truth.

4. Even the strongest of Christians do not have the power within themselves to have and sustain joy, peace, fulfillment, grace and the other fruit of the Spirit. Therefore, the apostle Peter explained, *"Forasmuch then as Christ hath suffered for us in* *the flesh, arm yourselves likewise with the same mind: for he that hath suffered in the flesh hath ceased from sin; That he no longer should live the rest of his time in the flesh to the lusts of men, but to the will of God,"* **1 Peter 4:1-2**. That's a call for recognition of the fact that in our own fleshly strength, we can never succeed spiritually. Without the working of the Holy Spirit in the life of a believer, that believer will live a barren, fruitless and generally frustrated life.

B. For believers and churches to experience the blessed life God wants for them, they must submit to the Holy Spirit.

1. Jesus said it: *"If any man will come after me, let him deny himself,"* **Luke 9:23**.

2. In discussing this reality, the apostle Peter said, *"Yea, all of you be subject one to another, and be clothed with humility: for God resisteth the proud, and giveth grace to the humble. Humble yourselves therefore under the mighty hand of God, that he may exalt you in due time."* He followed this call for genuine humility with these words, *"But the God of all grace, who hath called us unto his eternal glory by Christ Jesus, after that ye have suffered awhile, make you perfect, stablish, strengthen, settle you,"* **1 Peter 5:5-10**. Humility, self-control, submission!

3. The Holy Spirit will produce His natural fruit in us only as we submit to His control. Note well when the strengthening and settling come; they come only after the yielding or submitting. There are many great things the Spirit of God would do for God's children, but He will not do those things where the heart is rebellious and un-submitted. Israel's first king, Saul, is a foreshadow and illustration of this point. When he was humble and submitted to the Lord, God's Spirit worked in him to give victories over the Ammonites, Philistines, Moabites, Edomites and the kings of Zobah. See **1 Samuel 11-14**. Once he became proud and rebellious, the Spirit of the Lord no longer gave him victories. Instead, *"The Spirit of the Lord departed from Saul."* When the Spirit no longer strengthened him, he went from failure to failure to ruin. See **1 Samuel 16-31**. Let every one of us who knows Christ as personal Savior, learn from Saul's mistakes.

4. God, through His Spirit, wants our daily deliverance, victory and fruitfulness in life; but when we are proud and self-willed, He will not supply the strength apart from which spiritual victory is impossible. As Samuel said to Saul, *"Because thou hast rejected the word of the Lord, he hath also rejected thee from being king,"* **1 Samuel 15:23**. Jesus said, *"Whosoever exalteth himself shall be abased,"* **Luke 14:11**. This passage is customarily applied to the unsaved; however, it is not necessarily limited to them. The passage is very applicable to those believers who function in their own strength rather than in the strength of the Lord. God says, *"Because I have called, and ye refused; I have stretched out my hand, and no man regarded; But ye have set at nought all my counsel, and would none of my reproof: I also will laugh at your calamity; I will mock when your fear cometh: When your fear cometh as desolation, and your destruction cometh as a whirlwind; when distress and anguish cometh upon you. Then shall they call upon me, but I will not answer; they shall seek me early, but they shall not find me: For that they hated knowledge, and did not choose the fear of the Lord: They would none of my counsel: they despised all my reproof. Therefore shall they eat of the fruit of their own way, and be filled with their own devices,"* **Proverbs 1:24-31**.

5. Those who would claim the daily power of the Holy Spirit for victory and service must yield self to His control. Key to His power is yielding and submission. That's why Paul said, *"Neither yield ye your members as instruments of unrighteousness unto sin: but yield yourselves unto God, as those that are alive from the dead, and your members as instruments of righteousness unto God."* **Romans 6:13**. James wrote, *"God resisteth the proud, but giveth grace to the humble. Submit yourselves therefore to God,"* **James 4:6-7**. The Holy Spirit could overpower us and make us do right, but He won't. He could go ahead and empower and deliver us even in our self-will and rebellion; but He won't. To the contrary, such self-will withholds His power and blessings. As Isaiah put it, *"Behold, the Lord's hand is not shortened, that it cannot save neither his ear heavy, that it cannot hear: But your iniquities have separated between you and your God, and your sins have hid his face from you, that he will not hear,"* in **Isaiah 59:1-2**. When a believer ceases to humbly submit himself to God's control through

His Spirit, he loses his power to resist temptations, his compassion, his true godly zeal and boldness, his love, his joy, his patience, his objectivity, his impartiality, his meekness, his faith and every other virtue which is so necessary in the service of God. Thus, Paul warned, *"But I keep under my body, and bring it into subjection: lest that by any means, when I have preached to others, I myself should be a castaway,"* **1 Corinthians 9:27**. God promised *"There hath no temptation taken you but such as is common to man: but God is faithful, who will not suffer you to be tempted above that ye are able; but will with the temptation also make a way to escape, that ye may be able to bear it,"* **1 Corinthians 10:13**. That promise is only possible when the Holy Spirit who lives within gives us the power for victory. Apart from his delivering power, God's people fall into many needless defeats. For example, saved people go through the emptiness and disillusionment of worship and service done in the energy of the flesh; performance that does not grow out of a heart submitted to God and His glory alone. With the Holy Spirit living within, there is no reason for discouragement, timidity, impatience, resentments, bitterness and fruitlessness.

6. Paul warned, *"But they that will be rich fall in to temptation and a snare, and into many foolish and hurtful lusts, which drown men in destruction and perdition,"* **1 Timothy 6:9**. Multitudes of God's people have fallen into lying, deceit, immorality, pride, negativism, drunkenness, hatred, thievery, robbery, murder and every other imaginable sin. Yes, God's people! How and why did they do it? It was not because the Holy Spirit didn't live within them or because He couldn't deliver them. The answer is that they were not submitted to the Spirit, and He therefore would not provide the strength or power for spiritual victory which they needed. The believer who could have won lost. Why? Because the Holy Spirit only empowers and gives spiritual victory to those who are submitted to Him. This explains why the lives of so many of God's people consist of one continuous line of defeats void of spiritual victory and prosperity.

QUENCHING THE HOLY SPIRIT

A. This is the point of the key verse for this chapter. *"Quench not the Spirit,"* **1 Thessalonians 5:19**. *"Quench"* is from the Greek word **shennumi** (shen'-noo-mee). Strong's Greek Dictionary defines it to mean "to extinguish" as in putting out a fire. *Quench* is an imperative verb. We are not to suppress or stifle the Holy Spirit.[2] The Spirit controls our lives only to the extent that we voluntarily submit to Him. The rise of pride or self-will within us diminishes His control. Just as the light of a candle grows ever dimmer as oxygen supply is diminished, even so the Holy Spirit's power through our lives reduces as self grows. Quenching the spirit is failing to submit to Him. That failure limits His power in our lives, thus taking away spiritual success.

B. Quenching the Holy Spirit is the antithesis of being filled with the Holy Spirit. In the same message where Paul admonished us to not quench the Spirit, he also said, *"Be not drunk with wine, wherein is excess; but be filled with the Spirit,"* **Ephesians 5:18**. The phrase *"be filled with"* is from the Greek word **pleroo** (play-ro'-o) and means *to level up, be full, be complete.*[3] Every aspect of our lives is to be level full of the influence of the Holy Spirit. Instead of Him being forced into the small corners of our lives by self-will; He should be given full or complete control. Whatever He says in His Word should be obeyed. Whatever providential occurrences He allows into our lives, we should accept with thanksgiving. As Paul said *"I have learned, in whatsoever state I am, therewith to be content,"* **Philippians 4:11**. Our attitude should ever be *"not my will, but thine, be done,"* **Luke 22:42**. That means we submit to His will by speaking and acting honestly, by forgiving one another, in marriage, in relationships, by modest dress codes, with wholesome speech patterns, by job practices, in our priorities, with good attitudes and in every other way. That kind of practical submission does not result in depression, sorrow, emptiness, resentment, Stoicism, regrets and negative emotionless living. To the contrary, submission to the Holy Spirit produces fulfillment, richness and vibrance in life. The apostle Paul spoke

---

[2] James Strong, *Greek Dictionary of the New Testament,* (Nashville, Tennessee: Abingdon Press, 1958), ref. 4570.

[3] Ibid., ref. 4137.

of the *"love in the Spirit"* in the Colossian believers. He followed with these words to them: *"For this cause we also, since the day we heard it, do not cease to pray for you, and to desire that ye might be filled with the knowledge of his will in all wisdom and spiritual understanding; That ye might walk worthy of the Lord unto all pleasing, being fruitful in every good work, and increasing in the knowledge of God; Strengthened with all might, according to his glorious power, unto all patience and longsuffering with joyfulness,"* **Colossians 1:8-11**. Their lifestyle of joy and richness in life stands out like a beacon; and it was there because the Holy Spirit showed His power and produced His fruit in their submitted lives. He's the same as He has always been; and when given that kind of control, He will produce that kind of life in every believer and church.

C. Being *"filled with the Spirit"* is not having more or less of His person. No believer has one-half or one-third of the Holy Spirit. Nobody has only an arm or leg. He's a living person. It's not that we are like a glass, and He's like water. The idea of more or less of Him like water in a glass is a total misnomer. No believer can get more or less of His person. Every believer has all of the Holy Spirit. Being *"filled with the Spirit"* is about control. It's about letting Him have full control. He's to be the boss of our lives, our *"Master."* A *"Spirit filled"* life or church is one under the control of the Holy Spirit. Submission to Him is voluntary. We can give Him more or less influence or control. We have a choice in whether or not we submit, and how much. Oh, how much better off every believer would be under the full influence and control of the Holy Spirit of God! The power for Christian victory is there; yet few avail themselves of even a small part of that power. Paul insisted that our lives should be *"filled with the Spirit."*

D. Oh, how easily individuals and churches can be deceived by the showy, the emotional performances! Praise the Lord for passionate worship and church services; worship where people are not afraid to expose their hearts, emotions and feelings; however, these are only of God when they are conducted in truth with the right motives. For example, there are rip-roaring church services where people supposedly speak in tongues, heal sick people and perform miracles. The music is often top-of-the-line, there are tears and the place is jumping with excitement.

Someone has well said, *"All that glitters is not gold."*[4] Many things which people and churches do in the name of God and Christianity are not of God or Christian at all. The truth is that unknown tongues, miracle healings, prophesying and new revelation ended nearly 2,000 years ago with the completion of the Bible.[5]

E. The question to ask ourselves is not "How much of the Spirit do I have?" Rather we should ask, "How much of me does the Spirit control?" "Am I truly submitted to Him?" Today the Holy Spirit is very much alive and at work. He is doing many, many great things unilaterally of our involvement; but there are many other wonderful things which He wants to do in and through us. He will not do them apart from our submission to Him. He leads only those who are submitted to Him.

---

[4] https://en.wikipedia.org/wiki/All_that_glitters_is_not_gold

[5] See *What We Believe and Why 1* Chapters 28-33 by Lester Hutson. Available on Amazon.com.

Chapter 20

Results of the Indwelling Holy Spirit

Galatians 5:22-23

It is a mistake to focus on what the Holy Spirit doesn't do instead of focusing on what He does do. A negative approach to life on any front almost always results in a negative outlook.

SPONTANEOUS RESULTS OF SUBMISSION TO THE HOLY SPIRIT

A. Once the Holy Spirit is given control in the life of a believer, He will spontaneously produce many excellent qualities.

1. The most obvious results of His control are specifically named in Scripture. *"The fruit of the Spirit is love, joy, peace, longsuffering, gentleness, goodness, faith, meekness, temperance: against such there is no law,"* **Galatians 5:22-23**. Nine specific excellent character qualities are named. They are not qualities the believer can artificially manufacture in and of himself. They spontaneously emanate from the life of a submitted believer even as heat emanates from fire. When conditions are right in a believer's life, these nine qualities will automatically be there. Yes! *"Automatically!"* The presence or absence of these qualities in a believer's life testify of his/her submission to the Holy Spirit or of the lack thereof.

2. Peter was inspired of God to write a parallel passage about traits which characterize a submitted believer. He explained that it is God's *"divine power"* which *"hath given unto us all things that pertain unto life and godliness."* How does He give us *"all"* these *"things that pertain unto life and godliness?"* He does so primarily through *"the knowledge of Him that called us."* He has given us *"exceeding great and precious promises,"* and through these we can become *"partakers of the divine nature."* In other words, God the Holy Spirit through His Word works to strengthen us and make us more of what He wants us to be. In fact, as we delight in and abide by His Word, such qualities as *"faith"*, *"virtue"*, *"knowledge"*, *"temperance"*, *"patience"*, *"godliness"*, *"brotherly kindness"*, and *"charity"* increase and abound in us, **2 Peter 1:2-9**.

3. The qualities spontaneously produced by the Holy Spirit parallel those produced by the Word. Both Paul and Peter speak of *"love, temperance,"* and *"faith."* One mentions *"goodness"* while the other speaks of *"virtue."* One speaks of *"longsuffering"* while the other calls it *"patience."* Paul spoke of *"meekness"* and *"gentleness"* while Peter speaks of *"kindness"* and *"godliness."* There is no discrepancy or contradiction. This parallel makes clear that the Bible is not the same as the Holy Spirit; it is not a part of our triune God. The Holy Spirit is a person; the Bible is not. The Bible alone does not do all of the work in believers today. The point is that the Holy Spirit uses His Word, the Bible, to do much of His work in us. The Holy Spirit is the source of the power found in the Word of God. He is the person who makes the Word of God *"quick, and powerful, and sharper than any twoedged sword, piercing even to the dividing asunder of soul and spirit, and of the joints and marrow, and is a discerner of the thoughts and intents of the heart,"* **Hebrews 4:12**. *"Quick"* is translated from the Greek word **zao** meaning *alive* or *living*.[1] Who makes the Word of God alive? The Holy Spirit! He gives it the convicting power which it has.

---

[1] James Strong, *Greek Dictionary of the New Testament*, (Nashville, Tennessee: Abingdon Press, 1958), ref. 2198.

4. Today, in us the Holy Spirit produces *"love;"* not sensuous, fickle love; but true committed, caring, righteous love. The more a believer learns the Word, the deeper the Spirit will automatically make His love to be. He also produces *"joy."* True joy in the heart of believers rises or falls upon their commitment to the Holy Spirit. Those who yield to Him will have joy. *"Now the God of hope fill you with all joy and peace in believing, that ye may abound in hope, through the power of the Holy Ghost,"* **Romans 15:13**. Furthermore, in the hearts of all those who submit to Him, the Spirit spontaneously generates *"the peace of God, which passeth all understanding,"* **Philippians 4:7**. Abiding peace is a current result of Holy Spirit control. His fruit is *"peace,"* but it is also *"longsuffering"* which is patience. In building patience, the Holy Spirit often uses providential troubles: *"We glory in tribulations also: knowing that tribulation worketh patience,"* **Romans 5:3**. Patience spontaneously begins to grow where the Holy Spirit is in control. When you see a believer who is *"gentle,"* you are seeing evidence of what the Holy Spirit is doing in his life. The same is true when you see *"goodness, faith, meekness and temperance"* which is self-control. In any believer, these are testimonies of the Holy Spirit of God's current work. These traits are not natural to the flesh, which is prone to *"Adultery, fornication, uncleanness, lasciviousness, Idolatry, witchcraft, hatred, variance, emulations, wrath, strife, seditions, heresies, Envyings, murders, drunkenness, revellings, and such like,"* **Galatians 5:19-21**. The Spirit of God works in believers to replace these evil traits with the good qualities that only He can produce. Those qualities are evidence or confirmation that He is at work through His Word in that believer's life.

B. The Word (Bible) is the tool or channel by which the Spirit gets His truth into our hearts. The Holy Spirit then uses His Word in our hearts to demonstrate His power in and through us.

1. He produces the daily strength or power for service and fruitfulness in His work. This is not a reference to the special power to heal or perform miracles as generated by the Holy Spirit in the apostles and those upon whom they laid their hands. To the contrary, this is a reference about the strength or power to continue in acceptable service and fruitfulness

to God. *"Let us have grace whereby we may serve God acceptably with reverence and godly fear,"* **Hebrews 12:28**. It's His power that keeps us rejoicing in the blessings we have including the privilege to be a part of the service of the King of kings. His power keeps us from becoming *"weary in well doing,"* **Galatians 6:9**. The Holy Spirit of God can give courage, patience, stamina, meekness; and the ability to respond correctly to adversity, persecutions, and provocations. He can give the drive to win souls, and the zeal and boldness that transforms cowards into mighty warriors in the faith. He can produce wonderful spontaneous liberty in a believer's life. *"Where the Spirit of the Lord is, there is liberty,"* **2 Corinthians 3:17**. The Holy Spirit through the Word of God in our lives equips us for all we will ever face: *"Now the God of peace, that brought again from the dead our Lord Jesus, that great shepherd of the sheep, through the blood of the everlasting covenant, Make you perfect in every good work to do His will, working in you that which is well-pleasing in his sight, through Jesus Christ; to whom be glory for ever and ever,"* **Hebrews 13:20-21**.

In a very clear analogy, the Word of God is to us spiritually as natural food is to us physically. God's Word to us is, *"Desire the sincere milk of the word, that ye may grow thereby,"* **1 Peter 2:2**. As we take His Word into our spiritual being, the Holy Spirit uses it to make us stronger and more mature in the Lord. Ultimately the Word produces fruit in us as we allow the Holy Spirit of God to use it in our lives.

2. In a very real sense, the Holy Spirit is always at work in believers to strengthen and build their lives. He strengthens them, builds their character and gives them resistance to temptations. That's the desire of the heart of every believer who prays in truth, *"Lead us not into temptation, but deliver us from evil,"* **Mathew 6:13**. Through the Holy Spirit, he is looking to God for deliverance and defense against evil and temptation. Jude expressed the limitless power of the Holy Spirit to meet our needs when he wrote, *"Now unto Him that is able to keep you from falling, and to present you faultless before the presence of His glory with exceeding joy, To the only wise God our Savior, be glory and majesty, dominion and power, both now and ever,"* **Jude 24-25**.

3. Praise God for His Holy Spirit, who not only controls the universe; but who specializes in the lives of believers. He gives them power to serve, and He produces life's finest qualities in them. He uses His Word, His providence and His power to make God's people all they should be. Truly we must say with Jude, *"to . . . God . . . be the glory!"*

4. Why, oh why, do so many of God's children spend their lives in such doom and gloom? All of the power they need to be everything God wants for and of them lives within. Paul asked, *"If God be for us, who can be against us?"* **Romans 8:31**. The fact that the Holy Spirit lives within doesn't exempt us from life's trials and natural weaknesses and frailties. It does equip us to face and endure them with *"love, joy, peace, longsuffering, gentleness, goodness, faith, meekness* and *temperance."* Guaranteed! *"The fruit of the Spirit,"* **Galatians 5:22-23**. If you don't have this fruit, you need immediate, earnest and deep soul-searching. If your church is cold, stiff, lifeless and void of these traits; your church needs radical change. Not a new music style, program, sound-system or building; but a wake-up to the Holy Spirit and what submission to Him looks like.

UNILATERAL WORK ON OUR BEHALF THROUGH THE INDWELLING HOLY SPIRIT

Do not be mistaken, and assume that the Holy Spirit does nothing in or for the believer without the believer's consent and submission. Even when we, His children, do not know or care enough to ask or seek His help, in many ways He looks out for our welfare. Whether or not we know it or seek His help, *"We know that all things work together for good to them that love God, to them who are the called according to his purpose,"* **Romans 8:28**. Yes, He works for our *"good"* which we sometimes think is bad.

A. He *seals* us and guarantees our eternal security.

1. In view of faith in Christ as our personal Savior, God saved us from sin's penalty by His matchless grace. Wherefore, we are *"accepted in the beloved"* (Jesus Christ) *"in whom we have redemption through his blood, the forgiveness of sins, according to the riches of his* *grace,"* **Ephesians 1:6-7**. Because of our connection to Jesus Christ, *"We have obtained an inheritance, being predestinated according to the purpose of him who worketh all things after the counsel of his own will: That we should be to the praise of his glory, who first trusted in Christ. In whom ye also trusted, after that ye heard the word of truth, the gospel of your salvation: in whom also after that ye believed, ye were sealed with that holy Spirit of promise, Which is the earnest of our inheritance until the redemption of the purchased possession, unto the praise of his glory,"* **Ephesians 1:11-14**. Note well: *"Ye were sealed with that holy Spirit of promise."*

2. Not one of us, no not one is capable of keeping ourselves saved. If it were not for the Holy Spirit of God who keeps us saved in spite of ourselves, every one of us who had believed in Christ would be hopelessly lost forever; but we are not hopelessly lost. We do not live in moment-by-moment fear that at any given second we might sin in some way, lose our salvation, die and find ourselves in the Lake of Fire. As believers who have trusted the Blessed Redeemer, we are eternally secure. We are dead to self, *"and your life is hid with Christ in God,"* **Colossians 3:3**. We are *"kept by the power of God,"* **1 Peter 1:5**. Finally, we are *"sealed with that holy Spirit of promise,"* **Ephesians 1:13**. In Christ in God sealed with the Holy Spirit. The entire Godhead committed to our eternal welfare. No wonder Paul asked the rhetorical question, *"If God be for us, who can be against us?"* **Romans 8:31**. The answer is obvious.

B. He causes *Providence* to work for our good.

1. *Providence* is defined as *"Divine guidance or care . . . God conceived as the power sustaining and guiding human destiny."*[2]

2. The word *providence* occurs only one time in the King James Bible and is used to convey the idea of human-forethought or provision. Though the word is not used in the Bible to convey the idea of God's provision, the idea or concept is laced throughout the Bible.

3. The concept of *providence* is obvious in **Romans 8:28**: *"And we know that all things work together for good to them that love God,*

[2] https://www.merriam-webster.com/dictionary/providence

to them who are the called according to his purpose." It is God who makes all things work together for our good. Paul fully accepted human free agency, but behind it all and through it all runs God's sovereignty.[3]

4. The following Psalm is strong testimonial to the providential watch-care of God: *"I will lift up mine eyes unto the hills, from whence cometh my help. My help cometh from the LORD, which made heaven and earth. He will not suffer thy foot to be moved: he that keepeth thee will not slumber. Behold, he that keepeth Israel shall neither slumber nor sleep. The LORD is thy keeper: the LORD is thy shade upon thy right hand. The sun shall not smite thee by day, nor the moon by night. The LORD shall preserve thee from all evil: he shall preserve thy soul. The LORD shall preserve thy going out and thy coming in from this time forth, and even for evermore,"* **Psalm 121:1-8**.

5. God appeared to Abraham and said, *"I am the Almighty God,"* **Genesis 17:1**. There is no power equal to or above He who is *"Almighty."* Thus, in the Bible you read such statements as, *"Our God is in the heavens: he hath done whatsoever he hath pleased,"* **Psalm 115:3**. He opens doors that no other can close and closes doors that no other can open. *"These things saith he that is holy, he that is true, he that hath the key of David, he that openeth, and no man shutteth; and shutteth, and no man openeth,"* **Revelation 3:7**.

6. God is the ultimate power. He can do anything any time. He always has the final word. At times, it may not seem so, but all powers and things are subject to God. Listen to His own words: *"Remember the former things of old: for I am God, and there is none else; I am God, and there is none like me, Declaring the end from the beginning, and from ancient times the things that are not yet done, saying, My counsel shall stand, and I will do all my pleasure: Calling a ravenous bird from the east, the man that executeth my counsel from a far country: yea, I have spoken it, I will also bring it to pass; I have purposed it, I will also do it,"* **Isaiah 46:9-11**.

C. The Holy Spirit is God, and He is always working in us *"both to will and to do of his good pleasure,"* **Philippians 2:13**. He's working

[3] A.T. Robertson, *Word Pictures in the New Testament*, vol. 4, (Nashville, Tennessee: Broadman Press, 1931), 377.

in us, when we know it and when we don't, when we're submitted and when we aren't.

1. With or without our permission, our great God the Holy Spirit can and does do what's needed for us. It may or may not be pleasant, but He can and will work on our behalf. Sometimes that involves chastening, particularly when we grow stubborn, self-willed and rebellious: *"For whom the Lord loveth he chasteneth, and scourgeth every son whom he receiveth. If ye endure chastening, God dealeth with you as with sons; for what son is he whom the father chasteneth not? But if ye be without chastisement, whereof all are partakers, then are ye bastards, and not sons. Furthermore we have had fathers of our flesh which corrected us, and we gave them reverence: shall we not much rather be in subjection unto the Father of spirits, and live? For they verily for a few days chastened us after their own pleasure; but he for our profit, that we might be partakers of his holiness. Now no chastening for the present seemeth to be joyous, but grievous: nevertheless afterward it yieldeth the peaceable fruit of righteousness unto them which are exercised thereby,"* **Hebrews 12:6-11**.

2. He wants us to yield, submit to Him; and it is when we do that He can bless as well as use us most extensively; however, He knows quite well how to deal with self-willed, unsubmitted, rebellious children. He knows how to take away opportunities: shut doors right in our faces and block our paths. He can open them, but He can shut them. When it happens, most people call it *luck*.

3. It is the Lord, the Holy Spirit, who brings us through crises and who takes care of us in specific ways. When we pray that God will *lead us not into temptation, but deliver us from evil*; we are placing ourselves at the mercy of the Holy Spirit. He is the person of the Godhead who actually lives in us and works specifically for our deliverance. Sometimes deliverance means preventing factors which could take our health, our effectiveness and even our lives. It means removing or minimizing temptations which could wreck us spiritually. When we are at wit's end and do not know what we need or how to ask for it, *"The Spirit also helpeth our infirmities: for we know not what we should pray for as we ought: but the Spirit itself maketh intercession for us with groanings which cannot be uttered,"* **Romans 8:26**.

4. The Holy Spirit knows us and what we need. He cares individually and personally for us. *"Casting all your care upon him; for he careth for you,"* **1 Peter 5:7**. He wants us to live in light of His presence with the love, joy, peace and other fruit that He produces in lives; but if we are not willing to recognize Him and surrender control of our life to Him, He will take measures to bring us under His control. The measures can be extreme. He may very well use providence to wake us up and get our attention. If we run through His stop signs, His measures on our behalf are sure to intensify.

D. Every believer should make every effort to recognize the work of the Holy Spirit in his life.

1. We may be too occupied with the cares of this life to pay much attention to the Holy Spirit, but He is always paying close attention to the person in whose heart He lives. He's omniscient. He is God; He knows everything. *"The Spirit searcheth all things, yea, the deep things of God,"* **1 Corinthians 2:10**. Of God King David said, *"There is not a word in my tongue, but, lo, O LORD, thou knowest it altogether,"* **Psalm 139:4**. The Bible says of Him, *"Neither is there any creature that is not manifest in his sight: but all things are naked and opened unto the eyes of him with whom we have to do,"* **Hebrews 4:13**.

2. When He providentially allows things into our lives, we would do well to learn why. They are always for our good. How can we properly interpret these providential workings or deliverances on our behalf? Scripture makes the answer unmistakably clear. We can only do so through the light of the Word of God. In fact, these providential workings in us are not only designed to sustain us and make us fruitful; but also intended to turn us to the Word of God for further instruction and proper analysis.

3. The providential workings of the Spirit are within themselves not sufficient to teach us what God is doing. Their design is to get our attention. Then, we can go to His written Word for a clear and proper interpretation and understanding of what God is doing in us. The Bible says of the existing universe, *"The invisible things of him from the creation of the world are clearly seen, being understood by the things that are*

made, even his eternal power and Godhead; so that they are without excuse," **Romans 1:20**. The natural universe is an ever-present testimonial of the greatness of God. Yet, the things that *"are clearly seen"* in *"the creation of the world"* are not sufficient for one to adequately know and serve God. The creation and the providential working of God should send people to the written Word of God for proper understanding and interpretation of what He has done. It is a fact that *"Faith cometh by hearing, and hearing by the Word of God,"* **Romans 10:17**. The things which providentially happen in the life of a believer should get his/her attention and turn him to God's Word where he can be instructed in the ways of God. That's not always easy and clear-cut, but it is God's path to Holy Spirit leadership. Please do not misunderstand. I am not saying the Holy Spirit reveals truth to us apart from the Word of God. No! I am saying is that in delivering us, He arranges circumstances both for us and to us. Our only way to properly analyze these activities is in light of His written Word. No person gets God's will by promptings, impulses or other feelings alone. Promptings, impulses or other feelings must be evaluated in light of the written Word of God.

Through the opening and closing of doors in our life, the Holy Spirit seeks to improve the direction of our lives; but not through these providential events alone. It is only when the daily providential activities of God turn us to His Word for proper interpretations; and we yield and submit ourselves to the authority of His Word in these specific occurrences that we can claim to be led by the Spirit of God. Holy Spirit leadership is not following any or every whelm, feeling or inclination of the heart which might be thought to be of God. To the contrary, it is applying the principles of Scripture to the real-life situations that the Spirit brings to us through providence and circumstances.

4. A glorious thought is the fact that once our heart is filled with the truths of God's Word as recommended in **Psalms 119:11**, the Spirit of God can bring them to our remembrance on the spot. This enables us to make wise interpretations and decisions on the spot. Obviously, the Spirit can only bring to our memory what has been previously placed there. Thus, every child of God would do well to delight himself in the Word of God. *"Blessed is the man that walketh not in the counsel of the ungodly, nor standeth in the way of sinners, nor sitteth in the seat of the scornful. But his delight is in the law of the LORD; and in his law doth he meditate day and night. And he shall be like a tree planted by the rivers of water, that bringeth forth his fruit in his season; his leaf also shall not wither; and whatsoever he doeth shall prosper,"* **Psalms 1:1-3**.

5. So many of God's people are handicapped as they face the circumstances of life. They have neglected to fill their hearts with the Word of God. Maybe it was television, sports or too much busyness, but it didn't happen. Thus, they have no way to *"try the spirits,"* **1 John 4:1**, and properly analyze what's happening. In too many cases, believers can't decide whether the Holy Spirit is leading or Satan is enticing. Even when a matter is of the Holy Spirit, most cannot put the matter in proper perspective and gain its maximum benefit. They have failed to hide God's Word in their hearts. The Holy Spirit is thus hampered in the leading of such ones. Obviously the more one ingests the truths of the written Word, the more fully the Holy Spirit can lead him. As he grows in truth, he increasingly reaches positions to respond properly and speedily to the providential workings of the Spirit. Daily deliverance by the Holy Spirit of God is not always a matter of His unilateral, miraculously acts of deliverance. He can and often does act unilaterally, without our will or knowledge, deliver us. Most of the time, He introduces circumstances into our lives. If we fail to know and apply Biblical principles to these real-life situations, we are the losers. The fault is our own. The delivering power of the Spirit was there, but somehow by our blindness to the situation and ignorance of the principles of written truth which should have been applied to the situation, we fail to avail ourselves of the deliverance of the Holy Spirit which is available to us. This happens in our efforts to reach people with the gospel, in business ventures, in our marriage and across the spectrum of life.

6. We serve a great God. He asks, *"Am I a God at hand, saith the LORD, and not a God afar off?"* **Jeremiah 23:23**. He is very near, even in our hearts. In spite of our ignorance of Him and His Word, *"He daily loadeth us with benefits,"* **Psalms 68:19**. Do not think that you must be perfect for the Holy Spirit to work in and through you. That is not the case. Every one of us should seriously ponder the thought of surrender and of how much more the Spirit can and would use us. With our foot off the brake and with His unrestrained control, our lives would be so much richer and more fruitful.

7. Deliverance today! Our deliverance daily is the primary work of the Holy Spirit. Praise God for Him. Without His delivering and sustaining power, we could not survive in the work of the Lord. May God help us not to be blind to what He is doing to deliver, enrich and sustain us daily! When the good blessings of life come to us, let us recognize that it is the Holy Spirit of God who is their author. God forbid that we be like ancient Israel of whom God said, *"The ox knoweth his owner, and the ass his master's crib: but Israel doth not know, my people doth not consider,"* **Isaiah 1:3**.

Chapter 21

Holy Spirit Conviction

Acts 7:51

God in the person of the Holy Spirit plays the lead role in practical activities in today's world. God the Father took the lead role in creation. Today He is in heaven. We pray, *"Our Father which art in heaven,"* **Matthew 6:9**. God the Son *"is set down at the right hand of the throne of God,"* **Hebrews 12:2**. *"He is able also to save them to the uttermost that come unto God by him, seeing he ever liveth to make intercession for them,"* **Hebrews 7:25**. God the Holy Spirit lives on this earth in the hearts of those who are saved by the blood of Christ. *"If the Spirit of him that raised up Jesus from the dead dwell in you, he that raised up Christ from the dead shall also quicken your mortal bodies by his Spirit that dwelleth in you,"* **Romans 8:11**.

The Holy Spirit is right down here on planet earth, living in the saved; however, being God, He is omnipresent. He is not limited by location. People can be in only one spot at a time; the Holy Spirit is everywhere all of the time. He's in believers, but He also has a current work which is outside of believers.

Shortly before Jesus ascended back into heaven, He announced that He was departing, and that the Holy Spirit would follow Him as the dominate person of the Godhead on earth. Listen in on Jesus' words: *"Nevertheless I tell you the truth; It is expedient for you that I go away: for if I go not away, the Comforter will not come unto you; but if I depart, I will send him unto you. And when he is come, he will reprove the world of sin, and of righteousness, and of judgment: Of sin, because they believe not on me; Of righteousness, because I go to my Father, and ye see me no more; Of judgment, because the prince of this world is judged,"* **John 16:7-11**.

Few subjects within the ranks of professing Christians generate as much controversy as does the current work of the Holy Spirit: over who He is, what He does and what He does not do. People have many feelings they do not understand. Strange activities happen in church, and seemingly unexplainable events occur during the course of daily living. The tendency of many is to assume these feelings and activities to be the work of the Holy Spirit of God. Thus, the Holy Spirit gets credit for much He does not do.

The only authoritative source on the activities of the Holy Spirit is the Bible. There alone we are told much of what He does and does not do. We know the Holy Spirit never acts contrary to what the Word of God says of Him. Thus, to know whether any feeling or act is of the Holy Spirit, it must be analyzed in light of the Word of God. If the feeling or act is contrary to what the Scriptures say the Holy Spirit does or does not do, then the feeling or act is not the doing of the Holy Spirit of God. A sad human trait is the propensity to elevate experiences and feelings above all else, even above the Bible. Unfortunately, the theology of many people is largely based on what they feel, their experiences and what they've been taught. Embracing only what the Bible teaches, especially on the person and work of the Holy Spirit will quickly draw passionate accusations of, *"You don't believe in the Holy Spirit."*

This chapter will focus particularly on how the Holy Spirit convicts lost sinners as well as wayward believers.

THE HOLY SPIRIT CONVICTS TO BRING PEOPLE TO GOD

A. Being God, the Holy Spirit wants every lost person to be saved.

1. Few, if any, truths are more obvious than God's desire for the lost to be saved.

a. *"For God so loved the world, that he gave his only begotten Son, that whosoever believeth in him should not perish, but have* *everlasting life. For God sent not his Son into the world to condemn the world; but that the world through him might be saved,"* **John 3:16-17**.

b. *"The Son of man is come to seek and to save that which was lost,"* **Luke 19:10**.

c. To see how much God loves lost sinners and wants them to be saved and have eternal life, look at Jesus Christ, the God of heaven and earth hanging there in shame and agony, dying in the place of sinners, doing for them what they could not do for themselves. *"Hereby perceive we the love of God, because he laid down his life for us,"* **1 John 3:16**. Life for men may be cheap. It's not cheap to God. We may not care much for vile, fallen sinners, but God cares.

d. The Bible says, *"The Lord is not slack concerning his promise, as some men count slackness; but is longsuffering to us-ward, not willing that any should perish, but that all should come to repentance,"* **2 Peter 3:9**.

e. The heart of God for lost sinners is unmistakable. He wants every one of them to be saved, and He has gone to extreme lengths to see it happen.

2. God has done in Christ everything that is necessary for lost sinners to be forgiven and have eternal life.

a. Yes! *Everything!* In view of the work which He was doing to see sinners saved, Jesus while hanging on the cross said, *"It is finished,"* **John 19:30**.

b. God's penalty for sin is death; *"The wages of sin is death,"* **Romans 6:23**. God made that clear to Adam: *"Of the tree of the knowledge of good and evil, thou shalt not eat of it: for in the day that thou eatest thereof thou shalt surely die,"* **Genesis 2:17**.

c. On the cross, Jesus Christ *tasted death for every man. "But we see Jesus, who was made a little lower than the angels for the suffering of death, crowned with glory and honour; that he by the grace of God should taste death for every man"* **Hebrews 2:9**. He didn't deserve death. He was innocent, the sinless God of heaven and earth, yet He willingly, voluntarily gave His life for us, guilty sinners.

- **d.** He died, was buried and rose again on the third day. He shed and offered His innocent blood as a perfect sacrifice for sinners. *"Neither by the blood of goats and calves, but by his own blood he entered in once into the holy place, having obtained eternal redemption for us,"* **Hebrews 9:12**.

- **e.** That's it! It's a done deal. The work by which lost sinners can be forgiven and receive eternal life had been completed, finished. Now, it's up to the lost sinner to simply receive it by faith. *"He that believeth on the Son hath everlasting life: and he that believeth not the Son shall not see life; but the wrath of God abideth on him"* **John 3:36**.

3. In view of the heart of God and the work He has done to save sinners, the Holy Spirit works to bring conviction of their need of Christ and His salvation to the hearts of lost people.

B. Being God, the Holy Spirit wants every believer to turn from sin and live a righteous, holy life.

1. The Holy Spirit lives in the heart of every believer. He obviously knows the heart: the motives, the desires, the wishes, the plans and the deeds. He knows the thoughts and hears every word, even those unspoken. *"There is not a word in my tongue, but, lo, O LORD, thou knowest it altogether,"* **Psalm 139:4**. He knows every deed. *"Whither shall I go from thy spirit? or whither shall I flee from thy presence? If I ascend up into heaven, thou art there: if I make my bed in hell, behold, thou art there. If I take the wings of the morning, and dwell in the uttermost parts of the sea; Even there shall thy hand lead me, and thy right hand shall hold me. If I say, Surely the darkness shall cover me; even the night shall be light about me,"* **Psalm 139:7-11**.

2. God's Word, the Bible is packed with passages showing God's expectations that His children live sanctified, holy lives which are set apart from the evil of this world. *"Sanctify yourselves therefore, and be ye holy: for I am the LORD your God,"* **Leviticus 20:7**. That's not just an Old Testament thing. *"Be ye holy; for I am holy,"* **1 Peter 1:16**. *To sanctify* means to dedicate, consecrate, purify.[1] Notice that God started His sentence with

[1] James Strong, *Hebrew and Chaldee Dictionary*, (Nashville, Tennessee: Abingdon Press, 1958), ref. 6942.

the reflexive verb *"sanctify."* It's an imperative. The initiative rests on the subject which is understood to be *you. You sanctify yourself.* One of the great doctrines of the Bible is *sanctification.* It is woven throughout the Bible like a silver thread.

3. Surely, even the youngest spiritual baby in the Lord has an awareness that God's children are to *"abstain from fleshly lusts, which war against the soul,"* **1 Peter 2:11**, and live lifestyles set apart to Christ. *"Only let your conversation be as it becometh the gospel of Christ."* **Philippians 1:27**. *"Having your conversation honest among the Gentiles: that, whereas they speak against you as evildoers, they may by your good works, which they shall behold, glorify God in the day of visitation,"* **1 Peter 2:12**.

4. In order to turn believers from the evil in their lives, the Holy Spirit convicts their hearts.

   a. God's efforts to purify His people is easy to see as He dealt with Old Testament Israel. His efforts to turn them from evil to righteousness were incessant. Here is only one of multiple examples: *"As I live, saith the Lord GOD, I have no pleasure in the death of the wicked; but that the wicked turn from his way and live: turn ye, turn ye from your evil ways; for why will ye die, O house of Israel?"* **Ezekiel 33:11**.

   b. Here is but one of a great number of exhortations admonishing believers to turn from sinful living to holy, Christlike behavior. *"Let him that stole steal no more: but rather let him labour, working with his hands the thing which is good, that he may have to give to him that needeth. Let no corrupt communication proceed out of your mouth, but that which is good to the use of edifying, that it may minister grace unto the hearers. And grieve not the holy Spirit of God, whereby ye are sealed unto the day of redemption. Let all bitterness, and wrath, and anger, and clamour, and evil speaking, be put away from you, with all malice: And be ye kind one to another, tenderhearted, forgiving one another, even as God for Christ's sake hath forgiven you,"* **Ephesians 4:28-32**.

   Note well the statement embedded in this call for holiness in the lives of God's children. The Scriptures remind us that our evil motives, thoughts and words, *grieve the Holy Spirit* who *seals* us, thus guaranteeing our eternal security. *"And grieve not the holy Spirit of God, whereby ye are sealed unto the day of redemption."*

c. The Holy Spirit is always working to convict every believer to live a life of godliness. It seems to me that the truth expressed by Paul in his letter to the Church in Rome has application to both lost and saved people. *"Or despisest thou the riches of his goodness and forbearance and longsuffering; not knowing that the goodness of God leadeth thee to repentance?"* **Romans 2:4**. God wants all men and women who are on the wrong path to turn around. In light of the truth which is available to all men, Paul made the blanket statement, *"And the times of this ignorance God winked at; but now commandeth all men every where to repent,"* **Acts 17:30**.

THE INTRODUCION OF GOD'S WORD

At one time or another, most people have felt conviction. Many unsaved people have sat in church and listened to a sermon about the work of Christ. They knew they were lost and needed Him as Savior. Deep in their heart, they felt conviction. Before they trust Him in their heart, most people experience conviction. It's quite profound. It moves people very deeply; some openly weep.

Saved people know what conviction is. They know conviction deep in their heart as they contemplate doing something they know is wrong before God. Once a believer commits a sin, especially one that is obviously and blatantly wrong, the conviction of guilt can be extremely powerful. Guilt is a part of conviction, and it works on lost and saved alike.

A. The Holy Spirit does not convict people randomly or apart from the Word of God.

1. For many, the mental picture of conviction is that of the Holy Spirit in the form of a cartoon-type ghost penetrating the body into the heart where He puts pressure on sinners to turn from sin to righteousness. It's as though He enters into a mental conversation with the sinner, reasoning with him and pleading with him to turn.

2. Some mentally envision the Holy Spirit as quite selective in who He enters to convict. They think He enters only select ones while completely passing by others with no effort to reach them. Even of those whom they see the Spirit selecting for conviction, they think He convicts some more so than others.

3. The truth is that the Holy Spirit does not randomly enter and convict sinners apart from knowledge of truth. The Bible specifically speaks of *"The Spirit of truth; whom the world cannot receive, because it seeth Him not, neither knoweth Him,"* **John 14:17**. The Holy Spirit has a method for reaching into the hearts of men, lost or saved. He will not violate His own plan by some other arbitrary approach.

4. A church service provides an illustration of this erroneous mental concept. Those who think this way have a mental picture of a sinner who is under conviction. In their mental picture, they see the Holy Spirit having come to the heart where He has been denied entry. There He stands on the outside wooing, pleading and trying to break the stubborn will of the sinner.

B. How did God get His word to a world of lost sinners who could never come to a knowledge of God and His truth on their own? The apostle Paul addressed this specific issue.

1. In his letter to the Corinthian believers, he distinguished between worldly or human wisdom. *"And my speech and my preaching was not with enticing words of man's wisdom, but in demonstration of the Spirit and of power,"* **1 Corinthians 2:4**. His *speech* and *preaching* was not with *man's wisdom*. This very different message which he preached was confirmed by demonstrations of miraculous power. He continued and affirmed that the message he had was *"not the wisdom of this world,"* **1 Corinthians 2:6**.

2. He affirmed that the message he had was divine, not human. *"We speak the wisdom of God in a mystery, even the hidden wisdom, which God ordained before the world unto our glory: Which none of the princes of this world knew,"* **1 Corinthians 2:7-8**.

3. He also affirmed that on their own by any of the known ways of getting information, men would never figure out this message from God. *"But as it is written, Eye hath not seen, nor ear heard, neither have entered into the heart of man, the things which God hath prepared for them that love him,"* **1 Corinthians 2:9**. He continued, *"But the natural man receiveth not the things of the Spirit of God: for they are foolishness unto him: neither can he know them, because they are spiritually discerned,"* **1 Corinthians 2:14**. No *"natural man"* would have ever come up with God's great eternal plan of redemption.

4. The only way humanity would ever get this truth was directly from God. God had to unilaterally reveal these truths which are in the Bible. Paul affirmed that is how he and the others who wrote Scriptures got it. *"God hath revealed them unto us by his Spirit: for the Spirit searcheth all things, yea, the deep things of God,"* **1 Corinthians 2:10**. He continued the argument: *"Now we have received, not the spirit of the world, but the spirit which is of God; that we might know the things that are freely given to us of God. Which things also we speak, not in the words which man's wisdom teacheth, but which the Holy Ghost teacheth; comparing spiritual things with spiritual,"* **1 Corinthians 2:12-13**.

5. Humanity couldn't and didn't come up with the divine truths set forth in the Bible. God gave them to humanity through divine revelation. *"We have also a more sure word of prophecy; whereunto ye do well that ye take heed, as unto a light that shineth in a dark place, until the day dawn, and the day star arise in your hearts: Knowing this first, that no prophecy of the scripture is of any private interpretation. For the prophecy came not in old time by the will of man: but holy men of God spake as they were moved by the Holy Ghost,"* **2 Peter 1:19-21**.

6. Once they were divinely given, they became available and accessible to all mankind. Since God gave the Word of God, no person has to be specially endowed or chosen to get the truth. Lost people and saved people alike now have access to the Word of God. They have the capacity to receive or reject it. We have the message of God. Each individual must now decide what he or she will do with it.

C. The Holy Spirit convicts hearts through His Word which is His divine revelation.

1. Instead of the Holy Spirit working on the sinner apart from, ahead of or in addition to the Word of God, He works to convict the sinner through the Word of God. The Word of God is His product. He is the one who inspired it. It is a divinely inspired spiritual sword. It is *"quick,* (alive) *and powerful, and sharper than any twoedged sword, piercing even to the dividing asunder of soul and spirit, and of the joints and marrow, and is a discerner of the thoughts and intents of the heart,"* **Hebrews 4:12**. Whenever this Word of eternal truth is introduced into the heart of any person, it has a cutting, convicting effect. This is the Holy Spirit's way of convicting sinners.

2. Envision a church service where the Word of God is being preached. The living Word of the Spirit of God enters in through the spiritual ears into the heart where it begins to convict the sinner. The Word is no respecter of persons, and it enters each sinner in direct proportion to his individual mindset of receptiveness or resistance. Because the Word is the living Word of the Holy Spirit of God, it convicts; and that conviction is Holy Spirit conviction. This is how the Holy Spirit convicts sinners.

D. A clear example of how the Holy Spirit convicts hearts is seen in the Bible. Acts 7.

1. Shortly after the death, burial and resurrection of Jesus Christ, Stephen preached a tremendous sermon to the Jewish religious leadership in Jerusalem which had crucified Jesus Christ.

a. The scene and sermon are recorded in **Acts 7:2-53**.

b. It is noteworthy that Stephen was *"full of faith and power, did great wonders and miracles among the people,"* **Acts 6:8**. Stephen spoke the truth of this sermon (the Word of God) by the Holy Spirit.

2. As Stephen preached his Spirit-inspired sermon to them, they were convicted, *"When they heard these things, they were cut to the heart, and they gnashed on him with their teeth,"* **Acts 7:54**.

Their conviction was to the point of vicious anger. They proceeded to stone him to death. *"They cried out with a loud voice, and stopped their ears, and ran upon him with one accord, And cast him out of the city, and stoned him,"* **Acts 7:57-58**.

- **a.** How did the Holy Spirit convict these sinners?
- **b.** He did so through the Spirit-inspired Word which Stephen preached to them.
- **c.** The Holy Spirit used that Word to convict them.

3. As his hearers rejected his words and the words of other Spirit-inspired men who had spoken unto them, Stephen accused them of rejecting the Holy Spirit: *"Ye stiffnecked and uncircumcised in heart and ears, ye do always resist the Holy Ghost,"* **Acts 7:51**.

- **a.** The Word convicted them, but they rejected it.
- **b.** In so doing, they *resisted "the Holy Ghost?"*

E. Note well the statement of Stephen: *"As your fathers did, so do ye,"* **Acts 7:51**.

1. When they rejected the Word of truth which he preached, they rejected the Holy Spirit.

2. That's how the Holy Spirit has always convicted sinners.

- **a.** When the people in Noah's day heard the truth of God which he preached, they were hearing from God. They were convicted. When they rejected the truth they heard, they rejected the Holy Spirit.
- **b.** When the people in Moses's day heard the truth of God which he preached, they were hearing from God. They were convicted. When they rejected the truth they heard, they rejected the Holy Spirit.
- **c.** The same could be said of Samuel, David, Isaiah, Jeremiah, Daniel, John the Baptist and a host of others. It is not difficult to understand why Jesus said, *"O Jerusalem, Jerusalem, thou that killest the prophets, and stonest*

them which are sent unto thee, how often would I have gathered thy children together, even as a hen gathereth her chickens under her wings, and ye would not! Behold, your house is left unto you desolate," **Matthew 23:37-38**.

F. Regardless of the age or time, God uses His Word by His Spirit to reach the hearts of sinners, convict them and draw them to Himself. His plan has not changed; it has always been the same.

1. His Word must be introduced into the heart. *"Faith cometh by hearing, and hearing by the word of God,"* **Romans 10:17**. There is no shortcut. We can't *pray 'um in* or *wish 'um in*. William Carey said, *"They will not seek; they must be sought. They will not come; they must be brought. They will not learn; they must be taught."* Conviction may occur as the Word of God is being preached. It may reach a person in a song, prayer, a gospel tract or in years of input from a faithful mother, dad or friend. The Holy Spirit can use the Word of God like a long-dormant seed. The timing and circumstances may vary, but the constant is the Holy Spirit uses the Word of God to convict men and women.

2. He does not convict men in some mystical, helter-skelter way. He's not an imaginary ghost or esoteric, magical being who flits around like an unseen butterfly touching hearts without rhyme or reason. The biblical concept of Holy Spirit conviction never has been, nor is it now, His unilateral work in the heart of sinners apart from His revealed Word. Yes, He convicts sinners. He brings fear, contrition, guilt, anger, brokenness and many other strong feelings; but He does not do so separate or apart from His Word. His method of convicting sinners will always be according to the pattern set forth in His holy scriptures.

3. At this point I must say a word to you who do not know Christ as your personal Savior. Don't keep putting off salvation while you wait for the Holy Spirit to overpower you. Some preacher or other Christian may have led you to believe that the Holy Spirit will someday settle in on you and break your will in a great moment beyond your control. That just isn't going to happen; and if you wait for it, you'll die lost. No doubt, the Holy Spirit has already been convicting

you. You've heard His Word; and as you have, your heart has trembled, and you've felt Him drawing you to Himself. Friend, that is Holy Spirit conviction. You're not going to get something bigger, better and more powerful than that. Jesus said, *"The words that I speak unto you, they are spirit, and they are life,"* **John 6:63**. He concluded the 20th chapter of John by saying, *"These are written, that ye might believe that Jesus is the Christ, the Son of God; and that believing ye might have life through His name,"* **John 20:31**.

Chapter 22

My Spirit Shall Not Always Strive with Man

Genesis 6:3

God said there would come a day when *"My spirit shall not always strive with man,"* **Genesis 6:3**. That was a specific statement to Noah about the coming cataclysmic world-wide flood that would destroy the earth 120 years later. The day did come, and God destroyed this planet with water. Sedimentary deposits, fossil graveyards, the Grand Canyon and the world-wide distribution of fossils even on mountaintops are silent testimonies to a time of unparalleled judgment and chaos on this earth. Before the Great Flood, God's Spirit *strived* with the human race to turn from wholesale wickedness, but God made it clear to Noah that His patience has a limit. He told Noah that the day would come when He would quit trying to turn mankind from its love affair with evil. There would be no more *striving*. *"Strive"* is from the Hebrew word **diyn**. It means *to strive to turn as in a case at law, to contend, to plead a cause.*[1] God told Noah that He would stop pleading His case for righteousness with the evil, sex-crazed human race which was before Him. No more contending with sinners to turn! No more efforts to turn them from destruction! Instead of *striving*, there would be **judgment**!

---

[1] James Strong, *Hebrew and Chaldee Dictionary*, (Nashville, Tennessee: Abingdon Press, 1958), ref. 1777.

What happened back there is a warning to everyone! God's Spirit did quit *striving* with man, and the whole world perished. Every air-breathing thing outside of Noah's Ark died! Every one of them from people to fleas, from dinosaurs to cock-roaches drowned. The Bible says what happened back there is a prophetic prediction that it will happen again; not by water, but by fire. Another judgment day is on its way when God's Spirit *will no longer strive with man*. Listen to the divinely inspired apostle Peter: *"Knowing this first, that there shall come in the last days scoffers, walking after their own lusts, And saying, Where is the promise of his coming? for since the fathers fell asleep, all things continue as they were from the beginning of the creation. For this they willingly are ignorant of, that by the word of God the heavens were of old, and the earth standing out of the water and in the water: Whereby the world that then was, being overflowed with water, perished: But the heavens and the earth, which are now, by the same word are kept in store, reserved unto fire against the day of judgment and perdition of ungodly men. But, beloved, be not ignorant of this one thing, that one day is with the Lord as a thousand years, and a thousand years as one day. The Lord is not slack concerning his promise, as some men count slackness; but is longsuffering to us-ward, not willing that any should perish, but that all should come to repentance. But the day of the Lord will come as a thief in the night; in the which the heavens shall pass away with a great noise, and the elements shall melt with fervent heat, the earth also and the works that are therein shall be burned up,"* **2 Peter 3:3-10**.

The goal of this chapter is to help you understand ***how God's Spirit strives with man***. There is much misunderstanding on this issue. In this day of ghosts and goblins (and preachers who gloat in the sensational whether or not it's true), many people view God's Holy Spirit as a sort of comic-strip character, a Casper the Ghost. Nearly every strange, emotional impulse is accredited to Him, especially at church. He does *"reprove* (convict) *the world of sin, and of righteousness and of judgement,"* **John 16:8-11**. He does not convict sinful people in the way that most people suppose. This chapter will first show you three primary ways God has *striven* with man both before and after the Great Flood. The chapter will then show you that God's Spirit always *strives* with man in an impartial way. Finally, the chapter will show you that God does not arbitrarily select a few individuals and singularly *strive* with them more than He does other individuals.

THE WAYS GOD HAS *STRIVEN* WITH MEN BEFORE AND SINCE THE GREAT FLOOD

A. God strives to reach men through the natural world.

1. **Evidence** of God is everywhere. *"The heavens declare the glory of God; and the firmament sheweth his handywork. Day unto day uttereth speech, and night unto night sheweth knowledge. There is no speech nor language, where their voice is not heard,"* **Psalm 19:1-3**.

2. God's handiwork should turn men to Him; His forbearance is effort on His part to turn men from evil and to Him. *"Or despisest thou the riches of his goodness and forbearance and longsuffering; not knowing that the goodness of God leadeth thee to repentance?"* **Romans 2:4**.

3. In view of the massive evidence which testify of God, and in view of His patience in spite of continual rejection, those who refuse God are without excuse. *"The wrath of God is revealed from heaven against all ungodliness and unrighteousness of men, who hold the truth in unrighteousness; Because that which may be known of God is manifest in them; for God hath shewed it unto them. For the invisible things of him from the creation of the world are clearly seen, being understood by the things that are made, even his eternal power and Godhead; so that they are without excuse: Because that, when they knew God, they glorified him not as God, neither were thankful; but became vain in their imaginations, and their foolish heart was darkened. Professing themselves to be wise, they became fools, And changed the glory of the uncorruptible God into an image made like to corruptible man, and to birds, and fourfooted beasts, and creeping things. Wherefore God also gave them up to uncleanness through the lusts of their own hearts, to dishonour their own bodies between themselves: Who changed the truth of God into a lie, and worshipped and served the creature more than the Creator, who is blessed for ever. Amen,"* **Romans 1:18-25**. Note well, *"the invisible things of him from the creation of the world are clearly seen, being understood by the things that are made."* It is not at all difficult to see that there is a God, and that He is extremely gracious and merciful; evidence is everywhere in the natural world. Intelligent design is observable in every nook and cranny of the natural world, from the stars and other celestial beings to the brain, from the Periodic Table to the astounding reproductive processes observable in all living things.

4. The natural world is on public display 24 X 7. God is *striving* with man's intelligence. The natural world is silently screaming: *"Look for yourself. I'm not hidden away in some dark closet. Use your head. Evidence of intelligence and deliberate design are all around you, including your own highly designed body."*

B. God strives to reach men through the truth embedded within them.

1. When Adam and Eve did their evil, they knew it was wrong. *"When the woman saw that the tree was good for food, and that it was pleasant to the eyes, and a tree to be desired to make one wise, she took of the fruit thereof, and did eat, and gave also unto her husband with her; and he did eat. And the eyes of them both were opened, and they knew that they were naked; and they sewed fig leaves together, and made themselves aprons. And they heard the voice of the LORD God walking in the garden in the cool of the day: and Adam and his wife hid themselves from the presence of the LORD God amongst the trees of the garden,"* **Genesis 3:6-8**. Don't miss it: *"They knew that they were naked." "They sewed fig leaves together* and *"made themselves aprons."* When they realized God was close, *"they hid themselves."*

2. A fundamental sense of good and evil is a part of being a human. Though they are barely able to talk, and surely not skilled in morals, little children sense that some things are wrong: things such as lying, hurting others and sexual exploitation. The Bible speaks to this issue: *"For when the Gentiles, which have not the law, do by nature the things contained in the law, these, having not the law, are a law unto themselves: Which shew the work of the law written in their hearts, their conscience also bearing witness, and their thoughts the mean while accusing or else excusing one another,"* **Romans 2:14-15**.

3. When little children steal, hurt other children or break or ruin something, they are notorious for lying to their parents or other authorities. They don't have to be taught how to lie or cover-up evidence; it's built into their being. Country boys who steal watermelons, people who shop-lift and people of any age who engage in illicit sex do not need a lesson on stealing or morals to know it's wrong. Jesus said, *"Men loved darkness rather than light, because their deeds were evil,"* **John 3:19**. Have you noticed that most people who engage in robberies and other violent crimes wear hoodies? Have

you realized that the vast majority of rapes and murders happen after midnight? People instinctively hid their evil. Evil is in human nature, and an evil conscience is not an imaginary thing. Adolph Hitler, Joseph Stalin and Charles Manson all knew that what they were doing was wrong.

C. God strives to reach men through preachers and other messengers of His Word.

1. The Bible says, *"The preaching of the cross is to them that perish foolishness; but unto us which are saved it is the power of God,"* **1 Corinthians 1:18**. A growing number of earth's populace think Christianity and the message of salvation through Jesus Christ is nothing more than fables, fantasy and myth. The truth is that there is zero hope beyond the grave for all people who reject the redemptive work of Jesus Christ. By the preaching, the delivery of His message of deliverance and hope, God continually strives with men. He seeks to turn them from eternal destruction and to Himself. Here are His words: *"For after that in the wisdom of God the world by wisdom knew not God, it pleased God by the foolishness of preaching to save them that believe,"* **1 Corinthians 1:21**.

2. Before the Great Flood, Noah was the eighth *"preacher of righteousness,"* **2 Peter 2:5**. He preached 120 years. Obviously, there were other preachers. God was *striving*, constantly working to turn men and women from evil to good; however, they wouldn't listen. In spite of God's pleading and warnings through His messengers, the people of that day rejected Him and continued in their own evil ways. *"GOD saw that the wickedness of man was great in the earth, and that every imagination of the thoughts of his heart was only evil continually. And it repented the LORD that he had made man on the earth, and it grieved him at his heart. And the LORD said, I will destroy man whom I have created from the face of the earth; both man, and beast, and the creeping thing, and the fowls of the air; for it repenteth me that I have made them,"* **Genesis 6:5-7**.

   Continually since the Great Flood, God has had a parade of preachers: prophets like Moses and Isaiah, apostles like John and Paul and men like Polycarp, Hans Graebel, Charles Spurgeon, Billy Graham and thousands of others. This day, there are preachers of righteousness scattered across the planet. They are preaching God's Word, warning of eternity without God, telling people that the day of opportunity to get right with God will not stay open forever and pleading with men and women to come to Christ. Besides the vocational preachers, there are Sunday school teachers, caring dads and moms as well as friends at school and work. God is using them just like He used Noah before the flood. He is still *striving* with men to turn from evil to Him.

3. God's three ways of *striving* with man remain: the natural world, embedded truth and messengers of truth.

GOD ALWAYS *STRIVES* WITH MEN IN AN IMPARTIAL WAY

A. God desires the salvation of all men.

1. He made that fact clear when He said, *"For God so loved the world, that he gave his only begotten Son, that whosoever believeth in him should not perish, but have everlasting life,"* **John 3:16**.

2. God's substitutionary sacrifice was not for a select few; it was for all men. The divinely inspired apostle, John wrote, *"He is the propitiation for our sins: and not for ours only, but also for the sins of the whole world,"* **1 John 2:2**. Note well. John used the personal plural pronoun *"our."* He included himself in the group of people who have trusted Christ as Savior. He said Christ is the *"propitiation"* for the sins of believers. John then said Christ is the *"propitiation"* for *"the sins of the whole world."* That statement precludes the mistaken idea that the redemptive work of Christ was for the *elect* or a pre-select few. God loved all sinners, and Christ's work of salvation (*"propitiation"*) was for all of them. *Propitiation* is translated into English from the Greek word **hilasmos**. The word speaks of the sacrifice of Christ in the place of sinners by which He satisfied the justice of God against them making it possible for God to show mercy to the sinner who believes on Jesus Christ.[2] Every sinner who comes in faith to Christ

---

[2] W.E. Vine, Merrill F. Unger, William White, Jr., *Vine's Expository Dictionary of Biblical Words,* (Nashville, Tennessee: Thomas Nelson Publishers, 1985), 494.

is shown mercy and given eternal life, and every other sinner could come and experience God's mercy. In view of His death, burial and resurrection with all that entails, Christ Himself is *"the propitiation."* All human effort is excluded. The salvation of sinners rests solely on Him.

3. God's love and salvation for all sinners thunders throughout the Scriptures: *"The Lord is not slack concerning his promise, as some men count slackness; but is longsuffering to us-ward, not willing that any should perish, but that all should come to repentance,"* **2 Peter 3:9**. *"God sent not his Son into the world to condemn the world; but that the world through him might be saved,"* **John 3:17**. *"The Son of man is come to seek and to save that which was lost,"* **Luke 19:10**. To Israel and all mankind, God expressed His heart when He said, *"For I know the thoughts that I think toward you, saith the LORD, thoughts of peace, and not of evil, to give you an expected end,"* **Jeremiah 29:11**. *"The Spirit and the bride say, Come. And let him that heareth say, Come. And let him that is athirst come. And whosoever will, let him take the water of life freely,"* **Revelation 22:17**.

B. All men have access to the light, an equal exposure to truth.

1. The natural world is no respecter of persons; it's there for everyone to see and examine. Everywhere it points to God. Intelligent design is written in every atom and cell, especially the reproductive cells. *"The heavens declare the glory of God; and the firmament sheweth his handywork. Day unto day uttereth speech, and night unto night sheweth knowledge. There is no speech nor language, where their voice is not heard,"* **Psalm 19:1-3**. Evidence for God is strong and universal throughout the natural world. God's fingerprints are everywhere: as far as a telescope can see to as deep as a microscope can see. One invisible cell is a world within itself. The deeper you look the more obvious God becomes!

   The truth of God is absolutely unbiased. *"There is no respect of persons with God,"* **Romans 2:11**. The apostle Peter said, *"Of a truth I perceive that God is no respecter of persons,"* **Acts 10:34**. Nowhere is that clearer than in the natural world where every man has equal access to the limitless evidence which speaks of God. Every night and every day, God is *striving* to turn men to Himself.

2. The moral conscience is always there in every man. Deep down, all men know that good and evil exist. Some have hardened their hearts against God. The Bible predicts the time when many people will be viciously hardened against God and all for which He stands: *"Now the Spirit speaketh expressly, that in the latter times some shall depart from the faith, giving heed to seducing spirits, and doctrines of devils; Speaking lies in hypocrisy; having their conscience seared with a hot iron,"* **1 Timothy 4:1-2**. Regardless of how hard they get, men cannot escape their own conscience. In their hearts men still know there is right and wrong, good and evil. Speaking to hardened, God-rejecting men the Bible says, *"Despisest thou the riches of his goodness and forbearance and longsuffering; not knowing that the goodness of God leadeth thee to repentance?"* **Romans 2:4**. In a non-discriminatory way God continues to *strive*, to turn men to righteousness.

3. Also, God still has preachers who preach the truth. In thousands of churches world-wide, through radio and television, with gospel tracts in countless tracts, with tens of thousands of Christian books, through motion pictures and through world-wide Internet the message of the death, burial and resurrection of Jesus Christ is preached. Nobody is excluded. God is still pleading with sinners; striving. *"And the Spirit and the bride say, Come. And let him that heareth say, Come. And let him that is athirst come. And whosoever will, let him take the water of life freely,"* **Revelation 22:17**.

4. An old axiom of hermeneutics (Bible interpretation) says, *"If the literal sense makes sense, seek no other sense."*[3] In these great Bible passages, it's virtually impossible to miss the message of God. He literally wants people to come to Him and be saved. There is zero reason to seek any other sense.

5. Just like it was before the big Noahic Flood, the Spirit of God is *striving* with all men, the whole world. The world is a dark and sinful place, but there's still plenty of light everywhere. All men could be saved.

---

[3] https://jeanwilund.com/bible-study-tip-9-if-the-literal-sense-makes-sense-seek-no-other-sense

GOD'S EFFORTS ARE FOR ALL MEN

A. God's light and efforts are to all men.

1. Paul taught Christians to pray for all men, especially for civil leaders. He said, *"This is good and acceptable in the sight of God our Saviour; Who will have all men to be saved, and to come unto the knowledge of the truth,"* **1 Timothy 2:3-4**. How could anyone mistake the heart of God *"Who will have all men to be saved, and to come unto the knowledge of the truth?"* It takes lots of twisting and misuse of Scripture to come up with the idea that God is interested in the salvation of a select few, and not *"all men."*

2. His natural world is out there for everyone to see.

3. His Word is open to all people.

4. Note well! God's natural world, His truth of the knowledge of right and wrong and His Word will always be in perfect harmony. Anything contradictory to His Word is not of Him.

5. God's *striving* is on a non-discriminatory basis. He strives with a group approach. The Bible specifically says that *"God is no respecter of persons,"* **Acts 10:34**. He doesn't single-out some while ignoring and bypassing others. He's not Casper-the-Ghost flitting around like a butterfly discriminately landing here or there on a select few. No. God *"commandeth all men every where to repent,"* **Acts 17:30**.

6. Some well-intended people have jumped to a premature conclusion on God's statement in **Genesis 6:3**. They have assumed that God randomly convicts a few people here and there. They have then concluded that He might arbitrarily stop striving with them at any given moment. They presume that once He quits striving, that person will no longer be able to be saved. It's a fairly effective scare-tactic, but it is without biblical support. That is certainly not the correct interpretation of **Genesis 6:3**. Yet, it remains as a *proof-text*[4] for large numbers of sincere people.

---

[4] A *proof-text* is a passage of the Bible to which appeal is made in support of an argument or position in theology without regard to the context of the passage.

B. The idea of selective *striving* by the Spirit is erroneous.

1. God does not randomly pick and choose some with who to *strive* while damning all of the others to eternal hell. He does not *strive* with some more than others. He has made it abundantly clear that He wants *"all men to be saved,"* **1 Timothy 2:4**.

2. Acceptance or rejection in the heart of the individual will determine the degree of conviction. As a person pays attention to and seeks the God who gave the revelation, the greater His conviction will be.

3. Reader, don't wait for the Spirit to seek you out and overwhelm you. He won't. He's already been *striving* with you every day for a long time. Where things go from here will depend on you, not Him. It will depend on your response to the light you have. The Bible says, *"Seek the LORD while he may be found; call ye upon him while he is near,"* **Isaiah 55:6**.

C. As it was in the days of Noah, so shall it be at some point in the future.

1. One of these days, God will quit *striving* with mankind and with you.

2. One day, you will die. Your mortal life will be over. Finished! Forever! Your spirit will be in either heaven or hell. Forever! There will be no more *striving*. You will have had your opportunity. There will be no more efforts by God to turn you to Him.

3. In Noah's day, only 8 people heeded the *striving* of God, and followed Him. Every person who ignored the *striving* of the Spirit of God perished. Every one of them!

4. Jesus personally said, *"As it was in the days of Noe, so shall it be also in the days of the Son of man. They did eat, they drank, they married wives, they were given in marriage, until the day that Noe entered into the ark, and the flood came, and destroyed them all,"* **Luke 17:26-27**. They gave no heed to God's standards of morality. They took for granted the grand testimony of the natural world on which they lived and depended for their very existence. They didn't listen to Noah's message about God and coming judgment. The result? They perished. Yes! Perished! *"The world that then was, being overflowed with water, perished,"* **2 Peter 3:6**.

5. A repeat is on its way. This time, it will be destruction by fire. *"The day of the Lord will come as a thief in the night; in the which the heavens shall pass away with a great noise, and the elements shall melt with fervent heat, the earth also and the works that are therein shall be burned up,"* **2 Peter 3:10**. Paul said Jesus will come back, *"In flaming fire taking vengeance on them that know not God, and that obey not the gospel of our Lord Jesus Christ: Who shall be punished with everlasting destruction from the presence of the Lord, and from the glory of his power,"* **2 Thessalonians 1:8-9**.

You'd think that news would wake up people, and turn them to God. Peter said, *"Seeing then that all these things shall be dissolved, what manner of persons ought ye to be in all holy conversation and godliness,"* **2 Peter 3:11**. That is not at all the case. In spite of all the pleading, the *striving* of God, most of the population of this planet is going about day-to-day business as if there is no God.

6. Remember what God said, *"My spirit shall not always strive with man,"* **Genesis 6:3**. That warning is still in effect.

D. There is another application to God's warning: *"My spirit shall not always strive with man,"* **Genesis 6:3**.

1. Even if Jesus does not return in your lifetime, there will come a time when God's Spirit will no longer strive with you. You are mortal. Before long, you are going to die; and the world will go right on without you.

2. King Solomon wrote these bone-chilling words, *"There is no man that hath power over the spirit to retain the spirit; neither hath he power in the day of death: and there is no discharge in that war; neither shall wickedness deliver those that are given to it,"* **Ecclesiastes 8:8**. He also wrote, *"Whatsoever thy hand findeth to do, do it with thy might; for there is no work, nor device, nor knowledge, nor wisdom, in the grave, whither thou goest,"* **Ecclesiastes 9:10**. You know it's true. *"It is appointed unto men once to die, but after this the judgment,"* **Hebrews 9:27**. Every day, time keeps on verifying this reality.

3. When your day arrives, there will be no *striving*. Take a sheet of paper, and write these words: *"My spirit shall not always strive with man."* Leave out the word *"man,"* and write your name in the blank.

The *striving of the Spirit* is not a mystical, rolling of the dice by God to select His favorites. No. God loves everybody, and every day He is *striving* to turn them from evil to Himself. He's doing it today just like He did it before the Great Flood, and just like He has done it ever since. May all who have eyes open them to God's on-going efforts to save them! It will not always be this way.

Chapter 23

How to Know the Will of God for Your Life

Ephesians 5:14-17

Wouldn't you like to always know whether or not you are in *the will of God?* It's hard to believe that any true Christian wants to ever be outside of the will of God for his or her life; yet it is safe to say that most sincere Christians spend much if not most of their Christian lives outside the will of God. Throughout every day, there are decisions to be made about all sorts of things from which clothes to wear and how time will be spent. All along the Christian's trail are decisions which make a profound difference in life ahead: vocation, education, marriage mate, specific job, the right church, friendships, hobbies, housing, transportation, specific residence, children, investments, retirement and tens of thousands more. *How will I serve the Lord: teacher, music, deacon, pastor? How do I know God is calling me to preach? How do I know I am being called by God to another pastorate? Should I change jobs, move to another town or state, join this particular church? Should we have another baby, buy another car, move to a new house?* Life is an endless series of decisions.

Those who are committed to God want to do what He wants. That's not as easy as it may first seem. If the decision means lying versus telling the truth, it's a *no-brainer*; everybody knows God's will is to always *tell the truth.* The same is true with any decision where morals, character, integrity and any area of righteousness is at stake. The Bible is clearly against sex outside of marriage, abortions and irresponsible parenting, but where does the Bible say a couple should have four versus two children? Where does it tell you the town in which to live, the specific job you should take or the exact house for you?

The Bible addresses this matter of *"the will of God."* He does have a will for His people as to how they should live their lives. In view of His great work on behalf of all who know Him as Savior, He wants every child of His to do His will. *"Forasmuch then as Christ hath suffered for us in the flesh, arm yourselves likewise with the same mind: for he that hath suffered in the flesh hath ceased from sin; That he no longer should live the rest of his time in the flesh to the lusts of men, but to the will of God,"* **1 Peter 4:1-2**. He knows which decision is best, and His will is always that we make the best decisions. He wants us to live in His will all of the time.

This chapter deals with the will of God, and how to know it. *"Awake thou that sleepest, and arise from the dead, and Christ shall give thee light. See then that ye walk circumspectly, not as fools, but as wise, Redeeming the time, because the days are evil. Wherefore be ye not unwise, but understanding what the will of the Lord is. And be not drunk with wine, wherein is excess; but be filled with the Spirit,"* **Ephesians 5:14-17**. Paul spoke of *"understanding what the will of the Lord is,"* and connected that understanding to being *"filled with the Spirit."* It is certain that those who are not in submission to the control of the Holy Spirit are not doing *"the will of God."* No self-willed, stubborn or rebellious son of God is being *"led by the Spirit"* and doing *"the will of God."*

So many of God's people do Him great harm and dis-service by such claims as *"God led me"* or *"I knew it was God's will."* All kinds of bad choices and the messes that follow get blamed on God. People take jobs which take them out of church. For more money, people take jobs in another town where they can't find a good church. Preachers claim God is leading them to another church; but before long the new church is in a *knock-down and drag out.* The preacher rolls on down the road to the next church to which *God calls him*. Really? Is God the author of that kind of confusion? How about the missionary whom *God is calling* to another country. Two or three years later, he and his bitter family are back in the States. Is that sort of behavior *the will of God?* What about the young couple who fell madly in love, and insisted that it was the *will of God* that they marry? Not far down the road, they've had a nasty divorce; and are into their second marriage which is also *of God?*

It is certain that somewhere in this *woodpile* of thinking, there's a really big *rat.* God has said in His word that He *"is not the author of confusion, but of peace, as in all churches of the saints,"* **1 Corinthians 14:33**. He doesn't contradict Himself. He doesn't lead people to make fools out of themselves and Him.

Commandment #3 is, *"Thou shalt not take the name of the LORD thy God in vain; for the LORD will not hold him guiltless that taketh his name in vain"* **Exodus 20:7**. To blame God for what He didn't do is taking His name in vain just as sure as is misusing His name as a cuss word. It actually misuses His name in a more agrégés sense. A claim that you are being led of God; and that what is being done is His will, should never be a flippant, frivolous, superficial thing. God forbid. Very few things can be weightier than invoking the name of the creator God of this universe in support of what you say or do.

God wants every child of His to do His will, but never to abuse Him by ascribing His support for things that are not at all His doing. It's a serious offense against God to smear His name and reputation to justify and support our own selfish wills and interests. In the same letter in which he wrote of *"understanding what the will of the Lord is"* and of being *"filled with the Spirit,"* Paul also said, *"Not with eyeservice, as menpleasers; but as the servants of Christ, doing the will of God from the heart; With good will doing service, as to the Lord, and not to men,"* **Ephesians 6:6-7**. When people claim *the will of God*, they'd better be sure what they're doing is indeed God's will, and not their own will. John said, *"He that doeth the will of God abideth for ever,"* **1 John 2:17**. Moses said, *"The LORD will not hold him guiltless that taketh his name in vain,"* **Exodus 20:7**.

Sometimes the will of God is obvious; there is no reason to question or think twice about what *the will of God* is. For example, it is ALWAYS God's will that His people live holy or *"sanctified"* lives. *"For this is the will of God, even your sanctification, that ye should abstain from fornication,"* **1 Thessalonians 4:3**. It is God's will that we always be thankful: *"In every thing give thanks: for this is the will of God in Christ Jesus concerning you,"* **1 Thessalonians 5:18**. Peter said it is always the will of God that we stand up against error: *"For so is the will of God, that with well doing ye may put to silence the ignorance of foolish men,"* **1 Peter 2:15**.

The emphasis of this chapter is to focus on decisions which are not so obvious. What about those numerous decisions in life where a Bible verse or principle is not so clear-cut? The information given here will help you ascertain God's will for your life. In most cases, your decision may not be as *black and white* or definitive as you will want, but following the steps set forth here will keep you on solid, biblical grounds.

YOU MUST HAVE A SUBMITTED HEART

A. Jesus Christ is the perfect example in all things; and He was perfectly, wholly submitted to the will of the Father.

1. Hear Jesus' own words, *"For I came down from heaven, not to do mine own will, but the will of him that sent me,"* **John 6:38**. He continued in the next verse, *"I do always those things that please him,"* **John 6:39**.

2. God the Father affirmed twice that the entire time God the Son was on earth, the Son pleased the Father 100% of the time: *"This is my beloved Son, in whom I am well pleased,"* **Matthew 3:17; Matthew 17:5**. A third similar affirmation was made by the Father. Jesus prayed to the Father, *"Father, glorify thy name. Then came there a voice from heaven, saying, I have both glorified it, and will glorify it again,"* **John 12:28**.

3. No place shows the absolute submission of Jesus to the Father better than the Garden scene on the evening before the crucifixion. Knowing the agony that was just ahead, Jesus said to the Father, *"Father, if thou be willing, remove this cup from me: nevertheless not my will, but thine, be done,"* **Luke 22:43**.

B. Knowing you are in the will of God means getting *self* out of the picture.

1. Jesus said, *"For whosoever exalteth himself shall be abased,"* **Luke 14:11**. God rejects pride, self-will and arrogancy. *"God resisteth the proud, but giveth grace unto the humble,"* **James 4:6**.

2. The will of God demands a selfless, willing heart; *"Not my will, but thine, be done."*

3. *"Yea, all of you be subject one to another, and be clothed with humility: for God resisteth the proud, and giveth grace to the humble. Humble yourselves therefore under the mighty hand of God, that he may exalt you in due time,"* **1 Peter 5:5-6**.

4. Submission to His will should become the way of life for every child of God. Jesus taught us to pray, *"Thy will be done,"* **Matthew 6:10**. The Lord's will involves every nook and cranny of life. He has a will about the kind of persons to vote for, who to marry and not to marry, how to treat our employees or employer, how to dress, attitudes to have and not to have and plenty more. His will may be that you suffer and be poor, that you go to a hostile and foreign people as a missionary, that you change jobs or that you stay in the midst of your storm. He may have you lose your job, some of your friends and your health. A willing spirit says *"Alright Lord, I am willing for whatever you want. I'll go wherever you say, do whatever you want, marry whoever you choose, dress the way you say, (styles not withstanding); and suffer, give, or even die as you see fit."* No one with a willing spirit tries to tell the Lord what to do.

5. You can never know that you are in the will of God as long as self has a voice. You can have wishes and desires. God knows our hearts and what we want. He also knows when we want our way. The leadership of the Holy Spirit of God, and thus knowing we're in the will of God, demands true on submission in the heart of the child of God.

C. Brother, sister, always search your heart.

1. That should especially be the case in those weighty decisions of life: marriage mate, career, employer, home church and living environment.

2. The road to victory and true success and fruitfulness is in the purpose and power of God in what you do. Stay in His will, and He can make your life richer and fuller than you can possibly make it by following your own dreams in your own strength. James had it right when he wrote, *"Humble yourselves in the sight of the Lord, and he shall lift you up,"* **James 4:10**.

3. As brilliant as Paul the apostle was, he said, *"But I keep under my body, and bring it into subjection: lest that by any means, when I have preached to others, I myself should be a castaway,"* **1 Corinthians 9:27**. He wanted to live his life in the will of God. He also knew the only way to do it is by submission of life to the control and leadership of the Holy Spirit.

4. Get self out of the way. In honesty say with Jesus, *"Not my will, but thine be done."* The one who lives within you knows the deepest thoughts and intents of your heart. You're not in His will until He knows that you are willing for whatever He wants in your life. He may say, *"No."* If so, you are okay with that decision. He may bring you through suffering; but if that's what God wants, that's also what you want. You don't have the last say, and you accept that reality with thanksgiving and joy.

5. Brother/Sister, to be in God's will, here is where you start. Jesus personally said, *"If any man will come after me, let him deny himself, and take up his cross daily, and follow me,"* **Luke 9:23**.

YOUR DIRECTION MUST BE CONSISTENT WITH THE BIBLE

A. God is always in harmony with Himself.

1. The Bible describes Him as *"the Father of lights, with whom is no variableness, neither shadow of turning,"* **James 1:17**.

2. God is *"the same yesterday, and to day, and for ever,"* **Hebrews 13:8**.

3. He said to Israel, *"O house of Israel, are not my ways equal?"* **Ezekiel 18:29**. *"I am the LORD, I change not,"* **Malichi 3:6**.

B. One of the many great characteristics of God is His consistency.

1. Never has He been found inconsistent with Himself. Never! Not once!

2. The Father, the Son and the Holy Spirit are *"one." "Hear, O Israel: The LORD our God is one LORD,"* **Deuteronomy 6:4**. Every attribute (not most) of the Father is found in the Son and the Holy Spirit. They are never inconsistent with each other.

3. God made the universe, and it is consistent with itself and with God. Nothing in God's natural world contradicts Him. The laws of nature are always consistent with themselves and with other laws. The fact that the natural world is in a state of *stasis* is standing testimony to the consistency of

God. *"Stasis is a state in which something remains the same, and does not change or develop."*[1] The scientific world recognizes that apart from consistency, the natural world could not exist. The natural world is in *stasis* because God is consistent; it is a reflection of God who designed and made it. *"Of old hast thou laid the foundation of the earth: and the heavens are the work of thy hands. They shall perish, but thou shalt endure: yea, all of them shall wax old like a garment; as a vesture shalt thou change them, and they shall be changed: But thou art the same, and thy years shall have no end,"* **Psalm 102:25-27**.

4. Like the natural world, the written Word of God is consistent throughout, from **Genesis** to **the Revelation**. It is always in harmony with itself. Jesus expressed the consistency of the Word of God and the God of the Word when He said, *"Heaven and earth shall pass away, but my words shall not pass away,"* **Matthew 24:35**. No passage can be taken alone to build a case against the whole of the Bible. *"No prophecy of the scripture is of any private interpretation,"* **2 Peter 1:20**. To be correctly understood, every Scripture must be viewed in light of all other Scriptures. When viewed that way, the perfect harmony of the Bible will manifest itself.

C. The Holy Spirit never leads anybody in any way out of harmony with God's written Word.

1. God's Word, His world and His will are always in perfect harmony. Any motive, word or deed that is inconsistent with The Bible is not of God and not His will. The Holy Spirit of God never leads anyone to do anything inconsistent with His Word. Regardless of how sincere and good-spirited anyone is in what he does, if it is contrary to the written Word, God is not in it. He will not say something in His Word only to contradict it by leading someone contrary to it.

2. Great insight into the will of God is seen in what God said to Joshua when he was about to invade Canaan. He wanted to be sure he was doing God's will. He had been an eye-witness to what happened to Israel a generation earlier when self-will stymied the will of God. God said to Joshua, *"Only*

[1] https://www.collinsdictionary.com/us/dictionary/english/stasis

be thou strong and very courageous, that thou mayest observe to do according to all the law, which Moses my servant commanded thee: turn not from it to the right hand or to the left, that thou mayest prosper whithersoever thou goest. This book of the law shall not depart out of thy mouth; but thou shalt meditate therein day and night, that thou mayest observe to do according to all that is written therein: for then thou shalt make thy way prosperous, and then thou shalt have good success," **Joshua 1:7-8**. What a clear and practical powerhouse declaration! It's a timeless message for all people of all time who want to walk in the will of God. Note well God's insistence that Joshua stay true to the book, the revealed Word of God. It is never, never God's will that anyone act contrary to His written Word. God used Solomon to say, *"For the commandment is a lamp; and the law is a light: and the reproofs of instruction are the ways of life,"* **Proverbs 6:23**.

3. In front of us is an inescapable practical truth. No person can violate Scripture and honestly claim God led him to do so. Regardless of how earnestly he may claim God led him to do so, no believer is ever led of God to lie, commit an immoral act, date or marry an unsaved person, embrace a false doctrine, go to an unscriptural church, take up an offense against a brother or do many of the things people claim the Holy Spirit led them to do.

4. Where the Bible gives no specific statement on an issue, it gives guiding principles. Yes, principles such as honesty, integrity, humility, biblical morality, obedience to God-ordained authority, respect for the property of others, the sanctity of life, responsibility for one's words and actions, patience and many more. There are financial principles, marriage principles, work ethics, dress codes and principles on how to behave in relationships. Though the Bible may not specifically mention your particular situation, it will always give you a principle of truth. Books like the **Proverbs** and **Ecclesiastes** are full of principles stated in short, but potent nutshells. These books specialize in principles, but principles are salt and peppered throughout the Bible. Sometimes, they are stated; but they are revealed in the actions of Bible characters, and in biblical accounts where the hand of God is seen.

The Holy Spirit of God is always consistent with His stated principles. For one to be in the will of God and be led by the Holy Spirit, he must be acting in harmony with the statements and principles of the written Word. Violation of the written Word is undisputable testimony that the words, actions or course of action under consideration are not of God.

YOU MUST CONSIDER THE PROVIDENCE OF GOD

A. Sometimes, regardless of how submitted one is and in spite of how carefully he searches the Scriptures, he cannot find clear direction in the making of certain decisions.

1. For example, a godly, humble, submitted pastor receives a pastoral call from another church.

a. The pastor's heart is in submission and open to the will of God. He earnestly wants God's will to be done. Self-will is surrendered; he is willing to stay at the old church or go to the new church.

b. Neither choice would violate a biblical directive or principle. He has searched the Bible. It does not directly address his given situation.

c. How then can this earnest, godly man of God perceive the Holy Spirit's leadership in the matter? The answer must come from a careful, prayerful consideration of God's providential arrangements in the matter.

d. I personally saw it happen. For almost 12 years, I served as pastor of a wonderful church in a mid-sized Texas city. God blessed. People were saved and baptized. The church grew in numbers and the people grew spiritually in the Word. I loved those people, and they loved me.

A sister church in a large Texas city found itself in need of a pastor. For 13 years that church was plagued with division and decay. It had serious financial problems, lacked an acceptable meeting-place and had people who wanted to dominate, not follow.

This was a flag-ship church; a church with a great heritage with lots of influence over churches of like-faith and order. Doctrinally, we were compatible, like two peas in a pod. I knew the church quite well, and knew that there were no available potential pastors who fit the doctrinal, age, personality and other needs of this particular church. I knew that without compatible leadership, the old flag-ship church was likely to sink.

I prayed and searched my heart. Diligently. Before God, I knew I was willing to stay where I was or move to the new church. The dear people which had grown up with me for 12 years didn't want me to leave. There were lots of tears. We were happy, growing and in the midst of a time of revival. The new church was divided, had money problems and many other negative issues. Satan tried to tell me what a fool I was to even consider leaving where I was to go into a hornet's nest of problems.

I searched the Bible to find light on this decision. I knew that going or staying would not violate any Bible passage or principle. There were great needs and great opportunities in both cases. I earnestly searched my soul and the Bible for more than four months.

I couldn't miss the providence of God, the *handwriting on the wall.* As the days progressed, it became increasingly obvious that I should relocate. It was obvious that I could easily be replaced where I was. I knew the people were sound and well-grounded. They had property, facilities, money-in-the-bank and momentum.

I knew that I was of the right doctrine, the right age, the right temperament and the right backbone for the new church. I had known the new church since I was a young boy, they knew me: through youth camps, missionary cooperation and other mutual involvements. The Lord placed a great burden on my heart for the new church. Increasingly, I realized that I was the man for the job, and I felt a constraint. Long before a call was formally extended, time after time, pastors and friends from near and far said things to me like, *"I hear you're moving to Berean."* I remember thinking, *"I don't know that."* I began to sense that it was coming, but it didn't happen overnight. It took quite a while for God's will for me in this matter to become clear. The providential working of God over several months is what made the right decision clear. In my heart, long before the vote was taken and the call was extended by the new church, I knew what the decision would be.

2. Sometimes an objective consideration of the providential handiwork of God in a matter makes God's will and leadership obvious. Considerations such as job changes, geographical relocations, purchases, decisions related to your children, the timing on preaching specific sermons, the timing on when to bring up certain issues in conversation and the making of particular investments are examples of matters which can fall into this category.

B. The Holy Spirit of God controls providence.[2]

1. Keep in mind that the whole world is in the hands of God, and it is God the Holy Spirit whose controls providence. Acting as one with the Son and the Father, *"He is before all things, and by him all things consist,"* **Colossians 1:17**. *"And we know that all things work together for good to them that love God, to them who are the called according to his purpose,"* **Romans 8:28**. He is the one who *"openeth, and no man shutteth; and shutteth, and no man openeth,"* **Revelation 3:7**.

2. Most people call it *luck, chance* or say it *"just happened."* People who know God are aware that there is no such thing as *luck* or *chance*. *"The most High ruleth in the kingdom of men, and giveth it to whomsoever he will,"* **Daniel 4:32**.

3. What is likely the best known and loved of all Psalms speaks very loudly about the special providential care of God for His people. The tender, personal care of our great divine shepherd who ever works on behalf of His spiritual sheep is unmistakable: *"The LORD is my shepherd; I shall not want. He maketh me to lie down in green pastures: he leadeth me beside the still*

[2] See chapters 12 and 15.

waters. He restoreth my soul: he leadeth me in the paths of righteousness for his name's sake. Yea, though I walk through the valley of the shadow of death, I will fear no evil: for thou art with me; thy rod and thy staff they comfort me. Thou preparest a table before me in the presence of mine enemies: thou anointest my head with oil; my cup runneth over. Surely goodness and mercy shall follow me all the days of my life: and I will dwell in the house of the LORD for ever," **Psalm 23:1-6**.

4. God has not left His people alone to wander aimlessly in life always unsure that they are doing His will. Day by day, He is deeply and intimately involved in the lives of His children. He seeks their good even though sometimes the path is through pain, sorrow and suffering. His heart toward His people is expressed through the grand ole weeping prophet Jeremiah: *"For I know the thoughts that I think toward you, saith the LORD, thoughts of peace, and not of evil, to give you an expected end,"* **Jeremiah 29:11**. Sometimes that's hard to see, but it's always true. One of our dear brothers in Christ left us these words, *"Henceforth there is laid up for me a crown of righteousness, which the Lord, the righteous judge, shall give me at that day: and not to me only, but unto all them also that love his appearing,"* **2 Timothy 4:8**.

5. Take courage, dear brother/sister. God knows where you are. He wants you to do His will. Keep your heart humble and submitted to Him. Stay in His Word and don't stray from it. Pay attention to what He's doing day-by-day in your life. Follow the light He gives you. When you see our Blessed Redeemer face-to-face, you'll be so glad you let the Holy Spirit lead you to do the will of God from your heart.

APPLICATION

A simple story is told that many years ago, long before the days of electronic guidance systems, a man was aboard a large ship in the darkness of night as it approached the narrow entrance to a Norway harbor. The man was amazed that the captain would attempt to pilot the ship into port under such dark and dangerous conditions. As he inquired, the captain called his attention to three red beacon lights. Two were in the far distance, and one was on the bow of the ship. The captain explained to the passenger that entry to the port was not as hard and dangerous as it first appeared. He said he needed only to navigate the ship in the open sea until he got all three beacons lined up to appear as one light. Then the captain said he simply drove the ship straight to the light. As long as the three lights all stayed in a perfect line, the ship would go straight into port without danger.

Those who would know they're being led by the Holy Spirit of God have been provided a marvelous divine guidance system by our great God. He has allowed us to choose in our own hearts to submit to Him. He has given us His eternal, unwavering Word. It's full of information about how to navigate life. Every minute of every day, His divine providence is at work on our behalf. He wants us to walk with Him and pay attention to what He is doing to guide us.

Dear brother and sister, submit your heart to God. Let Him have full control. Search the Scriptures for they are the words of life. Pay attention to the providence of God in your life. Look at the happenings around you in light of the word: (1) a submitted heart, (2) strict conformity to the written Word and (3) recognition of and cooperation with the providential workings of God. Line up these three spiritual beacons and drive your ship toward the light.

Once we are led of the Holy Spirit and walking in the will of God, He will confirm His leadership of our lives by His fruit. Remember *"The fruit of the Spirit is love, joy, peace, longsuffering, gentleness, goodness, faith, meekness, temperance,"* **Galatians 5:22-28**. These are the natural, spontaneous results of the leadership of the Holy Spirit in a life. One who is led of the Spirit does not have to try to have these characteristics; they're automatic. Obviously, their absence is a strong message.

One of the strongest confirmations of a godly decision is peace. When you make the right decision and you know it's the will of God, there's an amazing peace. Regardless of how things go, the peace remains. It's not a peace that very many people understand, but it's extremely deep, wholesome and fortifying. I am confident it's the peace of which Paul wrote: *"Rejoice in the Lord alway: and again I say, Rejoice. Let your moderation be known unto all men. The Lord is at hand. Be careful for nothing; but in every thing by prayer and supplication with thanksgiving let your requests be made known unto God. And the peace of God, which passeth all understanding, shall keep your hearts and minds through Christ Jesus,"* **Philippians 4:4-7**.

I bear personal testimony to this great truth. I know that *"peace of God, which passeth all understanding."* There have been too many times when I took control of my life, and did things my way. That peace has been replaced with anxiety. Yet, time and again, I have faced life in the raw. Some of those times, I submitted my heart to Him, stayed true to His Word and followed His providential guidance. The results have aways been peace. Always! Many times, the valleys have been very deep, and the trials more than I could bear; but His peace has always been there; a deep, strange peace which I cannot adequately describe. It was there when I lay on the edge of life on Highway 90, broken by a head-on collision and unable to stand or speak one word. I was there when I moved to Berean Baptist Church, and faced many of the greatest challenges of my life.

Brother, sister, when you walk in the will of God, the peace of God in your heart will be your confirmation.

Chapter 24

Understanding the Promise of the Father

Acts 1:4-14

Shortly before Jesus ascended into Heaven, He specifically mentioned *"the promise of the Father"* and *"the baptism of the Holy Ghost." "And, being assembled together with them, commanded them that they should not depart from Jerusalem, but wait for the promise of the Father, which, saith he, ye have heard of me. For John truly baptized with water; but ye shall be baptized with the Holy Ghost not many days hence,"* **Acts 1:4-5**. Jesus told His apostles to *"wait"* in *"Jerusalem"* for *the baptism* to occur. Jesus went on to explain the results of *the baptism of the Holy Ghost. "Ye shall receive power, after that the Holy Ghost is come upon you: and ye shall be witnesses unto me both in Jerusalem, and in all Judaea, and in Samaria, and unto the uttermost part of the earth,"* **Acts 1:8**.

After Jesus' explanation of *the baptism of the Holy Ghost*, He miraculously ascended into a cloud and vanished from their sight. *"And when he had spoken these things, while they beheld, he was taken up; and a cloud received him out of their sight. And while they looked stedfastly toward heaven as he went up, behold, two men stood by them in white apparel; Which also said, Ye men of Galilee, why stand ye gazing up into heaven? this same Jesus, which is taken up from you into heaven, shall so come in like manner as ye have seen him go into heaven,"* **Acts 1:9-11**.

The astonished apostles heeded Jesus' words, and went into the City of Jerusalem, and waited for the promise to be fulfilled. *"Then returned they unto Jerusalem from the mount called Olivet, which is from Jerusalem a sabbath day's journey. And when they were come in, they went up into an upper room, where abode both Peter, and James, and John, and Andrew, Philip, and Thomas, Bartholomew, and Matthew, James the son of Alphaeus, and Simon Zelotes, and Judas the brother of James. These all continued with one accord in prayer and supplication, with the women, and Mary the mother of Jesus, and with his brethren,"* **Acts 1:12-14**.

This account of Jesus' ascension and His admonition to the apostles just before it happened is straight-forward and clearcut. There's no legitimate reason for confusion. Jesus' main theme was *the baptism of the Holy Ghost* and what was to happen once it occurred.

Within the ranks of Christendom, *the baptism of the Holy Ghost* is a hot-button issue. Some think it comes at the moment a person is saved; they think it is the same as being indwelt by the Holy Spirit. Others think it comes at some later point. The latter group thinks believers should *seek the baptism of the Holy Ghost*, and often collectively pray for it. The person seeking *the baptism* prays for it, and those gathered around passionately and with tears beg God for *the baptism*. When it happens, the candidate is to manifest it by speaking in an unknown tongue.

There are those of us who believe *the baptism of the Holy Ghost* happened as the Father promised, and it is not an on-going phenomenon which continues to occur. This chapter is intended to be a simple look at *"the promise of the Father."* The following chapter is a careful look at *the baptism of the Holy Ghost.*

Acts 1:4-14 raises three important issues regarding *"the promise of the Father."* These must be understood in order for one to have a correct view of *the baptism of the Holy Ghost,* the day of Pentecost and of the entire age of the apostles.

THE GIVING OF THE PROMISE OF THE FATHER

A. The promise was clearly the subject of Jesus:

1. *"For John truly baptized with water; but ye shall be baptized with the Holy Ghost not many days hence,"* **Acts 1:5**.

2. Jesus was speaking specifically about the coming *baptism of the Holy Ghost.*

B. Though it was *"the promise of the Father"* it was delivered through John the Baptist.

1. It happened at the baptism of Jesus, Here is what John said, *"I indeed baptize you with water unto repentance: but he that cometh after me is mightier than I, whose shoes I am not worthy to bear: he shall baptize you with the Holy Ghost, and with fire,"* **Matthew 3:11**.

2. Mark recorded the event. *"John was clothed with camel's hair, and with a girdle of a skin about his loins; and he did eat locusts and wild honey; And preached, saying, There cometh one mightier than I after me, the latchet of whose shoes I am not worthy to stoop down and unloose. I indeed have baptized you with water: but he shall baptize you with the Holy Ghost,"* **Mark 1:7-8**.

3. John also recorded the event. *"John bare record, saying, I saw the Spirit descending from heaven like a dove, and it abode upon him. And I knew him not: but he that sent me to baptize with water, the same said unto me, Upon whom thou shalt see the Spirit descending, and remaining on him, the same is he which baptizeth with the Holy Ghost. And I saw, and bare record that this is the Son of God,"* **John 1:32-34**.

C. When Jesus assembled with His apostles just prior to His ascension, He specifically spoke in reference to this event at which time the promise of the Father was delivered by John the Baptist.

1. He *"assembled together with them"* (His apostles) and reminded them of John's announcement of *"the promise of the Father,"* **Acts 1:4**.

2. In Luke's account of the life of Christ, he referenced this occasion and quoted Jesus: *"And, behold, I send the promise of my Father upon you: but tarry ye in the city of Jerusalem, until ye be endued with power from on high,"* **Luke 24:49**. Luke said that at some point after this meeting Jesus *"led them out as far as Bethany, and he lifted up his hands and blessed them. And it come to pass, while he blessed them, he was parted from them, and carried up into heaven,"* **Luke 24:50-51**. This corresponds exactly to **Acts 1:9-10**.

3. Just before he ascended from the Mount of Olives, His Apostles questioned Him about restoring again the kingdom to Israel. He told them that *"it is not for you to know the times or the seasons, which the Father hath put in his own power,"* **Acts 1:7**. He went on to say that once they received the promise of the Father (*baptism of the Holy Ghost*) they would have special power to enable them to accomplish the mission before them. *"But ye shall receive power after that the Holy Ghost is come upon you,"* **Acts 1:8**.

We now know what *the promise of the Father* was. Shortly after they returned to Jerusalem, the waiting apostles would be *baptized with the Holy Ghost.* The Father gave the promise through John the Baptist, and Jesus reaffirmed it. In fact, Jesus said the baptism would occur very soon.

THE PROMISE ITSELF

A. The promise was that Jesus would do the baptizing. Look again at the divinely inspired words of the apostle John. *"John bare record, saying, I saw the Spirit descending from heaven like a dove, and it abode upon him. And I knew him not: but he that sent me to baptize with water, the same said unto me, Upon whom thou shalt see the Spirit descending, and remaining on him, the same is he which baptizeth with the Holy Ghost. And I saw, and bare record that this is the Son of God,"* **John 1:32-34**.

1. Note well. *"Ye shall be baptized with the Holy Ghost,"* but by whom? John the Baptist left no doubt that the one who would do this baptizing was none other than Jesus Christ. When John spoke of *"the same is he which baptizeth with the Holy Ghost,"* he was clearly referring to Jesus Christ.

2. There is a major fallacy or false theology afloat today which claims that on *the day of Pentecost* (recorded in **Acts 2**) the Holy Ghost baptized the church. From this it is then projected (with the misapplication of **1 Corinthians 12:13**), that at the point of salvation all believers are baptized by the Holy Spirit into the church.

3. Note that *"the promise of the Father"* was that Jesus would baptize the apostles, the leaders of His church, with the Holy

Ghost. In no sense is there an inference that the Holy Ghost would baptize anybody. The Holy Ghost was metaphorically equivalent to water. The Apostles would be immersed in Him for a special purpose.

B. Jesus said the result of that Holy Ghost baptism would be *"power."*

1. This *"power"* was not that which a child of God has today through prayer, godliness or being filled with the Spirit. This was the miraculous power which the Apostles and certain ones associated with them had. It was specifically the power to heal, speak in languages they did not formerly know, work miracles and perform supernatural deeds.

a. This miraculous power which the apostles had and could give to others set them apart from all others. They had been baptized by Jesus with the Holy Ghost. The result was *"power"* that no other persons had unless it was given by an apostle. *"So then after the Lord had spoken unto them, he was received up into heaven, and sat on the right hand of God. And they went forth, and preached every where, the Lord working with them, and confirming the word with signs following. Amen,"* **Mark 16:19-20**. The *"signs"* which followed them were miracles. The *"signs"* were not merely natural talents on steroids; they were works which could not be done through any human abilities.

b. Philip who was a deacon in the church at Jerusalem, **Acts 6:5**, had been give this miraculous *"power"* by the apostles. He was evangelizing in Samaria and large numbers were coming to Christ. (*"Then Philip went down to the city of Samaria, and preached Christ unto them. And the people with one accord gave heed unto those things which Philip spake, hearing and seeing the miracles which he did,"* **Acts 8:5-6**. Note well that Philip did *"miracles;"* not merely superhuman deeds.) Philip was exercising this *"power."* When the apostles who were at Jerusalem heard what was happening in Samaria, they sent Peter and John to investigate. *"Now when the apostles which were at Jerusalem heard that Samaria had received the word of God, they sent unto them Peter and John,"* **Acts 8:14**.

Philip could exercise the power, but he could not give the power to someone else; however, the apostles could convey the *"power"* to a third person. *"Who, when they were come down, prayed for them, that they might receive the Holy Ghost: (For as yet he was fallen upon none of them: only they were baptized in the name of the Lord Jesus.) Then laid they their hands on them, and they received the Holy Ghost,"* **Acts 8:15-17**. Notice that Simon the sorcerer who was in Samaria quickly realized that only the apostles could give this awesome *"power"* to a third person. He wanted, not only the *"power;"* but also the power to give it to other persons. *"And when Simon saw that through laying on of the apostles' hands the Holy Ghost was given, he offered them money, Saying, Give me also this power, that on whomsoever I lay hands, he may receive the Holy Ghost,"* Notice also how this power was given to a third person: *"Through laying on of the apostles' hands the Holy Ghost was given,"* **Acts 8:18-19**. This scene is about the *"power"* of the Holy Ghost; not the *person.* As believers, they were already indwelt by the person of Holy Spirit. Peter quickly told Simon that he had no *"part"* in this special ministry of the conveyance of this divine *"power"* to another person. *"Peter said unto him, Thy money perish with thee, because thou hast thought that the gift of God may be purchased with money. Thou hast neither part nor lot in this matter,"* **Acts 8:20**.

c. The apostles were keenly aware that they had a special role not common to all believers. They were to complete the Scripture, the divine revelation of God which is now the New Testament. As they preached, taught and wrote the "*power*" which no other people had, testified that they were in truth of God, and the message they had was indeed the message of God. The Bible describes this phenomenon which lasted only until the Scriptures were completed. *"How shall we escape, if we neglect so great salvation; which at the first began to be spoken by the Lord, and was confirmed unto us by them that heard him; God also bearing them witness, both with signs and wonders, and with divers miracles, and gifts of the Holy Ghost, according to his own will?"* **Hebrews 2:3-4**. The *"signs and wonders, and with divers miracles, and gifts of the Holy Ghost"* constitute the *"power"* which Jesus said would accommodate the baptism of the Holy Ghost. He said, *"Ye shall receive power, after that the Holy Ghost is come upon you,"* **Acts 1:8**.

Paul said, *"Our gospel came not unto you in word only, but also in power, and in the Holy Ghost, and in much assurance,"* **1 Thessalonians 1:5**. There's that *"power"* again; and it assured those who heard Paul and the other apostles were legitimate men of God, and not imposters.

Paul emphasized the same point to the Corinthians: *"And I, brethren, when I came to you, came not with excellency of speech or of wisdom, declaring unto you the testimony of God. For I determined not to know any thing among you, save Jesus Christ, and him crucified. And I was with you in weakness, and in fear, and in much trembling. And my speech and my preaching was not with enticing words of man's wisdom, but in demonstration of the Spirit and of power: That your faith should not stand in the wisdom of men, but in the power of God,"* **1 Corinthians 2:1-5**. There it is again: *"in demonstration of the Spirit and of power."* This is not talking about getting eloquent, passionate or all lathered-up and sweaty in sermons. This is language about a demonstration of *"power"* that all could see was not something any human(s) could ever do.

2. Every believer needs power from God for life and service for we are all totally powerless without Him; however, we should never equate the power for everyday life and service with the *"power"* the Apostles received as a result of the baptism of the Holy Ghost. This writing is about two entirely different aspects or dimensions of the power of God.

C. In view of the tremendous assignment that lay just ahead for them, the apostles would need this special miracle-working *"power."*

1. Just ahead was the overwhelming task of leading this fledgling Christian movement forward *"in Jerusalem, and in all Judea, and in Samaria, and unto the uttermost part of the earth,"* **Acts 1:8**. They were the ones with the assignment of proving that it was a movement of God, and not of man. The miraculous *"power"* provided by the Holy Ghost was the divine evidence which they needed.

2. It is a joy to say that the New Testament records their success in each of these regions. These men used this special *"power"* to lay the groundwork which brought the glorious gospel of Christ to us.

At this point we know *the promise of the Father* was special, miraculous *power* to those who would soon experience *the baptism of the Holy Ghost.*

THE WAITING OF THE APOSTLES

A. Jesus specifically instructed the apostles to wait of the fulfillment of the promise.

1. Jesus' commandment to His apostles about waiting was specific. *"And, being assembled together with them, commanded them that they should not depart from Jerusalem, but wait for the promise of the Father, which, saith he, ye have heard of me,"* **Acts 1:4**. In his divine record of the life of Christ, Luke corroborated the historical account given in Acts. Jesus said to His apostles, *"Behold, I send the promise of my Father upon you: but tarry ye in the city of Jerusalem, until ye be endued with power from on high,"* **Luke 24:49**.

2. This is precisely what you find them doing in the inspired historical account: *"Then returned they unto Jerusalem from the mount called Olivet, which is from Jerusalem a sabbath day's journey. And when they were come in, they went up into an upper room, where abode both Peter, and James, and John, and Andrew, Philip, and Thomas, Bartholomew, and Matthew, James the son of Alphaeus, and Simon Zelotes, and Judas the brother of James. These all continued with one accord in prayer and supplication, with the women, and Mary the mother of Jesus, and with his brethren,"* **Acts 1:12-14**.

B. Do not be confused about what they were doing.

1. They were not in that upper room *praying through* or becoming exceedingly fervent or passionate so that God would give them this special power. No! They were simply *waiting* for that which God had promised. This text is routinely misapplied today.

2. Jesus had said the promise would be fulfilled *"not many days hence,"* **Acts 1:5**. The appointed day was *the day of Pentecost* which was 50 days after the Jewish feast of *First Fruits.* In fulfillment of His prophetic feast, God would baptize the leaders of His church 50 days after the resurrection of His Son. For these Apostles that was 10 days ahead. Like the fulfillment of the *Passover*, the fulfillment of *Pentecost* would be a one-time event. Thus, the Apostles were *waiting.*

3. They were waiting and sure enough it happened just as God had promised through John the Baptist. *"And when the day of Pentecost was fully come, they were all with one accord in one place. And suddenly there came a sound from heaven as of a rushing mighty wind, and it filled all the house where they were sitting. And there appeared unto them cloven tongues like as of fire, and it sat upon each of them. And they were all filled with the Holy Ghost, and began to speak with other tongues, as the Spirit gave them utterance,"* **Acts 2:1-4**.

We now know what was promised, how the promise was delivered and why the apostles were waiting. They were waiting for the special *"power"* of God to carry out their tremendous assignment. That's really what the fulfillment of *Pentecost* is about. It was not about how to be saved (that's what the *Passover* is about); *Pentecost* is about the Lord's church and the means He used to plant it. It's not about charismatic power for all believers; it's about the special *"power"* God gave His apostles to launch His church and world-wide evangelism. God expects every saved person to be an active member of one of His churches. No member needs Apostolic power to serve Him. What serving Him does take is submission, dependence on Him and faithfulness.

The next chapter in this book will be a direct look at *baptism of the Holy Ghost.*

Chapter 25

The Baptism of the Holy Ghost and Its Ramifications

Acts 2:1-15

The Baptism of the Holy Ghost. What's that? What is it? Was it limited to select people? Is it something that happens to all believers? If so, does it happen at the point of salvation? Does it happen at some point after salvation? Which point? If one is baptized with the Holy Ghost, how does he know? To say the least, this subject is controversial. It is also very divisive.

This chapter should be studied in conjunction with the previous chapter which dealt with the prediction of this event.

There are many who say, *"What difference does it make? This is a doctrinal issue, and doctrine is too divisive. Let's just forget our differences and be one happy people."*

Let us be reminded that definitions can make profound differences. Some years ago, in the Vatican our young guide pointed to a great marble statue from Pompeii and said, *"We rescued it from its owners."* I had never before realized that *rescue* and *stealing* were the same. Yes! Definitions matter. At the time of Christ and the apostles, *orthodoxy* was almost universally known to be the positions of the Scriptures on an issue. *Heresy* was any stance contrary to the Word of God. 200 years later, *orthodoxy* was generally known to be the position of *"the church"* and *heresy* was any stance contrary to the position of the church. Even if that position was in perfect harmony with the Scriptures! Define *stop* to mean *go,* and many things radically change. The definition of a human *baby* was redefined to *fetus tissue,* and the floodgate to the killing of millions of little people was suddenly opened. The fact is that what you believe and how you define things makes a difference. Satan is evil, but he's not stupid. He knows that by changing definitions, he can call evil good, and good evil.

Now that you understand the promise of the Father that at some point Jesus would baptize the apostles with the Holy Spirit, this chapter looks at what (1) the Baptism of the Holy Ghost is, (2) what it's not and (3) the difference what you believe on this subject makes.

To clearly establish the context of this chapter, please be reminded of the words of John the Baptist: *"I indeed baptize you with water unto repentance: but he that cometh after me is mightier than I, whose shoes I am not worthy to bear: he shall baptize you with the Holy Ghost, and with fire,"* **Matthew 3:11**. This event was so important that it was repeated in **Mark 1:6-8**, **Luke 3:16-17** and **John. 1:26-34**.

WHAT THE BAPTISM OF THE HOLY GHOST IS

A. It happened the day Jesus baptized His church with the Holy Ghost. (In Scripture *Holy Ghost* is often used interchangeably with *Holy Spirit.*)

1. John the Baptist made it unmistakably clear that Jesus Himself was the one who did the baptizing. *"John seeth Jesus coming unto him, and saith, Behold the Lamb of God,"* **John 1:29**. He then said of Jesus, *"the same is he which baptizeth with the Holy Ghost,"* **John 1:33**. Jesus, not the Holy Ghost, did the baptizing. *"He shall baptize you with the Holy Ghost, and with fire,"* **Matthew 3:11**. The truth is that the Holy Ghost has not baptized anybody or anything.

2. Metaphorically, the Holy Ghost was the substance (water) of the baptizing, and Jesus did the baptizing. Notice again **Matthew 3:11**. Jesus would baptize *"with the Holy Ghost."* See also **John 1:33**. Listen to Jesus' own words, *"John truly baptized with water; but ye shall be baptized with the Holy Ghost not*

many days hence," **Acts 1:5**. Do not miss Jesus' words, *"ye shall be baptized with the Holy Ghost." "Ye"* was the apostles. They were the ones baptized with the Holy Ghost.

3. The apostles were the first members of Jesus' newly established church. *"God hath set some in the church, first apostles,"* **1 Corinthians 12:28**. With the baptism of His apostles with the Holy Ghost which occurred on The Day of Pentecost, God officially credentialed His church as the place where He would meet with His people. God's first meeting-place with His people was the Tabernacle of Moses. The Tabernacle was superseded by the Temple. The Baptism of the Holy Ghost was God's official crowning of His church as His meeting-place with His people. He would no longer meet with His people in the Tabernacle or in the Temple.

4. Note well from the text of **Acts 1** that after His resurrection Jesus showed *"himself alive . . . by many infallible proofs."* Many saw Him, but His focus was clearly on the apostles. *"Until the day in which he was taken up, after that he through the Holy Ghost had given commandments unto the apostles whom he had chosen: To whom also he shewed himself alive after his passion by many infallible proofs, being seen of them forty days, and speaking of the things pertaining to the kingdom of God,"* **Acts 1:2-3**. Most of His post-resurrection ministry was to the Apostles. The *baptism of the Holy Ghost* was not on everyone; it was the apostles who were baptized with the Spirit. It was not an individual baptism, but rather a corporate baptism of apostles who were the chief leaders of His church. Through this baptism, Jesus' church as an institution was divinely credentialed.

B. This special baptism occurred on the day of Pentecost.

1. *"And when the day of Pentecost was fully come, they were all with one accord in one place. And suddenly there came a sound from heaven as of a rushing mighty wind, and it filled all the house where they were sitting. And there appeared unto them cloven tongues like as of fire, and it sat upon each of them. And they were all filled with the Holy Ghost, and began to speak with other tongues, as the Spirit gave them utterance,"* **Acts 2:1-4**. This was *the baptism of the Holy Ghost.* It was God's divine affirmation that His church was now His official meeting-place with man. No longer a tabernacle or temple, but now His church.

When His tabernacle was completed, *"Then a cloud covered the tent of the congregation, and the glory of the LORD filled the tabernacle. And Moses was not able to enter into the tent of the congregation, because the cloud abode thereon, and the glory of the LORD filled the tabernacle."* **Exodus 40:34-35**.

Centuries later, God's temple was completed. Once it was complete, Solomon and the people assembled to dedicate it to the LORD. *"Now when Solomon had made an end of praying, the fire came down from heaven, and consumed the burnt offering and the sacrifices; and the glory of the LORD filled the house. And the priests could not enter into the house of the LORD, because the glory of the LORD had filled the LORD'S house. And when all the children of Israel saw how the fire came down, and the glory of the LORD upon the house, they bowed themselves with their faces to the ground upon the pavement, and worshipped, and praised the LORD, saying, For he is good; for his mercy endureth for ever,"* **2 Chronicles 7:1-3**.

Jesus said, *"Upon this rock I will build my church; and the gates of hell shall not prevail against it,"* **Matthew 16:18**. He did it. The apostles are waiting along with the other members of Jesus' new church. *"And when the day of Pentecost was fully come, they were all with one accord in one place. And suddenly there came a sound from heaven as of a rushing mighty wind, and it filled all the house where they were sitting. And there appeared unto them cloven tongues like as of fire, and it sat upon each of them. And they were all filled with the Holy Ghost, and began to speak with other tongues, as the Spirit gave them utterance,"* **Acts 2:1-4**.

Upon their completion, He credentialed His Tabernacle and His Temple with spectacular glorious appearances. On the Pentecost He did the same for His church.

2. According to Jesus this was what the Father promised. When Jesus commanded those apostles to *"wait for the promise of the Father,"* **Luke 24:49**, **Acts 1:4**, He was telling them to wait for this event. He told His Apostles to *"wait"* in Jerusalem for it to happen which is precisely what they did. They were neither trying to *"pray through,"* nor coax God into the baptism. They were simply waiting for the promise to be fulfilled.

3. Jesus said *the baptism of the Holy Ghost* would be accompanied by divine *"power."* When the *baptism* happened, the majesty and power were there including *"fire."*

4. The *baptism* occurred in Jerusalem, and shortly thereafter at the house of Cornelius who was a Gentile. Through a miraculous series of events, the apostle Peter went to Cornelius' house, and preached to Cornelius the glorious saving message of Jesus Christ. *"While Peter yet spake these words, the Holy Ghost fell on all them which heard the word. And they of the circumcision which believed were astonished, as many as came with Peter, because that on the Gentiles also was poured out the gift of the Holy Ghost. For they heard them speak with tongues, and magnify God,"* **Acts 10:44-46**.

   With the conversion of Cornelius and all of the drama which surrounded the event, God made clear that salvation and His church is not only for Jews. All people can be saved, and the Lord's church is for everyone, Jews and Gentiles.

5. The baptism of the Holy Ghost was a two-phased event. What happened on the Day of Pentecost was completed at the house of Cornelius. Though it occurred in two separate locations on two separate days, God once and for all credentialed His church and made it clear that it is for both Jews and Gentiles. The baptism of the Holy Ghost occurred on the Day of Pentecost; and at Cornelius' house, God made it clear that what He did at Pentecost extends to all believers who become a part of one of His churches.

WHAT THE BAPTISM OF THE HOLY GHOST IS NOT

A. The baptism was not an individual baptism of believers by the Holy Ghost into one giant church made up of all saved people.

1. A current common and popular belief is that at the moment of salvation a person is spiritually baptized by the Holy Spirit into the church.

   a. The idea is that Holy Spirit does the baptizing, not Jesus.

   b. To make this stance viable, the Holy Spirit is both the baptizer and the water.

   c. The person baptized becomes a member of the *body* of Christ which is supposedly made up of all other believers.

d. At the moment of this *spirit baptism* the new believer also supposedly receives at least one *spiritual gift.*

2. The Scripture that is misused to support this concept is **1 Corinthians 12:13**: *"For by one Spirit are we all baptized into one body, whether we be Jews or Gentiles, whether we be bond or free; and have been all made to drink into one Spirit."* **1 Corinthians** is a divinely inspired letter by Paul to one local church, *"Paul, called to be an apostle of Jesus Christ through the will of God, and Sosthenes our brother, Unto the church of God which is at Corinth,"* **1 Corinthians 1:1-2**.

a. It is a mistake to read into this book a message bigger than to one local church. Through the Bible there are messages to individuals which apply to all people in all locations in all eras of time. They are timeless messages. **1 Corinthians 12:13** is one of those timeless messages to a church. What Paul wrote to the Church in Corinth applies to all churches in all ages. It's a letter to a local church which is the only kind of church there is.

b. Paul's use of the pronoun *"we"* does not mean that he was speaking of one big church made up of all saved people. He was expressing a universal truth related to membership in any true church regardless of its location or time in history. The means of entry into a church is always the same. It comes at the point of the water baptism of a true believer. Paul could use the pronoun *"we"* since the truth was incumbent on him and all other believers and churches.

c. In this verse, *"Spirit"* is capitalized to denote the Holy Spirit. Paul was divinely inspired to say that one must be *in the Spirit* before he can have a valid baptism. That is simply to say that a person must be saved before he can be baptized by any church. At salvation one is *"born of the Spirit,"* **John 3:5**, and *"sealed with the holy Spirit of promise,"* **Ephesians 1:13**. That person is thus *"in the Spirit,"* as indicated in **1 Corinthians 12:13**. It is noteworthy that *"by"* is from the Greek preposition **en** which can translate *by, in and at* depending on context. All saved persons are *"in the Spirit."* Both the immediate context and the overall context of Scripture confirm that all believers are *"in the Spirit."*

- **d.** Believers are to be baptized in water. *"They that gladly received his word were baptized,"* **Acts 2:41**. There is *"One Lord, one faith, one baptism,"* **Ephesians 4:5**. In the text at hand, Paul was talking about water baptism. The idea that the Holy Spirit baptizes people is not consistent with Scripture.
- **e.** A church is sometimes called the *"body"* of Christ. For example, *"And he is the head of the body, the church: who is the beginning, the firstborn from the dead; that in all things he might have the preeminence,"* **Colossians 1:18**. In the biblical sense of *"body,"* the Church in Corinth was representative local churches. When people trust Christ, they should be baptized into a local church or *"body."*
- **f.** Regardless of the location or time in history, this is how it's to be done. People who trust Christ are to follow the Lord in water baptism into a local church. It is not too difficult to see that when believers follow the Lord in water baptism, they are added to the church that baptizes them.

B. The idea of a personal baptism by the Holy Spirit into a giant universal church made up of all the saved is popular and sounds good. It's just not taught in the Bible.

1. The real baptism of the Holy Ghost occurred shortly after Jesus ascended into Heaven. There is no Bible evidence to support the assumption that it will ever happen again.
2. It was not a baptism of an individual; it was a baptism of a group of men in corporate relationship as members of the Lord's church at Jerusalem, Israel.
3. The Holy Spirit baptized no one; Jesus did the baptizing.
4. Its purpose was to stamp God's decision that He would henceforth meet with His people in His church.
5. The power which accompanied the baptism of the Holy Ghost was literal, miracle-working power which could be demonstrated and seen; not inner power or the power a believer can receive to successfully do the work of God.

WHAT DIFFERENCE DOES A PERSON'S VIEW OF THE BAPTISM OF THE HOLY GHOST MAKE?

A. On the issue of Holy Ghost baptism, there are essentially two options.

1. One option is that the Holy Spirit spiritually baptizes every person in Himself at the moment that person trusts Jesus Christ as personal Savior.

With this option, the believer is baptized into a spiritual body composed of all believers. That spiritual body is commonly recognized to be the true Church of Jesus Christ. At the point of faith in Christ, all believers become a member of this spiritual universal, invisible church. It is universal because all believers are in it including both living and dead believers. Of course, this position presents a problem with Old Testament believers. Since they all died before Jesus established His church, what about Old Testament believers? Are they members or not?

With this option comes the stance that there is only one true church, and all saved persons, both living and dead, are members of it. Local churches are merely small parts of the whole church. Since all believers are members, wherever and whenever the church meets, they are entitled to all rights and privileges of membership.

2. The other option is that Jesus Christ through its first leaders (the apostles) baptized His church with the Holy Ghost. By so doing, Christ made it clear that His people are to worship and serve Him through His church.

Church is the name of the institution which Christ personally established during His earthly ministry. The Greek word from which church is translated into English is **ekklesia** which literally means *a called-out assembly.*[1] The **ekklesia** which Jesus called *"My church,"* **Matthew 16:18**, is seen in the New Testament to be *a called-out assembly of baptized believers covenanted*

---

[1] James Strong, *Greek Dictionary of the New Testament*, (Nashville, Tennessee: Abingdon Press, 1958), ref. 1577.

together to keep the ordinances and carry out the Great Commission.

Only in an abstract or institutional sense does the church exist universally. Like all nouns, in the concrete sense *church/assembly* (**ekklesia**) is always local. Assemblies are always local and visible and, by definition, churches are assemblies. Only in the imagination do universal, invisible assemblies/churches exist.

At the point of faith, a believer is baptized individually in water as a public testimony of his faith in Christ in view of His finished work: His death, burial and resurrection. With his baptism, the believer becomes a member of the local church which administered the baptism. All of the rights and privileges of membership become his including participation in communion.

B. A person's idea of Holy Ghost baptism will dictate his view of what a church is.

1. If Holy Ghost baptism is a personal spiritual baptism of every believer into a universal invisible church at the point of his salvation, then all saved persons are members of the same church. Water baptism is only symbolic and has nothing to do with church membership, and any believer can float between congregations regardless of his baptismal status. All saved people can participate in communion at will in any church gathering. Because all churches constitute only one true church and all believers are members because of Holy Spirit baptism, then any believer at any congregation at any time can fully participate in any and all church activities. He can participate in communion, vote on the church budget, vote on a new pastor and exercise his voice in all church affairs by right of membership. That is the inescapable logic which follows a spiritual baptism of every believer by the Holy Ghost at the point of salvation.

2. Conversely, if Holy Ghost baptism refers to water baptism into one local congregation, then a believer is not a church member until he is baptized. Upon water baptism, a believer is added to the local congregation which administered the baptism. The newly baptized believer becomes a member of one local church; and thus has a right to take communion, to vote and to participate in all church activities. Each local church determines the validity of each member's baptism, votes on its budget and handles its own business including discipline. That is the inescapable logic which follows recognition of the fact that believers are added to the membership of a local church at the point of water baptism.

C. Holy Ghost baptism cannot be both ways. The positions are diametrically opposed.

1. Local church theology is the unwavering position of the Bible.

2. Truth is never self-contradictory. You have to decide where you stand on the matter of Holy Ghost Baptism; which position is Scriptural, and which is not.

3. The wise choice is to take God's position on every issue.

Chapter 26

A Straight-Forward Look at the Sinner's Prayer

Acts 16:30-31

There are sincere people who think those who do not ask lost people to pray to be saved are really off base and wrong. This chapter is intended to show why some of us do not ask lost sinners to pray a prayer to be saved from sin's penalty which is eternal death. In this rather simple and straightforward way, we will set forth what we believe about the quite popular *Sinner's Prayer* and why we believe it is a big mistake to use it in an effort to bring a lost person to Christ for salvation.

ASKING LOST SINNERS TO PRAY IN ORDER TO BE SAVED FROM SIN'S PENALTY

A. **The *prayer for salvation* approach is so common and widespread in the ranks of those who consider themselves to be fundamental, Bible-believing or conservative Christians that those who do not practice it appear to be peculiar and out of step with Bible Christianity.**

   1. Most well-known television and radio preachers tell lost people to bow their heads, confess their sins and ask Jesus to come into their hearts.

2. By far the vast majority of today's *Salvation tracts* end with a written prayer which the reader is asked to pray to cinch his salvation.

3. In thousands of southern, fundamentalist and unaffiliated Baptist churches, the invitation is always characterized by the preacher asking people to bow their heads and pray a prayer of confession and invitation of Jesus into one's heart for salvation.

4. Standard furniture in thousands of churches is a long prayer bench or *"altar" down front* where people are invited to kneel and pray for God's forgiveness and salvation. In numerous churches, as soon as a person *comes to the altar,* trained counselors immediately get him/her on the knees so the person can *get saved.*

5. *"Roman Road Evangelism"* takes lost people right to the prayer. The preplanned approach is: show them they're lost, show them they're going to hell, show them the work of Christ; then, have them pray *"the sinner's prayer"* which is a prayer requesting God to save them.

6. The sinner's prayer is to thousands of churches what water is to a well or wheels are to a car. People who have seen only the prayer approach for salvations all their lives are flabbergasted when they see a church that does not ask lost people to pray to get saved. To some it seems so peculiar that it is regarded as sacrilegious. Some even become angry and critical, and will not stop to find out why this church does not use the *"Sinner's Prayer."* They are so ensnared in a lifelong habit and tradition they do not even want to check to see if it is a sound, biblical tradition. Too often, emotion and anger rule and prevail in the hearts of good, sincere people.

B. Some think certain Scriptures teach prayer for salvation from the penalty of sin.

1. The most commonly cited verse is **Romans 10:13** which says, *"Whosoever shall call upon the name of the Lord shall be saved."* This is the verse that is quoted on the majority of salvation tracts. It is the clincher verse at invitations.

   At first it seems for sure that this verse is inviting lost people to pray in order to be saved; however, the verse just before quickly dispels the idea that **verse 13** is inviting lost, hell-bound sinners to pray to be saved. **Verse 12** discusses a place in which there is no difference between Jews and Greeks: *"For there is no difference between the Jew and the Greek: for the same Lord over all is rich unto all that call upon him."* The only place where there is no difference between Jews and Gentiles, males and females, rich and poor, old and young and sick and well people is *"in Christ."* Only when people come in faith to Jesus Christ as personal Savior are they *"in Christ,"* **Ephesians 1:3-7**.

Verse 12 is clearly about people who are already saved, and in a position to *"call upon him."* The only way any person can reach God is through a mediator, and Jesus Christ is the only mediator between God and man that there is. *"There is one God, and one mediator between God and men, the man Christ Jesus,"* **1 Timothy 2:5**. It is clear from **verse 12** that saved, not lost people, can *"call upon the Lord."* Only people who have been saved from sin's penalty are in a position where *"there is no difference,"* and only those people have an intercessor by which they can *"call upon the Lord."*

Should anyone doubt that interpretation, he can look to **verse 14** which leaves no doubt: *"How then shall they call on him in whom they have not believed?"* The answer is simple and obvious! They can't. There can be no calling or praying until there is belief in Christ as personal Savior. Furthermore, there can be no believing (faith) until there is hearing. **Verse 17** says it: *"Faith cometh by hearing, and hearing by the word of the Lord."*

Romans 10:13 is not instructing lost men to pray to be saved from sin's penalty; it is instructing God's saved people to pray for daily deliverance from sin's power or control over their lives.

2. Another Bible passage which some interpret to teach prayer for salvation is **Luke 18:9-14**. This passage talks about two men, a Pharisee and a publican, both of whom went up to the temple to pray. The publican smote on his breast and said, *"God, be merciful to me a sinner,"* **Luke 18:13**. Some see this as a case of a lost praying to be saved.

The fact is that both these men went up to the temple specifically to pray. Even the Pharisees knew that *"God heareth not sinners,"* which is specifically stated in **John 9:31**. By the law under which these men lived, they could not have entered the temple had they not first been professing embracers of the Jewish faith as evidenced by their circumcision, **Ezekiel 44:7**. In Jesus' parable, **verse 9**, He did not use men who symbolize the lost, who couldn't pray. He used men who symbolize the saved, who could pray. He made a point about those who are in a position to pray. Even men, who are saved and can pray, fail. When they do, they are to come in prayer asking mercy, **Hebrews 4:16**; not in arrogant pride gloating over how much better they are than their failing brothers.

Jesus' point in His parable was not at all about how lost men get saved. He was dealing with humility versus pride in the lives of His children. Those who would use this passage to support the *Sinner's Prayer* position are artificially forcing a passage to teach a point it is not teaching.

3. Cornelius of **Acts 10** is another case often cited in support of the *pray for salvation* position. There is no question that Cornelius was a lost man, and that he was praying in his lost condition. **Verse 2** says he prayed. **Verse 4** says his prayers came up as *"a memorial before God."* God did not save Cornelius because he prayed. The fact is that in spite of all his praying, he remained lost until God raised up Peter who went to Cornelius with *"words whereby thou and all thy house shall be saved,"* **Acts 11:14**. If praying could save a man, Cornelius would surely have gotten saved by praying. Few if any lost men have been more devout, good and faithful to pray than Cornelius, **Acts 10:1-2**. Yet, he didn't get saved until he believed on Christ.

In the case of Cornelius, who was a Gentile, God had promised *"I will say to them which were not my people, 'Thou art my people; and they shall say, Thou art my God,'"* **Hosea 2:23**. **Romans 9:24-26** specifically identifies this prophecy to be a promise of Gentile conversions. Before Cornelius, Peter and the early believers had limited their preaching of Christ to the Jews. Jesus confirmed that His redemptive work was for all people, Jews and Gentiles. He said, *"That repentance and remission of sins should be preached in his name among all nations, beginning at Jerusalem,"* **Luke 24:47**. With Cornelius, God began the fulfillment of His promise to open the door of salvation wide to the Gentiles. Cornelius' prayers were simply a memorial reminder before God that the time had come to fulfill His longstanding promise. God didn't save Cornelius because he prayed. He saved him because he believed in the finished work of Christ on the cross. God saved him only when he believed.

4. There are a few other passages similar to these. Upon careful examination each of these yields no support for prayer as the means of appropriating eternal life.

FAITH IN JESUS CHRIST AS ONE'S OWN PERSONAL SAVIOUR

As one searches the scriptures, it becomes increasingly clear that God has one and only one way of appropriating the merits of his finished work on the cross, and that is by faith in Jesus Christ as one's own personal Saviour.

A. No truth is presented more clearly or labored more diligently in the Holy Bible than salvation by grace through faith.

1. *"For by grace are ye saved through faith; and that not of yourselves: it is the gift of God: Not of works, lest any man should boast,"* **Ephesians 2:8-9**.

2. The apostle John put it this way. *"That whosoever believeth in him should not perish, but have eternal life. For God so loved the world, that he gave his only begotten Son, that whosoever believeth in him should not perish, but have everlasting life. For God sent not his Son into the world to condemn the world; but that the world through him might be saved. He that believeth on him is not condemned: but he that believeth not is condemned already, because he hath not believed in the name of the only begotten Son of God,"* **John 3:15-18**.

3. Jesus said, *"Verily, verily, I say unto you, He that heareth my word, and believeth on him that sent me, hath everlasting life, and shall not come into condemnation; but is passed from death unto life,"* **John 5:24**.

4. The apostle Paul said, *"For I am not ashamed of the gospel of Christ: for it is the power of God unto salvation to every one that believeth; to the Jew first, and also to the Greek,"* **Romans 1:16**.

5. A lost man asked the apostle Peter specifically how to be saved: *"What must I do to be saved?"* **Acts 16:30**. He answered the question in the clearest of mortal terms: *"Believe on the Lord Jesus Christ and thou shalt be saved,"* **Acts 16:31**.

B. There is no other way.

1. Jesus said, *"If ye believe not that I am he, ye shall die in your sins,"* **John 8:24**.

2. He also said, *"He that believeth not is condemned already because he has not believed on the name of the only begotten Son of God,"* **John 3:18**. Note well. Lost people are *"condemned"* specifically because they have *"not believed on the name of the only begotten Son of God."* For no other reason.

3. Listen to John's insistence. *"He that believeth on the Son hath everlasting life: and he that believeth not the Son shall not see life; but the wrath of God abideth on him,"* **John 3:36**. Why should anyone add to God's idea about how to be saved from the penalty of sin which is eternity in the Lake of Fire? That's exactly what those do who add in a prayer.

4. A person can go to church; but if he doesn't believe on Christ as his personal Savior, he will never be saved from eternal damnation. Good morals won't give salvation. A person can be baptized; but if in the heart he does not come in faith to Jesus Christ, he is not saved. With the deepest of emotions and remorse, a person can pray *the Sinner's Prayer* naming every sin he can remember; but if he does not believe in Christ in the heart, he is not saved. The Bible says, *"With the heart man believeth unto righteousness,"* **Romans 10:10**. Any person can do anything else he wants to do; but until he believes on Jesus Christ as personal Savior, he will never ever be saved. I hasten to add that the moment a person comes in faith in his heart to Jesus Christ, he will be saved that instant.

C. If this is true and it is, then what effect will *"asking Jesus into your heart"* have on your salvation?

1. The answer to that is quite simply, "None!" You can ask Him into your heart all you want; but if you do not in your heart believe on Him, He won't save you. On the other hand, if you believe on Him as your Savior, He will save you, even if you do not ask Him to save you.

   It is pretty obvious that your asking doesn't matter one way or the other. It is not the *asking* that makes the difference; it is the *believing* that makes the difference.

2. You ask, *"Can a person who asks Jesus into his heart be saved?"* The answer is *"Yes."* If in the heart, he believes on Christ as Savior, God will save him on the spot. God will save him because he *"believed on the Son;"* not because he prayed a prayer. God will not refuse to save a believing sinner just because he is asking. He will save him anyway, in spite of his asking. Of course, even if he had not asked at all, God would have saved him just the same. God saves all who believe; He saves no one who doesn't believe.

   Listen carefully. If the sinner thinks the asking/prayer is contributing to his salvation, then he won't be saved. It is believing in Christ, plus nothing and minus nothing, that produces eternal salvation. There is a big danger in asking a sinner to pray at the point of salvation. He is likely to think the prayer was a part of the saving process, but it's not. Salvation comes only when it's Christ alone; no works, no baptism, no church membership and no prayer. Adding anything to God's plan of salvation will nullify the whole redemption transaction. That includes a prayer.

3. The wisest thing a soulwinner can do is keep the message clear and simple. Just tell lost sinners to believe on Jesus Christ to be saved. That's all it takes. To tell them to do anything more is to confuse the issue. Such additions contribute nothing to the transaction, but run the grave risk of causing the lost person to make a false profession of faith. The one who thinks prayer, or baptism, or good works, or anything other than faith in the Lord Jesus Christ will result

in eternal salvation is still lost and damned to hell. Jesus saves only those who believe; not those who pray; not those who reform; not those who work good works and not those who are baptized. He saves only those who believe. Jesus will save those who do these things; but not because they do these things. God will save a sinner only when he gives up on all other things and in the heart trusts Christ alone as his only hope. Any time he thinks that doing these things helped him get saved, he is still lost. Jesus saves sinners only when they come to Him in faith, apart from trust in any other thing.

4. Some of us do not ask people to pray in order to be saved. Why should we? Prayer doesn't save; faith in Christ does. Why should we confuse the issue and muddy the water for a sinner by asking him to do something God doesn't ask him to do, something which has the potential of damning his soul to hell?

Why should those who keep the salvation message simple and clear be thought strange and unscriptural for taking such a wholehearted Bible position on the issue?

If you think you are saved because you prayed to be saved, you'd better think long and hard about where you stand with God. If you think that you are saved because you prayed a prayer, or that a prayer had a role in your salvation, why should you continue to think you are saved? To be saved from sin's death penalty God told you to believe on *"the Son."* He did not tell you to pray to be saved. If you examine your heart and find you've done anything short of or more than believe on the Lord Jesus Christ to be saved, you are lost. If you are, I urge you to believe on the Lord Jesus Christ right now and be saved.

Chapter 27

Don't Let a Prayer Keep You Out of Heaven

John 3:15-18

God wants people to be saved, really saved; not merely go through an empty intellectual or emotional exercise. No words could ever make that reality clearer than the words of God Himself. Listen to Him say it, *"As Moses lifted up the serpent in the wilderness, even so must the Son of man be lifted up: That whosoever believeth in him should not perish, but have eternal life. For God so loved the world, that he gave his only begotten Son, that whosoever believeth in him should not perish, but have everlasting life. For God sent not his Son into the world to condemn the world; but that the world through him might be saved. He that believeth on him is not condemned: but he that believeth not is condemned already, because he hath not believed in the name of the only begotten Son of God,"* **John 3:15-18**.

God does not want anyone to rest in a counterfeit hope. Sadly, nothing has been more counterfeited than God's plan of salvation: *Quit your sins. Be baptized. Baptize the babies. Join a church. Go to church. Be a good person. Be sincere. Be zealous. Work hard. Sacrifice yourself. Crawl on your bare knees a long way over rocks. Give lots of money. You don't need a church; just be spiritual. Pray The Sinner's Prayer.*

The issue at the heart of this matter is *connecting with God.* How does any mortal ever connect with God. The Bible makes it obvious that no person can connect with God on his or her own merit. On his own, nobody can get an audience with God. No one can petition Him, talk to Him or consequently argue a case with Him. The Bible book of **Job** is a big debate between Job and four *friends* who came to *comfort* him. (He called them *"miserable comforters,"* **Job 16:2**.) Having suddenly lost his great wealth, his health and his family, Job was truly in an awful condition. He wanted an audience with God. *"Oh that I knew where I might find him! that I might come even to his seat! I would order my cause before him, and fill my mouth with arguments. I would know the words which he would answer me, and understand what he would say unto me,"* **Job 23:3-5**. On his own, Job couldn't get there. He said, *"Behold, I go forward, but he is not there; and backward, but I cannot perceive him: On the left hand, where he doth work, but I cannot behold him: he hideth himself on the right hand, that I cannot see him,"* **Job 23:8-9**. Job realized that his only hope was an intercessor. *"If I wash myself with snow water, and make my hands never so clean; Yet shalt thou plunge me in the ditch, and mine own clothes shall abhor me. For he is not a man, as I am, that I should answer him, and we should come together in judgment. Neither is there any daysman betwixt us, that might lay his hand upon us both,"* **Job 9:30-33**.

That is still the way it is. Jesus personally said so, *"I am the way, the truth, and the life: no man cometh unto the Father, but by me,"* **John 14:6**. The only way to get to God the Father is through His Son. End of discussion! Until a person has Jesus Christ as his mediator, he/she cannot get to God. Period!

The purpose of this chapter is to help readers see the futility of great deeds, good works, pious worship however passionate, faithfulness, sincerity and prayer apart from the mediatorial or intercessory work of Jesus Christ. He is the only one who can gain any mortal an audience with God. *"For there is one God, and one mediator between God and men, the man Christ Jesus,"* **1 Timothy 2:5**.

HOW DOES A SINFUL MAN CONNECT WITH A PERFECTLY HOLY GOD?

A. This is the big, insurmountable hurdle for every human.

1. Honest people recognize their limitations even with other men. There are strong and mighty men whom we simply cannot touch on our own: heads of great corporations, heads of states, celebrities, very wealthy people and many more. They're too insulated. Their corporate veils, their security systems, their high positions put them out of our reach. We cannot simply walk into their offices or homes and have a conversation. Our only hope is a *contact,* someone we know who knows them, someone who can arrange an audience for us.

2. If there are mortals whom we cannot reach apart from external intervention, how much more the God of the Universe? He surely needs nobody. He is completely self-contained and needs nothing. He said to the ancient nation of Israel, and to all other humans, *"I will take no bullock out of thy house, nor he goats out of thy folds. For every beast of the forest is mine, and the cattle upon a thousand hills. I know all the fowls of the mountains: and the wild beasts of the field are mine. If I were hungry, I would not tell thee: for the world is mine, and the fulness thereof. Will I eat the flesh of bulls, or drink the blood of goats?"* **Psalm 50:9-13**. God cannot be bribed or corrupted in any way. He cannot be threatened, intimidated or touched with any human power including the combined military might of all nations. He is not getting old and is never subject to any needs. In our own right, we have zero basis upon which to approach Him for anything; He doesn't need us, and never will.

B. The Bible is insistent that no man can reach God on his own.

1. We are all sinners. *"There is not a just man upon earth, that doeth good, and sinneth not,"* **Ecclesiastes 7:20**. *"All we like sheep have gone astray; we have turned every one to his own way,"* **Isaiah 53:6**. *"Surely men of low degree are vanity, and men of high degree are a lie: to be laid in the balance, they are altogether lighter than vanity,"* **Psalm 62:9**. The truth is that in the sight of God all people are sinners. *"Now we know that what things soever the law saith, it saith to them who are under the law: that every mouth may be stopped, and all the world may become guilty before God,"* **Romans 3:19**. There are no exceptions. *"Verily every man at his best state is altogether vanity,"* **Psalm 39:5**. God is so holy that He can look upon sinful men only in judgment. *"Thou art of purer eyes than to behold evil, and canst not look on iniquity,"* **Habakkuk 1:13**. The only reason God can view believers with favor is because His judgment has already been executed against them. It happened when Christ bore their death penalty as He died in their place on the cross.

2. Outside of Jesus Christ, sinners simply do not have the ability to stand before God. Job expressed the plight of all of us. *"I am afraid of all my sorrows, I know that thou wilt not hold me innocent. If I be wicked, why then labour I in vain? If I wash myself with snow water, and make my hands never so clean; Yet shalt thou plunge me in the ditch, and mine own clothes shall abhor me. For he is not a man, as I am, that I should answer him, and we should come together in judgment. Neither is there any daysman betwixt us, that might lay his hand upon us both. Let him take his rod away from me, and let not his fear terrify me: Then would I speak, and not fear him; but it is not so with me,"* **Job 9:28-35.** Job admitted his helpless condition. He couldn't get to God. He wanted to plead his case, but he couldn't get an audience. There was nobody to intercede with God for him. Apart from external help, he was hopeless; and he is a picture, a prototype of every man and woman, including the very best, most elite of the human race.

C. For any man to have a chance with God, he must have a mediator, an intercessor, a go-between.

1. Job longed for someone who could reach both him and God, and somehow reconcile the two. He lamented his need for an arbitrator. *"Neither is there any daysman betwixt us, that might lay his hand upon us both,"* **Job 9:33**. His words about a *"daysman"* speak of *someone to make things right, to correct what's wrong, to justify*. The Hebrew word is **yakach**, someone who is capable of arguing another's case because the person can't argue for himself.[1]

2. The parallel Greek word is **mesites** which is translated six times in the King James Bible as *"mediator."* The most straightforward of those places is the passage mentioned earlier, *"For there is one God, and one mediator between God and men, the man Christ Jesus,"* **1 Timothy 2:5**. The masculine noun **mesites** speaks of an arbitrator, *"one who intervenes between two parties."*[2] Note carefully, that the only *"one"* capable of arbitrating man's case with God is Jesus Christ.

---

[1] James Strong, *Hebrew and Chaldee Dictionary*, (Nashville, Tennessee: Abingdon Press, 1958), ref. 3198.

[2] James Strong, *Greek Dictionary of the New Testament*, (Nashville, Tennessee: Abingdon Press, 1958), ref. 3316.

Furthermore, Jesus Christ cannot mediate, plead or argue man's case before God upon the basis of man's merit or worthiness. All men are lawbreakers, transgressors and guilty as charged. They deserve nothing but God's scorn and judgment, the death penalty.

D. Upon the basis of who He is and what He has done for that person, Jesus Christ mediates the case of each person who comes to Him in faith. He never argues any person's case upon the basis of any merit whatsoever in that person.

1. In spite of the sins of all sinners, God loved them anyway. *"For God so loved the world, that he gave his only begotten Son, that whosoever believeth in him should not perish, but have everlasting life,"* **John 3:16**. How much did God love sinners, including you and me? *"Hereby perceive we the love of God, because he laid down his life for us,"* **1 John 3:16**. Phenomenal! Unfathomable!

   "Amazing love! How can it be,

   That Thou, my God, shouldst die for me?"

2. Jesus Christ literally took the death penalty (God's judgment for sin) upon Himself and paid it in full once and for all. This one *"Who, being in the form of God, thought it not robbery to be equal with God,"* **Philippians 2:6**, *"who did no sin, neither was guile found in his mouth,"* **1 Peter 2:22**, came to this earth in an ordinary human body and dwelt among us. He *"made himself of no reputation, and took upon him the form of a servant, and was made in the likeness of men: And being found in fashion as a man, he humbled himself, and became obedient unto death, even the death of the cross,"* **Philippians 2:7-8**. This innocent, sinless Son of God *"his own self bare our sins in his own body on the tree, that we, being dead to sins, should live unto righteousness: by whose stripes ye were healed,"* **1 Peter 2:24**. *"Neither by the blood of goats and calves, but by his own blood he entered in once into the holy place, having obtained eternal redemption for us,"* **Hebrews 9:12**.

3. The greatest courtroom scene in all of time and eternity is unfolded in **Romans 8:31-39**. The question is posed in the great court of heaven, *"What shall we then say to these things? If God be for us, who can be against us?"* **Romans 8:31**. *Who is going to accuse this human who has absolutely no right to be standing before*

God? "Who shall lay any thing to the charge of God's elect?" **Romans 8:33**. Satan who is *"the accuser of our brethren,"* **Revelation 12:10**, stands ever ready to say: *Sinner! Guilty! Unworthy!* Every one of us knows he's right. We are sinners. We are guilty. Not one of us is worthy. In the court of our great God, we cannot stand. If we get justice, what we deserve, we will surely be cast into the abyss of eternal separation from God.

But then, we have an advocate, Jesus Christ, the Lamb of God who was slain in our place for our sins. He paid our penalty! Once, and for all! He paid with His own blood! This greatest of all defense attorneys is right there interceding for us. *"Who is he that condemneth? It is Christ that died, yea rather, that is risen again, who is even at the right hand of God, who also maketh intercession for us,"* **Romans 8:34**. Bring on all the charges you want. Say whatever you please. God our Father is our judge. Jesus Christ is our High Priest. Our sins are forgiven. We are His children. We, who have no right to be here on our own can come *"boldly unto the throne of grace"* at any time. *"Seeing then that we have a great high priest, that is passed into the heavens, Jesus the Son of God, let us hold fast our profession. For we have not an high priest which cannot be touched with the feeling of our infirmities; but was in all points tempted like as we are, yet without sin. Let us therefore come boldly unto the throne of grace, that we may obtain mercy, and find grace to help in time of need,"* **Hebrews 4:14-16**.

4. Did you see it? Our mediator is not there before the throne of the Father pleading our innocence or our case based on who we are. No! No! No! He's pleading for us upon the strength of who He is, and what He's already done for us. God *"spared not his own Son." "It is Christ that died."* He has already paid our sin penalty in full, fully met God's justice against us. Our mediator pleads our case upon the basis of mercy, grace and forgiveness based on His work, not ours.

E. It was God who took the initiative to bridge the great divide that separated Him from sinful man.

1. If we mortals were to ever connect with God, He had to come; and He did. We did not have the ability to come to where He was. He came to us, and He provided a way for us to meet with Him. It was a one-way move. Salvation was God's idea. Redemption was His plan. The work of the cross was His work. Salvation is a unilateral contract. God saved us and salvation's validity in no way depends on us. We contribute nothing to it. He contributes everything. It's a covenant of grace, not merit. *"For by grace are ye saved through faith; and that not of yourselves: it is the gift of God: Not of works, lest any man should boast,"* **Ephesians 2:8-9**.

2. The refrain of a glorious hymn says it like this:

He came to me, O, He came to me.

When I could not come to where He was, He came to me.

That's why He died on Calvary,

When I could not come to where He was, He came to me.

3. God makes it overwhelmingly clear that every person's only hope of ever meeting with Him is in one mediator, the Lord Jesus Christ. Jesus' words on the issue bear repeating, *"I am the way, the truth, and the life: no man cometh unto the Father, but by me,"* **John 14:6**. Regardless of what anybody might think to the contrary, that is the way it is. You can't get to the Father except through the Son.

HOW CAN A SINFUL MAN HAVE JESUS CHRIST AS HIS PERSONAL MEDIATOR?

A. The Bible is emphatic that the only way to have Christ is by faith in Him.

1. The clearest, simplest, most directly to the point words in all of literature are found **John 3:15-18**. *"And as Moses lifted up the serpent in the wilderness, even so must the Son of man be lifted up: That whosoever believeth in him should not perish, but have eternal life. For God so loved the world, that he gave his only begotten Son, that whosoever believeth in him should not perish, but have everlasting life. For God sent not his Son into the world to condemn the world; but that* *the world through him might be saved. He that believeth on him is not condemned: but he that believeth not is condemned already, because he hath not believed in the name of the only begotten Son of God."* In this passage alone, *believing* is mentioned 5 times as being the sole means by which a person is saved from eternal damnation. It's especially noteworthy that **verse 18** states the sole difference between eternal life and eternal condemnation to be *belief. "He that believeth on him is not condemned: but he that believeth not is condemned already, because he hath not believed in the name of the only begotten Son of God."* The last verse in the chapter is a profound statement: *"He that believeth on the Son hath everlasting life: and he that believeth not the Son shall not see life; but the wrath of God abideth on him,"* **John 3:36**.

2. Faith is trust, belief, genuine dependence on Him alone. Trusting Christ is facing-up to the reality that you're a sinner, and that the consequence of unaddressed sin is eternal separation from God in the lake of fire. It's the realization that you cannot address your own sin problem. Any and all efforts on your part are futile: good works, baptism, sincerity, prayers, piety, better character. Believing on Jesus Christ is grasping, truly comprehending the fact that He alone can save you. Jesus Christ is God who came to this earth and went to the cross to pay the sin penalty once and for all. He died, was buried and rose again in three days. Today, He's alive and saving all who trust Him. Yes! Trust Him! That's what *believing on Him* is. It's not merely believing the facts about Him. It's trusting Him, giving up on all other hope beyond the grave other than Him.

3. Getting saved is a cathartic, transforming event. It is not merely a shallow, emotional, *down-front-of-the-church* event. It is not simply an intellectual decision to change your lifestyle and become a Christian. No! No! No! It is a total sell-out to Christ.

B. Nothing short of trusting Him makes Him your mediator. Nothing else!

1. Not a reformation. Nor a baptism. Not a church membership. Not passion. Not zeal. Not religious activity. Not a spiritual or highly emotional feeling.

2. Not a prayer. Until a person has Christ to mediate for him, he simply can't get to God. An audience with God requires mediation, and a person without Jesus Christ has no mediator, no High Priest to intercede. The Bible is quite explicit about this very thing. *"He that turneth away his ear from hearing the law, even his prayer shall be abomination,"* **Proverbs 28:9**. The blind man, who received restored sight from Jesus, quoted this passage. *"Now we know that God heareth not sinners: but if any man be a worshipper of God, and doeth his will, him he heareth,"* **John 9:31**.

3. Because they have Jesus as their High Priest to mediate with them, believers are invited to come to God whenever they wish. No appointment is necessary or required. *"Seeing then that we have a great high priest, that is passed into the heavens, Jesus the Son of God, let us hold fast our profession. For we have not an high priest which cannot be touched with the feeling of our infirmities; but was in all points tempted like as we are, yet without sin. Let us therefore come boldly unto the throne of grace, that we may obtain mercy, and find grace to help in time of need,"* **Hebrews 4:14-16**. But, what about those who through ignorance, neglect, willful rejection of God or any other reason have no High Priest in place? It's clear and simple; they can't get to God. They have no one to mediate or intercede for them. Before a person can possibly pray, Christ must first be in place as High Priest. Without Jesus the High Priest in place, no person can have dealings with God.

4. Nobody can by-pass God's Son and talk to Him about anything. Trying to pray before getting saved and having the intercessor in place is like trying to carry on a long-distance phone conversation without a connection. You have to get a line and then talk, not talk and then get a line. God's approach is first get saved, then pray; not pray to get saved. The mediator gets in place only when men trust Him; not when they try to pray without first coming to Him in the heart. Get this picture into your head. A lost person wants to be saved and starts praying to God to save him/her. Instead of coming to Christ in faith and receiving Him as mediator or High Priest, he's trying to talk to God. What the lost person should have done is first come in faith (trust/belief) to Christ in the heart. God would instantly save him on the

spot, and Jesus Christ would become his mediator. He would then be in a position to talk to God. It's really not difficult to follow God's simple directions. The first thing God says is *"Believe on the Lord Jesus Christ, and thou shalt be saved,"* **Acts 16:31**. That's how you establish a connection to God; and until that connection is established, there is no way to reach God.

C. The instant a person believes in Jesus Christ as personal Savior, he will be saved; but not before.

1. In view of God's clarity that to be saved, a person must come in faith in the heart to Christ who died, was buried and rose again for the sinner, you have to wonder why so many start by telling lost people to pray. The right thing to do is first bring lost people to Christ. Have them trust Him in the heart *"for with the heart man believeth unto righteousness,"* **Romans 10:10**. After the lost person is saved, he can thank God for his/her salvation; and confess Him before men as his Savior for *"with the mouth confession is made unto salvation,"* **Romans 10:10**. To bypass this order of approach to God is eternally fatal. Unless in his heart somewhere along the trail a person truly comes to Christ in the heart and is saved, he will never get to God. Jesus Christ saves all who trust Him; He saves no person who does not trust Him. God knows the heart.

2. When a person trusts Christ, he/she will be saved even if he doesn't pray. That person will not be saved because he/she prayed, but because he/she believed on Christ. On the other hand, a person who does not trust Christ in the heart will not be saved even though he/she prays, begs and pleads with great sincerity and emotion.

3. It's believing, not praying that makes the eternal difference. The Bible says, *"That if thou shalt confess with thy mouth the Lord Jesus, and shalt believe in thine heart that God hath raised him from the dead, thou shalt be saved. For with the heart man believeth unto righteousness; and with the mouth confession is made unto salvation,"* **Romans 10:9-10**. **Verse 10** is the safeguard to correctly understanding **verse 9**. The person who *confesses* or faces the truth of who Jesus Christ is and *"shalt believe"* on Him in the heart *"shall be saved."* That's pretty straightforward; but just in

> case anyone is not clear on it, the next verse makes the point unmistakable: *"with the heart man believeth unto righteousness."* That's what salvation is, *righteousness* in the heart. Once the heart has been made *right* with God, the mouth can *confess* in truth the salvation that is in the heart. To *confess* that one has been made right with God (saved) when it hasn't truly happened is a lie and lies are abominable to God. He always knows the truth about where people really stand with Him. He's never deceived.

It is likely today that there are multitudes in hell who prayed a prayer to be saved. The words were there, but the reality in the heart wasn't. They attempted to approach God without a mediator. It was an empty exercise. Don't let a prayer keep you out of heaven. Go back to **John 3:14-18** where we started. *"And as Moses lifted up the serpent in the wilderness, even so must the Son of man be lifted up: That whosoever believeth in him should not perish, but have eternal life. For God so loved the world, that he gave his only begotten Son, that whosoever believeth in him should not perish, but have everlasting life. For God sent not his Son into the world to condemn the world; but that the world through him might be saved. He that believeth on him is not condemned: but he that believeth not is condemned already, because he hath not believed in the name of the only begotten Son of God."* This passage *cuts to the chase.* Your salvation depends solely on what you do in your heart with Jesus Christ, nothing else. In order to get to God and make heaven, you must have Jesus Christ as your mediator. The moment you trust Him in your heart, He will be there.

Chapter 28

An Exegetical Trip Through Romans 10

It seems to me that very few Bible verses are more misunderstood and misused than **Romans 10:13**. By many well-meaning people this is the number one Bible verse used to win lost people to Christ. I am convinced that this verse is often used out of context.

I am about to take a brief exegetical trip through **Romans 10**. In the process I will seek diligently to use good rules of hermeneutics. Please understand that *exegesis* has to do with the message that comes ***out of*** any text, and is the opposite of reading a message ***into*** a text. *Hermeneutics* has to do with the interpretation of a passage. Good hermeneutics means staying true to the text; such matters as:

- Honesty to the context both immediate and overall.
- Consideration of the audience to whom a passage is written.
- The correct definition of words in the passage.
- The use of wording by the author.
- The type of language in the passage.
- An understanding of the situation that prompted the passage.

No one can (1) approach a passage with preconceived positions and (2) move roughshod through it while ignoring rules of language and common sense and legitimately expect to ascertain the correct meaning.

Please keep in mind that this brief exegetical trip through **Romans 10** is not intended to be comprehensive. It is a general overview which is true to the message of the passage. A more in-depth study will simply confirm in greater detail what is presented here.

THE DEFINITION AND USE OF THE WORD *"SALVATION"*

To save means *to deliver from a danger or peril.* The Hebrew word is **yasha** (yah-shah') meaning *to preserve or rescue.*[1] It is used 205 times in the King James Version of the Old Testament. The Greek word for *salvation* is **sozo** (sode'-zo) meaning *to protect or deliver.*[2] It is used 110 times in the King James Version New Testament. From the infinitive verb comes such derivatives as *salvation, save, saved, deliver, savior,* etc.

In the Bible *to save* is used in 3 senses. *To save* (and its derivatives such as salvation) is sometimes used to speak of protection or deliverance from **the penalty of sin** which is eternal separation from God in the lake of fire. One such reference is **John 3:17** which says, *"For God sent not his Son into the world to condemn the world; but that the world through him might be saved."* The verses on both side of this verse speak of salvation from sin's penalty. This is the sense in which *"saved"* is used in this place. **John 3:15-16** say, *"That whosoever believeth in him should not perish, but have eternal life. For God so loved the world, that he gave his only begotten Son, that whosoever believeth in him should not perish, but have everlasting life."* **John 3:18** farther confirms this usage. *"He that believeth on him is not condemned: but he that believeth not is condemned already, because he hath not believed in the name of the only begotten Son of God."*

To save (and its derivatives such as salvation) sometimes speak of protection or deliverance from the power of sin to wreck and ruin the daily lives of believers. One such reference is **Matthew 16:25**. Which says, *"Whosoever will save his life shall lose it: and whosoever will lose his life for my sake shall find it."* Satan is ever the adversary of every saved person. The apostle Peter warned, *"Be sober, be vigilant; because*

---

[1] James Strong, *Hebrew and Chaldee Dictionary*, (Nashville, Tennessee: Abingdon Press, 1958), ref. 3467.

[2] James Strong, *Greek Dictionary of the New Testament*, (Nashville, Tennessee: Abingdon Press, 1958), ref. 4982.

your adversary the devil, as a roaring lion, walketh about, seeking whom he may devour," **1 Peter 5:8**. God's people need daily salvation (deliverance). Thank our great God who provides it.

To save (and its derivatives such as salvation) also speak of protection or deliverance from the presence of sin, the time when believers are with the Lord and sin cannot touch them. One such reference is **Romans 5:9**. It says, *"Much more then, being now justified by his blood, we shall be saved from wrath through him."* The day will come when Satan will no longer be able to touch God's people. The Bible says, *"The devil that deceived them was cast into the lake of fire and brimstone, where the beast and the false prophet are, and shall be tormented day and night for ever and ever,"* **Revelation 20:10**. There will be no more need for salvation from the presence of sin's propagator.

To properly exegete any Bible occurrence of *to save* or its derivatives, it is vital to ascertain the proper usage of the word. In what sense or application is the word being used?[3] Good, honest hermeneutics **must** be employed. Otherwise, an improper interpretation and understanding is almost guaranteed.

STEP BY STEP THROUGH ROMANS 10

Verses 1-8

In this section, Paul primarily addressed his Israeli brethren and their salvation from sin's penalty. Except for a few who had come to Christ and been saved, the Jews as a whole were lost sinners facing condemnation and the wrath of God in the Lake of Fire. For centuries, most Jews had missed the point of the Law. They thought keeping the Law was the means of justification (salvation) from the eternal death penalty against sin, but it was not. The truth is that "*. . . by the deeds of the law there shall no flesh be justified in his* (God's) *sight,"* **Romans 3:20**. Paul explained that *"the law was our schoolmaster to bring us unto Christ, that we might be justified by faith. But after that faith is come, we are no longer under a schoolmaster,"* **Galatians 3:24-25**; yet Christ the Messiah had come, and the vast majority of the Jews missed it. That grieved the heart of Paul.

---

[3] For more information on God's Threefold Salvation, see *Great Bible Truths Revisited* by Lester Hutson, ISBN 978-1-7324282-0-1, (Amazon), pp 132-142.

Look at verse 1. He wanted them to be saved from sin's penalty. His passion for his own people after the flesh is obvious. *"Brethren, my heart's desire and prayer to God for Israel is, that they might be saved,"* **Romans 10:1**. *"Saved"* is a reference to *salvation from sin's penalty.*

Look at verses 2-7. For centuries Israel had been passionately religious, *"For I bear them record that they have a zeal of God, but not according to knowledge,"* **Romans 10:2**. They missed God's message of salvation from sin's penalty, and went about to establish their own means of salvation by self-righteousness, *"For they being ignorant of God's righteousness, and going about to establish their own righteousness, have not submitted themselves unto the righteousness of God,"* **Romans 10:3**. The Law pointed them straight to Christ; the Law was only *"a shadow of good things to come,"* **Hebrews 10:1**. *"Christ is the end of the law for righteousness to every one that believeth,"* **Romans 10:4**. *"Moses describeth the righteousness which is of the law, That the man which doeth those things shall live by them,"* **Romans 10:5**. The fact was that no one could keep the Law; not one. *"All we like sheep have gone astray; we have turned every one to his own way,"* **Isaiah 53:6**. The Law demanded perfection, and no one is perfect. Jesus explained, *"Be ye therefore perfect, even as your Father which is in heaven is perfect,"* **Matthew 5:48**. Paul explained that true righteousness is by faith, and it is solely the work of God in Jesus Christ. *"The righteousness which is of faith speaketh on this wise, Say not in thine heart, Who shall ascend into heaven? (that is, to bring Christ down from above:) Or, Who shall descend into the deep? (that is, to bring up Christ again from the dead.),"* **Romans 10:6-7**.

Look at verse 8. The message of salvation from sin's penalty was clearly enunciated by Jesus, but as a whole the Jews rejected Jesus' message and crucified Him. Yet, salvation from sin's penalty was close and still available to them, but they were still in spiritual blindness and unsaved. *"But what saith it? The word is nigh thee, even in thy mouth, and in thy heart: that is, the word of faith, which we preach,"* **Romans 10:8**.

What is the clear, undisputable message of the passage, the context? It is Paul's deep desire for the salvation of the Jewish people from sin's penalty. It is the obvious message of the context.

Verses 9-11

In this passage Paul explained how a person is saved from the penalty of sin and how one who experiences salvation in that sense should respond.

In **verse 9**, Paul mentioned Jesus Christ and *confession of Him with the mouth* and *belief in Him in the heart.* Since Jesus is the exclusive means of salvation from sin's penalty, and since salvation in this sense is based on His death, burial and resurrection; it is essential that a lost person accept **the facts** of who Jesus was and what He did to save sinners. For all people, especially Jews of whom Paul spoke in **Romans 10**, accepting Jesus as the Messiah and Savior of men was difficult. He said to them (and all men), *"That if thou shalt confess with thy mouth the Lord Jesus, and shalt believe in thine heart that God hath raised him from the dead, thou shalt be saved,"* **Romans 10:9**. To receive God's salvation from sin's penalty, every person must both accept the facts and trust Christ as personal Savior (*"believe in thine heart"*).

The following verse sets forth the order of *believing* and *confessing*. *"For with the heart man believeth unto righteousness; and with the mouth confession is made unto salvation,"* **Romans 10:10**. *Belief* in the heart brings the righteousness (salvation) of God; *confession* with the mouth is how bystanders hear and know a person has been saved.

That's really not hard to follow. *Belief* is in the heart which only God sees. When belief in Christ occurs God sees it, and at that point the righteousness of Jesus Christ is *"imputed"* (credited) to the believer. *"But to him that worketh not, but believeth on him that justifieth the ungodly, his faith is counted for righteousness. Even as David also describeth the blessedness of the man, unto whom God imputeth righteousness without works, Saying, Blessed are they whose iniquities are forgiven, and whose sins are covered. Blessed is the man to whom the Lord will not impute sin,"* **Romans 4:5-8**. *"I through the law am dead to the law, that I might live unto God. I am crucified with Christ: nevertheless I live; yet not I, but Christ liveth in me: and the life which I now live in the flesh I live by the faith of the Son of God, who loved me, and gave himself for me,"* **Galatians 2:19-20**. It is at that point that a sinner is saved *from sin's penalty*. Furthermore, no sinner will be saved until the point of belief occurs.

Once a person *believeth unto righteousness* and thus has everlasting life, that person can confess that he/she is saved and tell the truth. You can rest assured that regardless of how much *confessing* or claiming salvation one does apart from *belief in the heart,* there is no *"righteousness"* or salvation. It's a false *confession* or profession. Bystanders may not know it, but God knows. *Confession* is by the mouth which bystanders hear and observe. Once a person is made *righteous* (saved), he can then *confess* it; but if it is not true, he cannot honestly *confess* it. No amount of confession means anything until *righteousness* or *salvation* is first there.

Confession with the mouth is not the means of attaining salvation from sin's penalty; *believing* in the heart is. *Confession* merely acknowledges what is already there. The divine order is first salvation by believing in the heart, and then confession with the mouth of salvation's reality.

Look at **verse 11**. According to God, every person who receives salvation from sin's penalty should not be ashamed, but should confess it. *"For the scripture saith, Whosoever believeth on him shall not be ashamed,"* **Romans 10:11**. Confession is an outward manifestation of inward reality; however, there can be no true confession until there is inward reality.

Verses 12-13

Paul next enunciated the common ground of all believers. He said there is a place where there is no difference between people. *"For there is no difference between the Jew and the Greek,"* **Romans 10:12**. That place is *"in Christ."* All who have *believed unto righteousness* are in Christ. *"Ye are dead, and your life is hid with Christ in God,"* **Colossians 3:3**. There is only one place where people are all on the same ground. No person who is *in Christ* is there by merit. Every one of them is there exclusively by the person and work of Jesus Christ. They are all on that common ground. Between Jews and Greeks, males and females, rich and poor, sick and well; and in every other comparison, there are multiple differences; but not *in Christ.* Regardless of who they are every one of them is saved by the blood of Christ and there exclusively by grace. This verse is talking about people who have been saved from sin's penalty.

Paul continued his words about salvation from sin's penalty. He brought up the matter of *calling on the Lord.* He said, *"For the same Lord over all is rich unto all that call upon him. For whosoever shall call upon the name of the Lord shall be saved,"* **Romans 10:12-13**. Once a person *"believeth unto righteousness,"* that person is on the common ground of being *"in Christ."* Christ is now that person's Savior and *"Lord."* The moment that person trusted Him as Savior, He became that person's *"High Priest."* The new believer is now in a position where he can talk to God. Before the person got saved, he had no High Priest, no intercessor. He had no right, and couldn't talk to God. *"The LORD is far from the wicked: but he heareth the prayer of the righteous,"* **Proverbs 15:29**. *"Now we know that God heareth not sinners: but if any man be a worshipper of God, and doeth his will, him he heareth,"* **John 9:31**.

All that changed when he believed on Christ. Now he can call upon the Lord and receive *salvation* in the second sense or usage of the word: salvation from sin's power, the moment-by-moment help of God against Satan's incessant efforts to wreck and ruin our everyday lives. Here is the blessed invitation of God to every person who is *"in Christ"* and thus in the place where *"there is no difference." "Seeing then that we have a great high priest, that is passed into the heavens, Jesus the Son of God, let us hold fast our profession. For we have not an high priest which cannot be touched with the feeling of our infirmities; but was in all points tempted like as we are, yet without sin. Let us therefore come boldly unto the throne of grace, that we may obtain mercy, and find grace to help in time of need,"* **Hebrews 4:14-16**. Those who are invited in **Romans 10:13** to *"call upon the Lord"* and *"be saved"* **already have** salvation from sin's penalty. Otherwise, they would not be in the place where *there is no difference*. All of those who are saved from the penalty of sin now need the daily help of God which is salvation from the power of sin.

Verses 14-17

Paul explained that hearing the facts of Christ and His redemptive work is essential to believing on Him. The set of rhetorical questions followed by God's commendation of those who carry the gospel message to lost sinner make clear that *calling* on God is impossible apart from *believing* on Him. *"How then shall they call on him in whom they have not believed? and how shall they believe in him of whom they have not heard? and how shall they hear without a preacher? And how shall they preach, except they be sent? as it is written, How beautiful are the feet of them that preach the gospel of peace, and bring glad tidings of good things!"* **Romans 10:14-15**.

It would be hard to make the necessity of *believing* before *calling* clearer: *"How then shall they call on him in whom they have not believed?"* It is obvious from the question that a person who hasn't *believed* cannot *call*; yet many well-meaning people do not tell lost sinners to *"Believe on the Lord Jesus Christ, and thou shall be saved,"* **Acts 16:31**. Instead, they tell them to pray a prayer to be saved. The necessity of carrying the gospel of Christ to lost sinners is unmistakable. There is no other way for them to be saved from the penalty of sin which is the subject of this Bible passage.

In order to *believe* and be saved, people must hear and accept the facts of Christ and His redemptive work. It is then that they can come to Him in *"faith"* and be saved from sin's penalty. That's what Paul wanted for the Jews, but he also wanted salvation from sin's penalty for all men.

Verses 18-21

The last verse of this passage summarizes well the position of Israel which was the focus of Paul's concern. *"But to Israel he saith, All day long I have stretched forth my hands unto a disobedient and gainsaying people,"* **Romans 10:21**

Israel illustrates the reality that hearing the facts is not equivalent to accepting them. When Adam and Eve were in the presence of God, they knew the facts, the truth. Israel knew the facts in the days of Moses. It's hard to imagine the means of salvation from sin's penalty clearer than **Isaiah 53**. Yet, for the most part Israel missed the message. *"But I say, Have they not heard? Yes verily, their sound went into all the earth, and their words unto the ends of the world. But I say, Did not Israel know? First Moses saith, I will provoke you to jealousy by them that are no people, and by a foolish nation I will anger you. But Esaias is very bold, and saith, I was found of them that sought me not; I was made manifest unto them that asked not after me,"* **Romans 10:18-20**.

A few Jews saw it and put their faith in the coming Messiah, the Redeemer. Jesus said to the Jews of His day, most of whom were blind to who He was, *"Your father Abraham rejoiced to see my day: and he saw it, and was glad,"* **John 8:56**. Most of them were still holding onto a legal system of human merit for their salvation and hope. They kept on rejecting the effort of God to bring them to Him on the basis of His work for them. Yet, He kept His arm *"stretched out"* to reach them. *"But to Israel he saith, All day long I have stretched forth my hands unto a disobedient and gainsaying people,"* **Romans 10:21**.

That's still how it is with most Jews and Gentiles, yet today God continues to say, *"And the Spirit and the bride say, Come. And let him that heareth say, Come. And let him that is athirst come. And whosoever will, let him take the water of life freely,"* **Revelation 22:17**.

Chapter 29

Justification by Works

James 2:14-26

James 2:14-26 is the hotbed proof-text for all who argue that you must continue in good works in order to both be saved and stay saved from sin's penalty. Very few passages are misinterpreted and misapplied more frequently, and to a greater extent than this one. There is a sense in which men are justified by works, but not before God. The Bible is not silent on justification by works. To the contrary, it clarifies justification by works in three distinct ways. It first explains justification by works. It then illustrates justification by works. Finally, it applies justification by works. This chapter will examine the three ways men are justified by works.

THIS TEXT FIRST EXPLAINS JUSTIFICATION BY WORKS

A. Here is what the text passage actually says, *"What doth it profit, my brethren, though a man say he hath faith, and have not works? can faith save him? If a brother or sister be naked, and destitute of daily food, And one of you say unto them, Depart in peace, be ye warmed and filled; notwithstanding ye give them not those things which are needful to the body; what doth it profit? Even so faith, if it hath not works, is dead, being alone. Yea, a man may say, Thou hast faith, and I have works: shew me thy faith without thy works, and I will shew thee my faith by my works. Thou believest that there is one God; thou doest well: the devils also believe, and tremble. But wilt thou know, O vain man, that faith without works is dead?"* **James 2:14-20**.

B. Can a man be justified by faith alone in the eyes of another man? In the sense in which James speaks in this passage, the answer to this question is a resounding "**NO**."

1. The argument is that in your dealings with humans there is no *"profit"* in *"faith"* void of *"works,"* **Verse 14**.

2. No honest Bible scholar can escape the fact that in this text James argues justification before men by works.

C. James labored the argument in unmistakable terms.

1. *"What doth it profit?"* is equivalent to *What good is it?* The divine argument is clear and unmistakable: faith that fails to produce works is no good. It's simply vain, worthless talk, rhetoric. *"Though a man say he hath faith, and have not works? can faith save him?"* The answer is clearly "No." Faith that is sterile and intellectual only, and that does not produce action helps or saves no other human from whatever problem he has.

2. God stated a well-established reality, *"Man looketh on the outward appearance, but the LORD looketh on the heart,"* **1 Samuel 16:7**. The only way men can see *faith* is by the action *faith* produces. James stated the obvious, the universally observable, the great reality of human perception: apart from the words and actions it produces, people can't see faith. *"Even so faith, if it hath not works, is dead, being alone . . . But wilt thou know, O vain man, that faith without works is dead?"* **James 2:17, 20**. That's true because faith is in the heart, and no man can see into the heart of another man. They only know by the words and actions which come from the heart. Jesus said it: *"A good man out of the good treasure of his heart bringeth forth that which is good; and an evil man out of the evil treasure of his heart bringeth forth that which is evil: for of the abundance of the heart his mouth speaketh,"* **Luke 6:45**.

3. What a vivid way of making this point! James argued that *"the body without the spirit is dead;"* (a corpse, a dead man), and likewise *"faith without works faith is dead also,"* **James 2:26**.

4. James issued a bold challenge. *"Yea, a man may say, Thou hast faith, and I have works: shew me thy faith without thy works, and I will shew thee my faith by my works,"* **James 2:18**. The challenge still stands unmet: *I can prove my faith by my works, but I defy you to prove to me the existence of your faith without your works. We both know that you cannot do it.*

5. James brought the *"devils"* into the argument. *"Thou believest that there is one God; thou doest well: the devils also believe, and tremble,"* **James 2:19**. They *"believe"* in an intellectual sense, they know the facts; but there is no personal faith in Christ. Not one of them is saved. Only personal faith saves, and a personal faith in the living Savior will evidence itself in your life.

6. You can talk loud and long about how much you love God, and about your faith in Him; but until there is evidence in your life (works) to prove it, you will never be just in the eyes of other people. They will only know you by the fruit you bear. Jesus said it, *"Ye shall know them by their fruits. Do men gather grapes of thorns, or figs of thistles?"* **Matthew 7:16**.

D. James then explained justification by works by use of a hypothetical case.

1. *"If a brother or sister be naked, and destitute of daily food, And one of you say unto them, Depart in peace, be ye warmed and filled; notwithstanding ye give them not those things which are needful to the body; what doth it profit?"* **James 2:15-16**.

2. This is a hypothesis followed by a conclusion. It is called an *if - then* or conditional statement.[1] James' scenario is straightforward: *You find a Christian brother or sister nude, in rags and starving. Instead of meeting the need, you curtly dismiss them with the empty words, "Be ye warmed and filled."* It is noteworthy that *"filled"* is a vulgarism literally meaning *to eat well or gorge oneself* like a beast, especially a cow. You tell this needy person how much you care, how much you love, how important he/she is to you, that you're a Christian bringing him/her the love of God. Tell the person with all of the syrupy sincerity you can muster, but give him/her no food, no clothes, nothing to help. *"What doeth it profit?"* What good is all the lofty talk of love and faith without works to prove it? Worthless! Absolutely worthless! Hypocritical! Downright insulting! The irony is unmistakable! Words without clothing, food, actions are worthless, like a body without a spirit.

3. This passage clarifies justification by works by explaining that works are evidence of true faith.

---

[1] https://www.mathplanet.com/education/geometry/proof/if-then-statement

THIS TEXT ILLUSTRATES JUSTIFICATION BY WORKS

A. Here are the two Old Testament illustrations given by James. *"Was not Abraham our father justified by works, when he had offered Isaac his son upon the altar? Seest thou how faith wrought with his works, and by works was faith made perfect? And the scripture was fulfilled which saith, Abraham believed God, and it was imputed unto him for righteousness: and he was called the Friend of God. Ye see then how that by works a man is justified, and not by faith only. Likewise also was not Rahab the harlot justified by works, when she had received the messengers, and had sent them out another way?"* **James 2:21-25**.

B. Justification by works is illustrated in Abraham.

1. Abraham is the Bible's undisputed, true hero of faith. He believed God and was justified before God by his faith. When Abraham was 75 years old, God had promised that He would raise up *"a great nation"* through Abraham. See **Genesis 12:1-3**. Many years have passed, and Abraham is childless. He's now an old man, and his wife is getting too old to have a child; from a human standpoint, the odds of seeing nations rise up through him are growing ever slimmer. He's running out of time. Suddenly, God appeared to him. One of the benchmark junctions in the history of humanity is recorded with these words, *"And, behold, the word of the LORD came unto him, saying, This shall not be thine heir; but he that shall come forth out of thine own bowels shall be thine heir. And he brought him forth abroad, and said, Look now toward heaven, and tell the stars, if thou be able to number them: and he said unto him, So shall thy seed be. And he believed in the LORD; and he counted it to him for righteousness,"* **Genesis 15:4-6**.

2. In spite of the odds against it happening, Abraham believed God, and the apostle Paul referenced him as the father of faith. Here is the divine account of the justification of Abraham by faith in God. *"What shall we say then that Abraham our father, as pertaining to the flesh, hath found? For if Abraham were justified by works, he hath whereof to glory; but not before God. For what saith the scripture? Abraham believed God, and it was counted unto him for righteousness,"* **Romans 4:1-3**. **Verse 2** makes it clear that Abraham was justified before God by faith at the time he believed God's promise about a coming lineage. At

that time, God who knew his heart declared Abraham righteous and justified. That occurred at least 25 years before he offered Isaac.

C. While Abraham was justified before God by faith, he is also one of God's examples of a man who was justified before men by his works.

1. *"Was not Abraham our father justified by works, when he had offered Isaac his son upon the altar? Seest thou how faith wrought with his works, and by works was faith made perfect? And the scripture was fulfilled which saith, Abraham believed God, and it was imputed unto him for righteousness: and he was called the Friend of God. Ye see then how that by works a man is justified, and not by faith only,"* **James 2:21-24**.

2. God (yes, God) was careful to make it a clear fact that Abraham was justified and declared righteous well before Abraham was circumcised, and before he offered up Isaac his son. *"Cometh this blessedness then upon the circumcision only, or upon the uncircumcision also? for we say that faith was reckoned to Abraham for righteousness. How was it then reckoned? when he was in circumcision, or in uncircumcision? Not in circumcision, but in uncircumcision, And he received the sign of circumcision, a seal of the righteousness of the faith which he had yet being uncircumcised: that he might be the father of all them that believe, though they be not circumcised; that righteousness might be imputed unto them also,"* **Romans 4:9-11**. The offering of Isaac occurred more than 25 years after God declared Abraham just with Him. Do the math; it's not difficult.

3. Even so, God also said that Abraham was justified in a second sense. Through James God asked, *"Was not Abraham our father justified by works, when he had offered Isaac his son upon the altar?"* **James 2:21**. Yes, he was. He was justified in the eyes of all us bystanders. It was the offering of Isaac which showed the world that Abraham was a just, righteous man. God knew it all the time. He's the one who made Abraham just with Him; and He did it at the time Abraham believed His promise long before he offered Isaac.

4. Abraham was justified in two distinct senses. He was justified in the eyes of God by faith, **Genesis 15:5-6**. He was

justified in the eyes of man when he offered up Isaac, **Genesis 22:1-14**. There is no conflict in the Bible; there never is. Paul was talking about justification before God, and that comes by faith. James was talking about justification before men, and that comes by works. The true personal faith Abraham had in God produced obvious obedience to God by action that could be seen by all. The offering of *"his only begotten son"* Isaac, **Hebrews 11:17**. That offering was unmistakable proof to men of all ages of the faith Abraham had in God. James' argument is air-tight; real faith in God produces visible works which men can see.

D. Justification by works illustrated in Rahab.

1. *"Likewise also was not Rahab the harlot justified by works, when she had received the messengers, and had sent them out another way?"* **James 2:25**.

2. Rahab, *"the harlot"* was bereft of all the obvious glitz of Abraham. Rahab was a heathen Gentile (Canaanite) *woman* (not man) proselyte who was once a prostitute. When Joshua's messengers came to Jericho on the brink of its destruction, Rahab placed herself at the mercy of the God of the invading Jews. How do we know? God who knows all things tells us. **Joshua 2** is the moving story of Rahab, and how she believed in the great God who was doing those marvelous things through His people, the Israelis. In faith, Rahab trusted Him. *"By faith the harlot Rahab perished not with them that believed not, when she had received the spies with peace,"* **Hebrews 11:31**. In spite of her immoral, heathen lifestyle, by faith Rahab got right with God.

3. Then, by her conduct in sheltering God's people, she was *"justified by works, when she had received the messengers, and sent them out another way."* What a great example and compelling proof that true faith expresses itself in works! A genuine conversion makes a difference that others can see!

4. What does this say to saucer-deep *"Christians"* who speak of how they love God, and who put on a religious show on Sunday; but who live and act just like the rest of the world on Monday? What about the smug pretenders who hide behind *"You can't see my heart?"*

THIS TEXT CLARIFIES JUSTIFICATION BY WORKS BY APPLYING IT PROPERLY

A. James spoke primarily of justification before men, and that comes by works.

1. James was not speaking here of how a person receives eternal life. Instead, he spoke mainly of how a man appears just or right to other men. He spoke of feeding and clothing people, and those are clearly human to human business. He said, *"Shew me thy faith without thy works, and I will shew thee my faith by my works,"* **James 2:18**. That is the talk of humans to humans.

2. God *"knoweth the secrets of the heart,"* **Psalm 44:21**. God needs no works to show Him anything; however, with men it's a totally different story. No person can see into the heart of another person. God can see *faith,* but man can't. Men can only see the works which faith produces. If there are no works, men will conclude that there is no faith. That the idea of **James 2:18**: *"Yea, a man may say, Thou hast faith, and I have works: shew me thy faith without thy works, and I will shew thee my faith by my works."* No man will be justified before other men by his faith alone; justification before other men **requires** works.

B. The Judgment Seat of Christ is also a part of this picture.

1. Ultimate accountability, judgment is inherent in **James 2**. Though works never bring a person to God's forgiveness and justification in His sight, nevertheless works are extremely important to God. As clearly as it is possible for language to express any idea, God says, *"For by grace are ye saved through faith; and that not of yourselves: it is the gift of God: Not of works, lest any man should boast,"* **Ephesians 2:8-9**. Though that is where many people stop, the idea doesn't stop there. The very purpose of God's amazing salvation by grace though faith is to produce good works in the saved person. *"For we are his workmanship, created in Christ Jesus unto good works, which God hath before ordained that we should walk in them,"* **Ephesians 2:10**.

2. One day every believer will stand before the Judgment Seat of Christ. *"As I live, saith the Lord, every knee shall bow to me, and*

every tongue shall confess to God. So then every one of us shall give account of himself to God," **Romans 14:11-12**. On that day every believer will be judged *"according to that he hath done"* (his works). *"For we must all appear before the judgment seat of Christ; that every one may receive the things done in his body, according to that he hath done, whether it be good or bad,"* **2 Corinthians 5:10**.

3. You can be certain that when that day comes, there will be no bickering and arguing over whether a person is justified by works or by faith. Every person who is present at the Judgement Seat of Christ will have been justified by grace through faith in Jesus Christ alone as personal Savior. Not one lost or unsaved person will be present. What will be on every mind? Works! Yes, works! *How did I serve the one who saved me by His marvelous grace?* Every reward that is given at that great time will be based on *works*. Yes! You got it! Works!

4. Peter spoke at length about abounding in good works *"that ye shall neither be barren nor unfruitful"* in order that *"an entrance shall be ministered unto you abundantly into the everlasting kingdom of our Lord and Saviour Jesus Christ,"* **2 Peter 1:8, 11**. I tell you that *We'll Work till Jesus Comes* should not be merely a lovely song. At the Judgment Seat of Christ, every believer will get hold of how important justification by works really is. No believer void of works will fare very well on that great day.

5. You tell me that you are a believer, that you have trusted Jesus Christ as your Savior. Great! Tell me about your works. Let's talk about the people you have clothed and fed. I'd like to see your spiritual children: those you've won to Christ and those you have mentored. I'd like to see your credit report, your church attendance record and talk to your mate, to your neighbors and to the people where you work. I can't help wondering how you are going to fare when you come face-to-face with the one *"Who gave himself for us, that he might redeem us from all iniquity, and purify unto himself a peculiar people, zealous of good works,"* **Titus 2:14**.

Chapter 30

The Justification of Abraham

Genesis 15 and 22

In the on-going debate over justification before God by faith versus justification before God by works, Abraham is a key player. The debate hangs on whether or not his justification before God occurred when God first promised him longevity or when he offered Isaac on Mount Moriah. If Abraham was saved from sin's penalty when he offered Isaac, then forgiveness of sins and eternal life is by works, doing something good enough to merit salvation. Conversely, if Abraham was saved from sin's penalty when he first believed God's promise of longevity, then forgiveness of sins and eternal life is by grace through faith in God; not by works or by doing something good enough to merit salvation.

The purpose of this chapter is to establish conclusively from the Bible that Abraham was justified before God more than 25 years before he offered his son Isaac on Mount Moriah. Here are the two biblical accounts commonly used in the debate over when and how Abraham was justified before God. This is really the battle-ground. Abraham was justified before God either by grace or by works. It can't be both ways. *"If by grace, then is it no more of works: otherwise grace is no more grace. But if it be of works, then is it no more grace: otherwise work is no more work,"* **Romans 11:6**.

There are those who contend that justification before God is by grace through faith in the finished work of God on behalf of fallen sinners. The passage they cite as proof is **Genesis 15:4-6**: *"And, behold, the word of the LORD came unto him, saying, This shall not be thine heir; but he that shall come forth out of thine own bowels shall be thine heir. And he brought him forth abroad, and said, Look now toward heaven, and tell the stars, if thou be able to number them: and he said unto him, So shall thy seed be. And he believed in the LORD; and he counted it to him for righteousness."*

There are others who contend that justification before God is by some sort of meritorious work by the lost, fallen sinner that will make him or her just with God. The passage they cite as proof is **Genesis 22:9-14**: *"And they came to the place which God had told him of; and Abraham built an altar there, and laid the wood in order, and bound Isaac his son, and laid him on the altar upon the wood. And Abraham stretched forth his hand, and took the knife to slay his son. And the angel of the LORD called unto him out of heaven, and said, Abraham, Abraham: and he said, Here am I. And he said, Lay not thine hand upon the lad, neither do thou any thing unto him: for now I know that thou fearest God, seeing thou hast not withheld thy son, thine only son from me. And Abraham lifted up his eyes, and looked, and behold behind him a ram caught in a thicket by his horns: and Abraham went and took the ram, and offered him up for a burnt offering in the stead of his son."*

THE BIBLE GIVES US A TIMELINE OF KEY EVENTS IN THE LIFE OF ABRAHAM

A. The total mortal lifetime of Abraham was 175 years. *"And these are the days of the years of Abraham's life which he lived, an hundred threescore and fifteen years. Then Abraham gave up the ghost, and died in a good old age, an old man, and full of years; and was gathered to his people,"* **Genesis 25:7-8**.

B. Abraham was 99 years old when he was circumcised. *"And Abraham was ninety years old and nine, when he was circumcised in the flesh of his foreskin,"* **Genesis 17:24**.

C. Abraham was 86 when his first son, Ishmael was born.

1. *"And Ishmael his son was thirteen years old, when he was circumcised in the flesh of his foreskin. In the selfsame day was Abraham circumcised, and Ishmael his son,"* **Genesis 17:25-26**.

2. Since Abraham's son Ishmael was 13 at Abraham's circumcision, Abraham had to be 86 when Ishmael was born. (99 - 13 = 86)

D. Abraham's second son, Isaac was born when Abraham was 100 years old.

1. *"And Abraham was an hundred years old, when his son Isaac was born unto him,"* **Genesis 21:5**.

2. That establishes Isaac's birth to be a year after Abraham's circumcision, and 14 years after Ishmael's birth.

E. When Isaac was weaned, Abraham made a great celebration feast.

1. *"And the child grew, and was weaned: and Abraham made a great feast the same day that Isaac was weaned,"* **Genesis 21:8**.

2. Studies confirm that ancient middle-eastern women normally weaned their children between 2 and 3 years of age. *"While this textual evidence is not conclusive, it suggests that complete weaning in the Near East could have been expected between 2 and 3 years. There could be substantial differences in the length of the breastfeeding period between girls and boys."*[1]

3. This corresponds with the age of young Samuel when he was taken by Hannah, and left with Eli at the House of God at Shiloh. *"And when she had weaned him, she took him up with her, with three bullocks, and one ephah of flour, and a bottle of wine, and brought him unto the house of the LORD in Shiloh: and the child was young,"* **1 Samuel 1:24**. Obviously, when Samuel was *"weaned,"* he had been potty-trained; and he was old enough to successfully function independently of his mother.

4. This gives us a Bible basic to accurately estimate Isaac's age at his weaning to have been not less than 2 years old, and possibly years older.

F. The Bible does not give the precise age of Isaac when his father Abraham took him to be sacrificed on Mount Moriah; however, it does give us insight.

1. Abraham called Isaac *"the lad,"* **Genesis 22:5**. The Hebrew masculine noun for *"lad"* is **na'ar**. It is translated *"lad"* 33 times,

---

[1] https://onlinelibrary.wiley.com/doi/pdf/10.1002/ajpa.23980

"youth" 6 times and *"young man"* 76 times[2] as in **Genesis 14:24** where Abraham referred to his young soldiers as *"young men." "Save only that which the young men have eaten, and the portion of the men which went with me, Aner, Eshcol, and Mamre; let them take their portion."*

2. Isaac was old enough, and sufficiently mature to talk and discuss in detail burnt sacrifices, carry a sizeable load of wood and walk a rugged two days from Beer-Sheba to Mount Moriah. See **Genesis 22:1-9**.

3. It is certain that at the time of the offering on Mount Moriah, Isaac was neither an infant nor a small boy. He was a well-developed and very capable young man. The contextual information strongly suggests that he was at least into his teens.

G. Inescapable conclusions regarding Abraham's age.

1. Abraham was 99 when he was circumcised.

2. Abraham was 100 when Isaac was born.

3. If Isaac was 15 when he was offered on Mount Moriah, Abraham would have been 115 years old.

4. At the time God made His promise to Abraham about a lineage, Abraham was *"childless,"* **Genesis 15:2**. Ishmael had not been born.

5. From Ishmael's birth until Abraham's circumcision was 13 years. Another year passed before Isaac was born which brought the total to 14 years after Abraham's circumcision. Conservatively speaking, Isaac was 15 years old when he was offered by Abraham. This brought the years to not less than 29 years after the promise of longevity and 16 years after Abraham's circumcision. Even if Isaac's age at the time of the Moriah sacrifice is lowered to 13, the sacrifice still occurred 14 years after Abraham's circumcision.

---

[2] James Strong, *Hebrew and Chaldee Dictionary*, (Nashville, Tennessee: Abingdon Press, 1958), ref. 5288.

THE BIBLE SPECIFICALLY SAYS ABRAHAM WAS JUSTIFIED IN UNCIRCUMCISION

A. In the midst of a lengthy discussion about justification, the apostle Paul said this, *"Blessed is the man to whom the Lord will not impute sin. Cometh this blessedness then upon the circumcision only, or upon the uncircumcision also? for we say that faith was reckoned to Abraham for righteousness. How was it then reckoned? when he was in circumcision, or in uncircumcision? Not in circumcision, but in uncircumcision. And he received the sign of circumcision, a seal of the righteousness of the faith which he had yet being uncircumcised: that he might be the father of all them that believe, though they be not circumcised; that righteousness might be imputed unto them also,"* **Romans 4:9-11**.

B. The Bible is clear about when Abraham's justification before God happened.

1. To start this chapter, we viewed the account from **Genesis 15**. It merits a revisit.

2. Abram (Abraham) was concerned because he had no child, no son to be his heir. He said to God, *"Behold, to me thou hast given no seed: and, lo, one born in my house is mine heir,"* **Genesis 15:3**.

3. God responded to Abraham: *"And, behold, the word of the LORD came unto him, saying, This shall not be thine heir; but he that shall come forth out of thine own bowels shall be thine heir. And he brought him forth abroad, and said, Look now toward heaven, and tell the stars, if thou be able to number them: and he said unto him, So shall thy seed be,"* **Genesis 15:4-5**.

4. That's when Abraham was justified before God. The Bible specifically says so. *"And he believed in the LORD; and he counted it to him for righteousness,"* **Genesis 15:6**.

a. Did you hear that? Don't miss it. This is when it happened, when Abraham was justified before God by faith, and not works.

b. In case you think we're misinterpreting this Scripture, God (yes, God) made sure honest people would never miss the point when He inspired the apostle Paul to write these words, *"What shall we say then that Abraham our* *father, as pertaining to the flesh, hath found? For if Abraham were justified by works, he hath whereof to glory; but not before God. For what saith the scripture? Abraham believed God, and it was counted unto him for righteousness,"* **Romans 4:1-3**. The best commentary on Scripture is Scripture. God made sure the world would know that Abraham was justified by faith, and not by works.

c. Not because He forgot that He had already said it (God NEVER forgets what He said), but to emphasize His point He said it again: *"Even as Abraham believed God, and it was accounted to him for righteousness. Know ye therefore that they which are of faith, the same are the children of Abraham. And the scripture, foreseeing that God would justify the heathen through faith, preached before the gospel unto Abraham, saying, In thee shall all nations be blessed. So then they which be of faith are blessed with faithful Abraham,"* **Galatians 3:6-9**. If that's not enough, God said it still again. *"And the scripture was fulfilled which saith, Abraham believed God, and it was imputed unto him for righteousness: and he was called the Friend of God,"* **James 2:23**.

5. Note very well!

a. Abraham was justified with God by faith 13 years before he was circumcised.

b. Abraham was justified with God by faith 14 years before Isaac was born.

c. Isaac was at least a teenager when Abraham offered him as a sacrifice.

d. Abraham offered Isaac as a sacrifice not less than 14 years after he (Abraham) was circumcised (probably more).

e. Abraham was justified (saved) at least 28 years before he offered Isaac (probably more).

C. Yet, there are those who say Abraham was justified with God when and because he offered Isaac as a sacrifice on Mount Moriah.

1. They cite **James 2:21** as proof: *"Was not Abraham our father justified by works, when he had offered Isaac his son upon the altar?"*

2. Under divine inspiration, James was quick to explain that faith produces good works. Abraham offered Isaac, not in order to be just with God, but because he was already just with God. How do we know that's true? The answer is *because in the next verse God told us. "Seest thou how faith wrought with his works, and by works was faith made perfect?"* **James 2:22**. Abraham's faith produced works, a testimony to all men of his faith.

3. It was not his work of offering Isaac that justified him; it was his faith, and God repeatedly emphasized that fact. God labored the point with evidence that Abraham had already been just with God for many, many years before the offering of Isaac.

HOW MEN BECOME JUST WITH GOD

A. Though the example of Abraham's justification with God is cited often in the Bible as the model of how sinners are made right with God, Abraham's example is discussed in great detail in **Romans 3-5**. In the midst of a discussion on the fallen estate of all men, and their inability to save themselves from their fallen condition, the Holy Spirit of God through the apostle Paul brought up Abraham as an example of how a hopeless man can become just with God. Abraham is God's poster child on how to be saved.

B. It was Abraham's faith, not his faithfulness, that made him right with God.

1. *"If Abraham were justified by works, he hath whereof to glory; but not before God,"* **Romans 4:2**.

2. The reality of Abraham was that he was a fallen sinner, damned before God and with no ability to save or rescue himself from his fallen condition. Abraham was like every human described in **Romans 3:9-20**.

3. Abraham was not justified before God because he was good or worthy. He was just as evil and unworthy as any other sinner.

C. In spite of Abraham's sinful condition, he believed God.

1. He had all of the reasons other skeptics and other unbelievers have to reject God. From agnosticism to atheism there were plenty of alternatives to believing God.

2. God said to Abraham, *"I have made thee a father of many nations,"* **Romans 4:17**. For an old man with a barren wife, that's hard to believe. The rest of the verse explains how impossible it seemed to Abraham. *". . . before him whom he believed, even God, who quickeneth the dead, and calleth those things which be not as though they were."* Abraham knew he and his wife were past childbearing, yet he believed God could do the impossible, even give a child in an impossible situation.

3. The next verses explain the thinking in the heart of Abraham: *"Who against hope believed in hope, that he might become the father of many nations, according to that which was spoken, So shall thy seed be. And being not weak in faith, he considered not his own body now dead, when he was about an hundred years old, neither yet the deadness of Sara's womb: He staggered not at the promise of God through unbelief; but was strong in faith, giving glory to God; And being fully persuaded that, what he had promised, he was able also to perform,"* **Romans 4:18-21**.

4. Believing is never easy: trusting a God you cannot see to save you from eternal damnation seems like a figment of someone's wild imagination based upon a clandestine redemption story that the vast majority of people see as a fable, mythology! Wow! Really? It's not so easy in a church to give lip-service to this Christian thing; but to believe it in your heart to the point of risking everything, your eternal destiny; that's huge.

5. Abraham did it. He believed in what, from a human viewpoint, seemed like the impossible. *"By faith Abraham, when he was called to go out into a place which he should after receive for an inheritance, obeyed; and he went out, not knowing whither he went. By faith he sojourned in the land of promise, as in a strange country, dwelling in tabernacles with Isaac and Jacob, the heirs with him of the same promise: For he looked for a city which hath foundations, whose builder and maker is God,"* **Hebrews 11:8-10**.

6. God was watching; He always is. Listen well to the crowning verse in **Romans 4**. It's **verse 22**. *"And therefore it was imputed to him for righteousness."* Because he believed in the promise of God, Abraham was made right with God.

D. Abraham is God's example of how any person gets right with God.

1. There never has been or ever will be but one way to get right with God, and Abraham illustrates that way. After introducing the example of Abraham, the Spirit of God then turned to all men. Look back to **Romans 4**. *"Now to him that worketh is the reward not reckoned of grace, but of debt. But to him that worketh not, but believeth on him that justifieth the ungodly, his faith is counted for righteousness,"* **Romans 4:4-5**. That's how it happens! Every time! There are no exceptions! Every justified person that has ever existed, exists or ever will exist is there only by the grace of God who gives His own righteousness to those who come to Him in faith. His righteousness is imputed (given without merit) without works. *"Even as David also describeth the blessedness of the man, unto whom God imputeth righteousness without works, Saying, Blessed are they whose iniquities are forgiven, and whose sins are covered. Blessed is the man to whom the Lord will not impute sin,"* **Romans 4:6-8**.

2. Everybody? Yes, everybody! Isn't this a Jewish thing? No, it's God's way of justification for all men. *"Cometh this blessedness then upon the circumcision only, or upon the uncircumcision also?"* **Romans 4:9**. Abraham *"received the sign of circumcision,* (Jewish) *a seal of the righteousness of the faith which he had yet being uncircumcised: that he might be the father of all them that believe, though they be not circumcised; that righteousness might be imputed unto them also:* (Note it well: To Jews and all who are not Jews!) *And the father of circumcision to them who are not of the circumcision only, but who also walk in the steps of that faith of our father Abraham, which he had being yet uncircumcised,"* **Romans 4:11-12**. God *"now commandeth all men every where to repent,"* **Acts 17:30**. Salvation is for all people, and all of them are saved the same way: by faith, and not by works. Abraham's faith *"was imputed to him for righteousness,"* but this divine record *"was not written for his sake alone, that it was imputed to him; But for us also, to whom it shall be imputed, if we believe on him that raised up Jesus our Lord from the dead; Who was delivered for our offences, and was raised again for our justification,"* **Romans 4:22-25**. Note it well: *"For us also, to whom it shall be imputed, if we believe on him that raised up Jesus our Lord from the dead!"*

3. Hallelujah! This story is not merely about Abraham. It has a point to it. It's about us, all of us! *"Abraham believed God, and it was accounted to him for righteousness. Know ye therefore that they which are of faith, the same are the children of Abraham. And the scripture, foreseeing that God would justify the heathen through faith, preached before the gospel unto Abraham, saying, In thee shall all nations be blessed. So then they which be of faith are blessed with faithful Abraham,"* **Galatians 3:6-9**.

4. One plan of eternal redemption! *"For by grace are ye saved through faith; and that not of yourselves: it is the gift of God: Not of works, lest any man should boast,"* **Ephesians 2:8-9**. One plan based upon a work that only God could do. He knew none of us could do it for ourselves, so He did it Himself. The work of salvation for sinners like us is His idea, not ours. He planned His work and worked His plan in the person and work of Jesus Christ. Like Abraham, we simply trust Him. He does the saving! Thank Him, and praise His holy name forever! *"Now unto the King eternal, immortal, invisible, the only wise God, be honour and glory for ever and ever. Amen,"* **1 Timothy 1:17**.

Chapter 31

Once Saved, Always Saved

2 Timothy 1:12

The Apostle Paul wrote these blessed words in "*I know whom I have believed, and am persuaded that he is able to keep that which I have committed unto him against that day*," **2 Timothy 1:12**. With this statement he was stating his confidence in the one who saved him. Paul, like all believers, was dependent upon the grace and trustworthiness of God for his salvation. His claim was that Christ the Savior was more than capable of getting him to heaven. He also believed that Jesus Christ was committed to doing just that. By faith Paul had committed himself to Christ; and Christ had committed Himself and all of His resources to the deliverance of Paul and every believer to heaven.

This belief is commonly and Theologically called **The Eternal Security of the Believer**. It's the Bible truth commonly known as ***once saved, always saved***.

WHAT A GLORIOUS TRUTH ONCE SAVED, ALWAYS SAVED IS!

Once saved, always saved means salvation is altogether by grace; not by works

The Bible words it like this, *"For by grace are ye saved through faith; and that not of yourselves: it is the gift of God: Not of works, lest any man should boast,"*

Ephesians 2:8-9. That's what God says on the issue. He also said on the matter of being saved, *"If by grace, then is it no more of works: otherwise, grace is no more grace. But if it be of works, then is it no more grace: otherwise, work is no more work,"* **Romans 11:6**. According to God, salvation is either by faith or it's by works. It's one way or the other; it's not a combination of faith and works. Listen to Him elaborate: *"Being justified freely by his grace through the redemption that is in Christ Jesus: Whom God hath set forth to be a propitiation through faith in his blood, to declare his righteousness for the remission of sins that are past, through the forbearance of God; To declare, I say, at this time his righteousness: that he might be just, and the justifier of him which believeth in Jesus. Where is boasting then? It is excluded. By what law? of works? Nay: but by the law of faith. Therefore, we conclude that a man is justified by faith without the deeds of the law,"* **Romans 3:24-28**.

Once saved, always saved says salvation is not predicated on behavior, good or bad

Everybody on this planet knows behavior has to do with how well you get along with somebody; not whether or not you are kin to that person by blood. The best possible son or daughter is no more or no less a son or daughter than the worst son or daughter. Everybody knows people do not become sons or daughters by being good or bad. Relationship in a family is not a behavioral matter. One thing, and one thing alone makes a person a bloodline member of a family, and that's a birth. That's an observable objective fact. It's provable. The New Birth alone makes people children of God's spiritual family; not how they live. The Bible says, *"Not by works of righteousness which we have done, but according to his mercy he saved us, by the washing of regeneration, and renewing of the Holy Ghost,"* **Titus 3:5**. Oh, what a glorious thing it is to know that salvation does not depend upon behavior! If it did, nobody would be saved because all people are sinners. *"For there is not a just man upon earth, that doeth good, and sinneth not,"* **Ecclesiastes 7:20**. Once saved, always saved means you don't have to go through life in dread and worry.

Once saved, always saved is worth having

In view of our weak and sinful natures, if it's not *once saved, always saved,* then not one of us will ever make it. Every one of us knows that a salvation that is only good as long as you're good isn't worth a thing.

Many years ago, I made a house call to a VERY religious man who lived in constant dread and fear. He was faithful in church, and very sincere. He was trying very hard to *"be good enough."* His church kept telling him that he had to *"live it."* Otherwise, he'd be lost again. This man had to daily drive the streets of Houston. He told me that he planned to live a very good life right up to the moment of his death. He envisioned himself getting into a fatal car wreck. He lived in fear that the wreck would stress him into saying a cuss word. He was sure that last-minute sin would cause him to lose his salvation and send him straight to hell where he'd spend eternity. What a terrible concept! How hopeless! Every one of us knows that if making heaven is based on our performance, we won't make it. We must have a Savior who saves us in spite of ourselves.

In spite of these irrefutable truths from the Bible, few beliefs are rejected more than *once saved, always saved,* **the eternal security of the believer**. Every single one of us knows that behavior impacts only our fellowship with others, yet people insist in inserting behavior into the mix of eternal life and the family of God.

SEVEN COMPOUND BIBLE PROOFS THAT ONCE A PERSON IS SAVED, HE IS SAVED FOREVER

A birth is irreversible

Some things cannot be undone: your birth date, a murder, even one day of your life. We do not have power to go back in time. We may get a second opportunity to do something again (we know them as second chances); but we can't erase the first time. It stands forever in the eternal records of God.

At the instant of salvation, believers are *"born again"* into the family of God. *"Whosoever believeth that Jesus is the Christ is born of God,"* **1 John 5:1**. To lose salvation (eternal life), a person would have to reverse time; and go back into their pre-birth condition. We all know that is not a possibility in the natural sense. Neither is an option in the spiritual sense. The concept of losing salvation makes no sense. A birth is irreversible.

The Bible says every believer has *"everlasting* (eternal) *life;"* not *temporary* life, but *"everlasting"* life

Listen to Jesus' own words: *"As Moses lifted up the serpent in the wilderness, even so must the Son of man be lifted up: That whosoever believeth in him should not perish, but have eternal life. For God so loved the world, that he gave his only begotten Son, that whosoever believeth in him should not perish, but have everlasting life. For God sent not his Son into the world to condemn the world; but that the world through him might be saved. He that believeth on him is not condemned: but he that believeth not is condemned already, because he hath not believed in the name of the only begotten Son of God,"* **John 3:14-18**.

Jesus repeated this claim many times. He said, *"Whosoever drinketh of the water that I shall give him shall never thirst; but the water that I shall give him shall be in him a well of water springing up into everlasting life,"* **John 4:14**. *"Verily, verily, I say unto you, He that heareth my word, and believeth on him that sent me, hath everlasting life, and shall not come into condemnation; but is passed from death unto life,"* **John 5:24**. Jesus never referred to the spiritual life which He gives as *temporary*. It's *permanent*, *"eternal," "everlasting."*

That means nothing can ever make a believer lost again

If a person can lose his/her spiritual life, then it was only temporary. Jesus said, *"This is the Father's will which hath sent me, that of all which he hath given me I should lose nothing, but should raise it up again at the last day,"* **John 6:39**. Did you hear that? He said He would *"lose nothing."* Of all who believe on Him as personal Savior, He said, *"I give unto them eternal life; and they shall never perish, neither shall any man pluck them out of my hand. My Father, which gave them me, is greater than all; and no man is able to pluck them out of my Father's hand,"* **John 10:28-29**. If even one person was born again into the family of God, then lost his eternal life, these claims by Jesus simply would not be true; however, they are true. God *"cannot lie,"* **Titus 1:2**. Once a person is saved, he is always saved.

Believers are kept by the power of God, not by their own powers or abilities

Of every believer, the Bible says, *"Ye are dead, and your life is hid with Christ in God,"* **Colossians 3:3**. Believers are *"sealed with the Holy Spirit of promise,"* **Ephesians 1:13**. Not one of us is capable of keeping ourself saved. God keeps us. *"Blessed be the God and Father of our Lord*

Jesus Christ, which according to his abundant mercy hath begotten us again unto a lively hope by the resurrection of Jesus Christ from the dead, To an inheritance incorruptible, and undefiled, and that fadeth not away, reserved in heaven for you, who are kept by the power of God through faith unto salvation ready to be revealed in the last time," **1 Peter 1:3-5**.

Praise God that's true! Not one of us can keep ourselves pure and sinless. Jesus said, *"All power is given unto me in heaven and in earth,"* **Matthew 28:18**. He said, *"I am Alpha and Omega, the beginning and the ending, saith the Lord, which is, and which was, and which is to come, the Almighty,"* **Revelation 1:8**. Note well: *"The Almighty!"* Only He has the power to keep people saved in spite of their sins, but He has it. The security of believers does not depend on their abilities; their security depends on His abilities, His power.

No believer can be put into double jeopardy

Before a person is saved, he is condemned by God because of his sins. "*He that believeth not is condemned already, because he hath not believed in the name of the only begotten Son of God,"* **John 3:18**. At the moment a person is saved, God forgives all of that person's sins. The Bible says, *"As far as the east is from the west, so far hath he removed our transgressions from us,"* **Psalm 103:12**. No believer must face his sins again. Jesus was judged on the cross for those sins. He paid the penalty. He died in the place of the sinner. *"Surely he hath borne our griefs, and carried our sorrows: yet we did esteem him stricken, smitten of God, and afflicted. But he was wounded for our transgressions, he was bruised for our iniquities: the chastisement of our peace was upon him; and with his stripes we are healed. All we like sheep have gone astray; we have turned every one to his own way; and the LORD hath laid on him the iniquity of us all,"* **Isaiah 53:4-6**. The apostle Peter put it this way, *"For Christ also hath once suffered for sins, the just for the unjust, that he might bring us to God, being put to death in the flesh, but quickened by the Spirit,"* **1 Peter 3:18**.

In the court of Almighty God, we've already been tried and convicted. God knew we didn't stand a chance; but *"God so loved the world, that he gave his only begotten Son, that whosoever believeth in him should not perish, but have everlasting life. For God sent not his Son into the world to condemn the world; but that the world through him might be saved. He that believeth on him is not condemned: but he that believeth not is condemned already, because he hath not believed in the name of the only begotten Son of God,"* **John 3:16-18**. It's not difficult to see why the Bible says, *"There is therefore now no condemnation to them which are in Christ Jesus,"* **Romans 8:1**. No believer must face eternal death for his sins. Jesus Christ has already died for them, paid the death penalty in full. Those sins will NEVER again have to be faced. There is no double jeopardy.

Jesus Christ is the personal defender of every believer

Yes! That's exactly what God claims. *"If God be for us, who can be against us?"* **Romans 8:31**. Every believer can say with the Psalmist who said, *"The LORD is on my side; I will not fear: what can man do unto me?"* **Psalm 118:6**.

In God's Court, Satan is the accuser of every believer including you and me. God the Father is the righteous judge of all things. The Lord Jesus Christ is our defense attorney. We're all guilty and have no defense; but Jesus our great Redeemer defends us upon the strength of His death, burial and resurrection. He makes no attempt to defend us upon the strength of our record. He puts His work on the line for us. Listen to God's own explanation of why every believer has eternal security. *"What shall we then say to these things? If God be for us, who can be against us? He that spared not his own Son, but delivered him up for us all, how shall he not with him also freely give us all things? Who shall lay any thing to the charge of God's elect? It is God that justifieth. Who is he that condemneth? It is Christ that died, yea rather, that is risen again, who is even at the right hand of God, who also maketh intercession for us,"* **Romans 8:31-34**. Note well: *"It is Christ that died, yea rather, that is risen again, who is even at the right hand of God, who also maketh intercession for us."* The death, burial and resurrection of Jesus Christ is the gospel *"by which also ye are saved,"* **1 Corinthians 15:1-4**. It *"is the power of God unto salvation to every one that believeth,"* **Romans 1:16**. When Satan brings us into question before God because of our sins, Jesus defends us upon the strength of His death, burial and resurrection.

The great apostle Paul thus asked this question, *"Who shall separate us from the love of Christ? shall tribulation, or distress, or persecution, or famine, or nakedness, or peril, or sword?"* **Romans 8:35**. Just who could make you lost again? Satan? People who hate you? Yourself? Simon Peter went so far as to renounce Jesus Christ. In the terror of Jesus' horrible crucifixion, Peter began *"to curse and to swear, saying, I know not the man,"* **Matthew 26:74**. The word *"curse"* is from the Greek word meaning *anathema.* It means to violently, passionately renounce. Did that renunciation make Peter lose his salvation? The answer is *No.* Absolutely not! Follow the life of Peter after he renounced his connection with Christ. The evidence is overwhelming that he was still as much a child of God as he had ever been.

According to the Bible, you can't lose your salvation. Once you're saved, you're always saved. Listen to the divine argument of the apostle Paul who wrote under the inspiration of the Holy Spirit, *"I am persuaded, that neither death, nor life, nor angels, nor principalities, nor powers, nor things present, nor things to come, Nor height, nor depth, nor any other creature, shall be able to separate us from the love of God, which is in Christ Jesus our Lord,"* **Romans 8:38-39**.

God puts the final word on the matter. He says that once you're saved, you cannot be lost again

Jesus who was *"God with us!"* **Matthew 1:23**. Here are His words, *"Verily, verily, I say unto you, He that heareth my word, and believeth on him that sent me, hath everlasting life, and shall not come into condemnation; but is passed from death unto life,"* **John 5:24**. Once you're saved, you can't go back and be lost again.

HEBREWS 10:1-14 AFFIRMS GOD'S POSITION ON THE MATTER OF ONCE SAVED, ALWAYS SAVED

Verses 1-8 talk about mankind's best efforts to be right with God

Verse 1 mentions, *"those sacrifices which they offered year by year continually."* The Israeli religious system which prevailed for centuries prior to Jesus Christ was the epitome of man's best efforts. Under this system, there was wholesale bloody sacrificing of sheep, goats, bullocks, pigeons and turtle doves. **Verse 1** also says those bloody sacrifices, *"can never . . . make the comers thereunto perfect."*

If those human efforts had been capable of solving the sin problem which condemns every person, Jew and Gentile, then the problem would have been solved. No more sacrifices would have been necessary. Listen to the divine explanation, *"For then would they not have ceased to be offered? because that the worshippers once purged should have had no more conscience of sins,"* **Hebrews 10:2**. The truth is, they didn't work. As the next two verses explain, *"In those sacrifices there is a remembrance again made of sins every year. For it is not possible that the blood of bulls and of goats should take away sins,"* **Hebrews 10:3-4**.

The fact is, those sacrifices were not designed to solve the sin problem; they were intended to turn lost sinners to Jesus Christ who would offer Himself as the ultimate sacrifice for their sins. **Verse 1** says the Law with all of its sacrifices and exacting rules was *"a shadow of good things to come."* A *"shadow"* is not the real thing; it's only a reflection of the real thing. The sacrifice of Jesus Christ is the real thing *"which taketh away the sin of the world,"* **John 1:29**. The Law, which is so typical of all human efforts for salvation, was never intended to forgive sins and give men eternal life. *"The law was our schoolmaster to bring us unto Christ, that we might be justified by faith,"* **Galatians 3:24**. The Law told every man that he couldn't be good enough; his only hope was in the long-predicted Messiah, the Savior who is Jesus Christ. All of that legal stuff including the animal sacrifices was and is not good enough with God. Listen to God's explanation. *"Wherefore when he cometh into the world, he saith, Sacrifice and offering thou wouldest not, but a body hast thou prepared me: In burnt offerings and sacrifices for sin thou hast had no pleasure. Then said I, Lo, I come (in the volume of the book it is written of me,) to do thy will, O God. Above when he said, Sacrifice and offering and burnt offerings and offering for sin thou wouldest not, neither hadst pleasure therein; which are offered by the law,"* **Hebrews 10:5-8**.

All of those sacrifices failed both individually and collectively. Not one person ever was saved from sin's penalty by keeping the law with all of its sacrifices. *"By the deeds of the law there shall no flesh be justified in his sight,"* **Romans 3:20**. Every human effort failed to save even one man, let alone keep him saved.

Verses 9-11 introduce Jesus Christ

He came to do what nobody else, including all righteous holy living, could do. *"Then said he, Lo, I come to do thy will, O God. He taketh away the first, that he may establish the second,"* **Hebrews 10:9**. Jesus had a new and better way.

Did it work? Absolutely it did! By what Jesus Christ did by the sacrifice of Himself, all who believe in Him *"are sanctified through the offering of the body of Jesus Christ once for all,"* **Hebrews 10:10**. His work stands in stark contrast to the work of the entire Levitical priesthood. *"Every priest standeth daily ministering and offering oftentimes the same sacrifices, which can never take away sins,"* **Hebrews 10:11**. Those Old Testament priests *stood "daily ministering and offering oftentimes the same sacrifices."* Why? The answer is clear. They couldn't get the job done. They couldn't fully address the sin problem. No sooner had they offered one animal sacrifice for sins, there was more sins which had to be addressed. The man who offered a sheep for yesterday's sins had to come back to address his new sins. They knew it and thus offered a *"continual burnt offering,"* **Exodus 29:42**. Imagine that! A *"continual burnt offering."* They couldn't get it done. It was a futile, hopeless process; yet most of them missed the point, and thought that they were saved from sin's penalty by offering these sacrifices.

Verses 12-14 Whereas the best efforts of humans failed, the work of Jesus Christ offers hope and eternal security to every man

He willingly, freely went to the cross and shed His own sinless blood to pay the guilt of every sinner. *"But this man, after he had offered one sacrifice for sins for ever, sat down on the right hand of God; From henceforth expecting till his enemies be made his footstool,"* **Hebrews 10:12-13**. Note well! He *"offered one sacrifice for sins forever."* That means he died, was buried and raised one, and only one time. He will never have to do it again. Never again! Jesus Christ personally addressed the sin problem, and solved it forever! Forever! Once a sinner by faith receives Christ's provision for his/her sins, the problem is forever solved. The sins of that person have been paid once and forever. He/she will never need to be saved again.

Note well the divine reasoning of this text. *"This man, after he had offered one sacrifice for sins for ever, sat down on the right hand of God,"* **Hebrews 10:12**. Note the contrast with the Levitical priests: *"Every priest standeth daily ministering and offering oftentimes the same sacrifices, which can never take away sins,"* **Hebrews 10:11**. Those priest *"standeth;"* Jesus *"sat down."* They couldn't get the job done; Jesus did. Here is how the text puts it: *"For by one offering he hath perfected for ever them that are sanctified,"* **Hebrews 10:14**. *"Perfected for ever!"* That's the eternal status of every person who has given up on all hope for the forgiveness of sins and eternal life; and who has come by faith in the heart to Jesus Christ depending on Him and Him alone for forgiveness of sins and eternal life.

A beautiful truth is in the heart of this passage. **Verse 10** says of all who have come to Christ as their hope, *"We are sanctified through the offering of the body of Christ once for all."* That little phrase *"once for all"* is translated from the Greek adverb **ephapax**. It literally means, *"once for all"* or one time with perpetual validity.[1] Hallelujah! Christ will never have to die again, and nobody who has been saved will ever have to get saved again. His *"one sacrifice for sins forever"* was enough to permanently solve the sin problem. Praise God, once we're saved, we're always saved.

---

[1] James Strong, *Greek Dictionary of the New Testament*, (Nashville, Tennessee: Abingdon Press, 1958), ref. 2178.

About the Author

LESTER HUTSON served as a Baptist pastor for over 60 years. He has also served as a national field representative for the Christian Law Association, a conference and revival speaker and the author of numerous books. He is committed to first-century Christianity, the inerrancy of the Scriptures and personal evangelism.

www.lesterhutson.org

www.ingramcontent.com/pod-product-compliance
Lightning Source LLC
LaVergne TN
LVHW020528100826
845148LV00010B/1394

* 9 7 8 1 7 3 2 4 2 8 2 9 4 *